THE AI DESIGN REVOLUTION

FROM REPRESENTATION TO AGENTIC ARCHITECTURE

Neil Leach, Wanyu He,
Daniel Bolojan and Theodoros Galanos

Routledge
Taylor & Francis Group
LONDON AND NEW YORK

Designed cover image: Neil Leach, Monolith in the Alps, generated using Midjourney, 2025. This image has been chosen to illustrate the subject of the book.

First published 2027
by Routledge
4 Park Square, Milton Park, Abingdon, Oxon OX14 4RN

and by Routledge
605 Third Avenue, New York, NY 10158

Routledge is an imprint of the Taylor & Francis Group, an informa business

British Library Cataloguing-in-Publication Data
A catalogue record for this book is available from the British Library

Library of Congress Cataloging-in-Publication Data
Names: Leach, Neil contributor
Title: The AI design revolution : how artificial intelligence will transform architecture / Neil Leach, Wanyu He, Daniel Bolojan and Theodoros Galanos.
Description: Abingdon, Oxon : Routledge, 2026. | Includes bibliographical references and index.
Identifiers: LCCN 2026017083 | ISBN 9781032388939 hardback | ISBN 9781032388861 paperback | ISBN 9781003347330 ebook
Subjects: LCSH: Architecture and technology | Generative artificial intelligence
Classification: LCC NA2543.T43 A39 2026
LC record available at https://lccn.loc.gov/2026017083

ISBN: 978-1-032-38893-9 (hbk)
ISBN: 978-1-032-38886-1 (pbk)
ISBN: 978-1-003-34733-0 (ebk)

DOI: 10.4324/9781003347330

Typeset in Garamond
by Apex CoVantage, LLC

CONTENTS

THE AI DESIGN REVOLUTION

The AI revolution is here. Now that AI has been unleashed, nothing will be the same again. But what will be the impact of AI on architectural design? *The AI Design Revolution* offers an accessible and engaging introduction to the relevance of artificial intelligence to architecture and how it is transforming the field.

The book brings together four of the world's leading experts on AI and architecture: Neil Leach, Wanyu He, Daniel Bolojan, and Theodoros Galanos. Together they look at the impact of AI on architecture, each from their own perspective, to offer a comprehensive overview of how AI is already leading to a profound and deep-rooted revolution in architectural design. This is essential reading for students of architecture and professional architects alike.

Neil Leach is a professor of architecture from the UK. He directs the Doctor of Design program at FIU, and has also taught at the AA, Harvard, Columbia, Cornell, IAAC, and SCI-Arc. He is a co-founder of DigitalFUTURES, and a former researcher for NASA developing a 3D printer for the Moon and Mars. He has published over 50 books, including most recently *Architecture in the Age of Artificial Intelligence: An Introduction to AI for Architects*, 2nd edition.

Wanyu He is Founder and CEO of XKool Tech, bridging architecture and AI. She holds a Doctor of Design degree from Florida International University and is a PhD candidate at Tongji University. She is a former OMA Senior Project Architect on various projects including the SZSE HQ. In addition to being the author of *AI for Architects* (Tongji University Press, 2021) and 20+ papers, she holds dozens of patents and mentors at leading universities. She has been featured on both the Hurun U40 List and the Fortune China Business Women lists.

Daniel Bolojan is an architect, researcher, and entrepreneur, working at the forefront of Creative AI and Agentic AI in architecture. He is an Associate Professor at Florida Atlantic University and Director of the Creative AI Lab. At Coop Himmelb(l)au he serves as Senior Architect and Computational Design Specialist, and has developed the DeepHimmelblau AI research project since 2018. He is also the creator of Versur, the first agentic AI platform built specifically for architects and designers.

Theodoros Galanos is the Generative AI Leader and Advanced Design Lead at Aurecon, where he develops AI-driven workflows for engineering and advisory teams, and contributes to initiatives such as Aurecon's strategic partnership with Nomic to accelerate complex problem-solving across the asset lifecycle. He is also the Chief Scientific Officer and Co-Founder of Infrared.city, leading the development of AI-powered environmental simulation tools that make advanced environmental analysis accessible to designers and engineers.

Greg Tate, Golf Force One, generated using Midjourney, 2025

David Alf, Vertical Living Above the Cherry Blossoms, generated using Midjourney, 2025

PREFACE

HOW AI WILL TRANSFORM ARCHITECTURE

The AI revolution is here. Now that AI has been unleashed, nothing will be the same again. But what impact will AI have on architectural design?

The AI Design Revolution offers an accessible and engaging introduction to the relevance of AI to architecture and offers a comprehensive overview of how AI will transform the field.

The volume brings together four of the world's leading experts on AI and architecture: Wanyu He, architect and AI pioneer, and CEO of AI architectural software developer, XKool; Daniel Bolojan, architectural designer and technologist, Associate Professor at Florida Atlantic University, CEO of Versur, and AI lead for Coop Himmelb(l)au; Neil Leach, architectural theorist and author of several books on AI and architecture, Professor at Florida International University, and co-founder of DigitalFUTURES; and Theodoros Galanos, Deep Learning expert, Chief Scientific Officer and co-founder of Infrared.city and generative AI lead for Aurecon Consulting Engineers.

Together they look at the impact of AI on architecture – each from their own perspective – to offer an informed overview of how AI is going to lead to a profound and deep-rooted revolution in architectural design.

This will be essential reading for all students of architecture, as well as professional architects eager to find out what the future might be like.

Figure 0.1 Robert Cha, Futurist Fiction Civic Center, digital rendering, generated with Midjourney, Magnific, and Photoshop, 2025

INTRODUCTION
THE AI DESIGN REVOLUTION

We live in the age of AI.

AI is everywhere. It's in our homes, on our phones, in our offices, in our cars – literally everywhere. But we might not be aware of it, because AI is essentially invisible.

Think of AI a little like electricity. Electricity can power a toaster, just as AI can drive a car. But we cannot see electricity, although we can see its effects. The same with AI. And electricity is also everywhere. It is often said, 'AI is the new electricity'. But unlike electricity, AI is continually learning.

When we order an Uber, we are using AI. When we use facial recognition to open our phones, we are using AI. Even when we are just using spellcheck, we are using AI. But most architects do not realise this. For example, in a survey conducted by the Royal Institute of British Architects (RIBA) in 2024, 41% of RIBA architects claimed that they did use AI, while the other 59% claimed that they did not use AI at all.[1] What is abundantly clear, however, is that we are all using AI, all the time.

Moreover, even those architects who did claim to be using AI were almost certainly only using a certain limited set of tools for generating images or videos, such as Midjourney, Stable Diffusion, LookX, Runway, or Veo2. Indeed, it would appear that for many architects, Midjourney is synonymous with AI. These models, however, serve as little more than sketching tools for brainstorming ideas – or 'ideating', as it is termed – and have fairly limited applications within the overall design process. However, the eventual impact of AI on architecture is going to be much deeper than this. AI is going to automate the entire design process, from form generation through to performance optimisation and fabrication itself. And everything will be based on data.

Welcome to the AI Design Revolution.

DOI: 10.4324/9781003347330-1

Figure 0.2 David Alf, Curious Reindeer Passing Through the Shou Sugi Ban Cabin, generated using Midjourney, 2025

WHAT IS AI?

What exactly is AI? We all use the term, but very few, it would seem, really understand what it means.

Let us start with a very basic definition. AI is a little like a 'digital brain'. Indeed, an artificial neural network is loosely modelled on the neural network of the brain, and – like the brain – it is composed of 'neurons' and 'synapses'. However, AI is not really like a brain, because AI is nowhere near as complex as the brain. For example, whereas systems like ChatGPT might have over a trillion connections, the brain has up to 1000 trillion connections – almost 1000 times more. Moreover, the neurons and synapses of AI are very different to the neurons and synapses of the brain. The neurons and synapses of the artificial neural networks of AI are part of an abstract, rigid, mechanical system, where the flow of information along the synapses is governed by the weights, which can be adjusted. By contrast, the neurons and synapses of the neural network of the brain are part of a living, evolving biological system, and are capable of complex behaviours. In short, the 'neurons' and 'synapses' of AI only mimic the neurons and synapses of the brain. AI is mechanical, whereas our brains are biological.

Moreover, there is a further important difference between AI and the brain. Unlike the brain, AI is not conscious – at least not yet. Nor is it sentient or self-aware. Nor can we say with any confidence just yet that AI has the capacity to 'think'. But we would be wrong to discount AI, simply because it is not quite the same as a brain. AI is capable of extraordinary feats. ChatGPT, for example, knows around 10,000 times more than any human being, and, as the technology advances, that ratio will only increase. Moreover, AI has far greater capacity to learn and share information than the human brain. AI is improving at an exponential rate, and inevitably the time will come when AI will prove far superior to the brain in many domains. Indeed, in certain domains, that moment has already arrived.

However, although AI constitutes a mechanical form of intelligence, quite different to the biological intelligence of the brain, it does similar things. As Margaret Boden puts it, '[Research in] AI seeks to make computers do the sorts of things that minds can do'.[2] In other words, AI is used to do things that would normally require human intelligence. Moreover, although the mechanical intelligence of AI is quite different to the biological intelligence of the brain, it is a form of intelligence nonetheless.

Then comes the crucial question: is consciousness really so important? We have always clung to this as being the essential difference between us and machines, despite their growing intelligence. As Max Tegmark notes, 'We humans have built our identity of being *Homo sapiens*, the smartest entities around. As we prepare to be humbled by ever smarter machines, I suggest that we rebrand ourselves as Homo sentiens!'[3] However, many scholars are now beginning to question the importance of consciousness. If, as most neuroscientists claim, consciousness is highly subjective, just how reliable is it? But aside from that, is it even that relevant? As Yuval Harari puts it, 'Which of the two is really important, intelligence or consciousness?'[4] For corporations and armies, at any rate, '[I]ntelligence is mandatory, but consciousness is optional'.[5] What really matters, surely, is not whether or not a machine is conscious so much as whether or not it can be effective. Provided my toaster can produce good toast, who cares whether it is conscious or not? As such, provided AI does its job well, the issue of consciousness is perhaps less important than previously thought.

Figure 0.3 Hera Kim, Heart-Shaped Pop-Up Store in New York City, generated using Midjourney, 2024

AI AND ROBOTS

AI is not a robot.

A robot might be controlled by AI, just as a Tesla car might be controlled by AI, but a robot is no more AI than a Tesla car is AI. In fact, AI is essentially software. But it is a special kind of software. AI refers to software systems designed to perform certain tasks that normally would require human intelligence, like understanding language, recognising images, making decisions, and learning from data. Unlike traditional software, which follows fixed rules and logic explicitly programmed by humans, AI today learns patterns from data and adapts over time. AI is therefore very sophisticated software, but it is software nonetheless.

AI is incapable of actually making things. In this respect, it is just like a brain, which also cannot make things. Rather, a brain sends signals to the body through a complex system of nerves and signalling pathways, and it is the body – the hands, especially – that makes things, based on those commands. With AI something similar happens. AI uses control algorithms that send precise instructions to actuators (motors, joints, and so on) to execute certain physical actions. Thus, although AI cannot actually make things, it can control a robotic arm that does, in the same way that the brain controls a biological arm.

Nonetheless, AI can be involved in construction. One strategy, as Wanyu He points out, is to create an AI-driven architectural workflow, using digital tagging and prefabrication.[6] Digital tagging assigns a unique identity to every component. This enables a continuous data flow from design through manufacturing to on-site assembly, allowing AI systems to analyse, optimise, and coordinate complex combinations of standardised components, while reducing errors and ensuring traceability. Prefabrication then acts as the physical realisation of this data logic, shifting construction from a labour-intensive, on-site process to a precision-driven assembly of factory-made elements. By increasing the proportion of off-site production, projects improve in terms of speed, quality control, cost predictability, and environmental efficiency.

Figure 0.4 Angela Gronitz, Tectonic Continuum, generated using Midjourney, 2025

A BRIEF HISTORY OF AI

The term 'Artificial Intelligence' was coined by John McCarthy for a summer workshop held in Dartmouth College in 1956, where some of the smartest minds in computer science and related disciplines in the States got together to explore the potential of AI.

In fact, what we now call AI already existed at the time. It was part of the field of cybernetics.[7] But the problem was that cybernetics meant so much more besides. It effectively combined control theory, feedback systems, biology, and early computing. It had become 'a grand unifying theory of the biological, the technological and even the social'.[8] In short, the term *cybernetics* was too broad, and covered too many unrelated topics; and, for many, it was too biological, with its emphasis on feedback and adaptation. By contrast, McCarthy's vision of AI was rooted in formal logic and mathematics – what would later become Symbolic AI. McCarthy wanted the term to emphasise intelligence as a property of machines that could be formally defined and engineered, rather than mimicked from biology or natural systems.[9] The coining of the new term AI was therefore a very deliberate strategic move, aimed at making a distinction between AI and cybernetics, and establishing a clearly delineated new field of research. As a result, the two overlapping research fields began to split into two distinct branches: cybernetics and AI. As Margaret Boden puts it, 'Those interested in life stayed in cybernetics, and those interested in the mind turned to symbolic computing'.[10]

The initial aspirations of this group of AI pioneers were somewhat overoptimistic. Their aim was nothing less than to solve the basic problems of AI within a few years. This never happened. AI proved far more challenging that had first been thought. Indeed, despite the initial high expectations, AI simply did not live up to the hype. As a result of this – and other factors – research into AI went through a series of 'AI winters', where confidence in the potential of AI collapsed and funding was withdrawn.

An important factor in this lack of progress could have been the fact that researchers had been pursuing the wrong approach to AI.[11] In the early days, the two dominant approaches were Symbolic AI, which followed an approach based on Logic, and Connectionist AI, which was based on neural networks and modelled on the brain. Neural networks had actually been explored from the very early days of computation by Pitts and McCulloch.[12] There is also evidence to suggest that two other leading figures, Alan Turing and John von Neumann, were also in favour of neural networks, and had both developed an interest in cybernetics and the brain. Also, some progress was being made by Frank Rosenblatt, who had developed the

Figure 0.5 Marcelo Ertorteguy, School of Architecture Reimagined, Universidad Central de Venezuela, Caracas, generated using Midjourney, 2025

Perceptron, an early neural network.[13] These three – Turing, von Neumann, and Rosenblatt – represented this alternative approach, based on neural networks.

A HISTORY OF ACCIDENTS

The history of AI can be understood as a history of 'accidents', and it could be argued that one of the factors that condemned AI to relative unproductivity during its first 50 years of existence was the deaths of all three of these key players who otherwise might have taken AI along a different path.

Tragically, all three died early, Turing by suicide in 1954, von Neumann from cancer in 1957, and Rosenblatt in a boating accident in 1971.[14] Had they lived longer, they might have shifted the balance in favour of neural networks. But alongside this, what sealed the fate of neural networks was the publication of a book written by Marvin Minsky and Seymour Papert, where they argued broadly that neural networks had severe limitations.[15] Many took the book as a critique of Connectionism, and it had the unintended effect of slowing down research on neural networks for over a decade.

This left Symbolic AI as the dominant approach. But Symbolic AI failed to deliver. Indeed, by the time the survivors of the initial workshop on AI in 1956 got back together for a reunion on the 50th anniversary of that historic event, they had to confess that they had precious little to show for all their work. Not only that, but they also predicted that there would be little to show in the next 50 years.[16] By a curious coincidence, however, 2006 – the year of their reunion – was roughly the time when AI was beginning to work.

What saved AI was also something of an accident, but a happy one. By far the biggest reason for this lack of progress had been the limited computation power available at the time. By a pure coincidence, it was discovered that graphic processing units (GPUs), although initially developed for the gaming industry before the turn of the millennium, had the additional capacity to transform computers into powerful machines capable of performing complex and resource-intensive tasks efficiently.[17] With the discovery of GPUs, computers were at last powerful enough to support the lofty expectations in terms of AI. Partly as a result of this, neural networks started to work, and became far more effective than approaches based on symbolic AI. In backing Symbolic AI, it would seem, the AI community had backed the wrong horse.

There were other reasons why AI had made so little progress initially. Early AI systems did not really 'learn'. They had to be hand-coded with rules. This limited their ability to adapt or generalise to new problems. Likewise, modern machine learning thrives on huge amounts of data. But in the early years of AI, digital data was scarce. There were no internet-scale datasets on which to train models. Indeed, the internet itself did not yet exist. As the internet took off, however, companies started to digitise more of their processes, and systematically store the resulting information. It was only then that 'big data' took off, and there was a sufficient abundance of data on which to train AI models. It was with this 'perfect storm' of conditions that the scene was set for the eventual triumph of the long overlooked approach based on neural networks – Connectionist AI – over the preferred, rival approach, Symbolic AI.

Figure 0.6 David Alf, Open Plan Living Carved into the Cast Concrete Mass, generated using Midjourney, 2025

THE DEEP LEARNING REVOLUTION

With the eventual success of neural networks, the Deep Learning revolution had begun. Deep Learning can be understood as a subset of Machine Learning, which is itself a subset of the broader category of AI. Think of these three categories like Russian dolls nested inside each other. These days, if anyone is referring to AI, chances are that they are referring to Deep Learning. Chatbots, such as ChatGPT and Claude, and Diffusion Models, such as Midjourney, are all based on Deep Learning. Deep Learning represents a significant advance on Machine Learning. Whereas Machine Learning used algorithms, Deep Learning uses neural networks, and whereas Machine Learning relies on manual engineering, Deep Learning learns directly from raw data. Deep Learning gets its name – 'deep' – from the vast number of layers – anything up to 1000 layers – in a neural network.

If there is one figure that we could point to as being highly instrumental in initiating the Deep Learning revolution, it is surely Geoffrey Hinton, who had drifted into AI almost by accident, through his interest in how the brain works. Hinton stubbornly persisted with neural networks, in the belief that for AI to work properly, it needed to be modelled loosely on the brain.[18] Eventually his persistence paid off. And this is what set the scene for the Deep Learning Revolution.

Figure 0.7 Massimo Russo, Visions of New Buildings 1 – Decompositions, generated using Stable Diffusion, 2025

In 2018, Hinton – often referred to as the 'Godfather of AI' – received the Turing Award along with his two doctoral researchers, Yann LeCun and Yoshua Bengio, for their work on Deep Learning.[19] In 2024, Hinton was awarded the Nobel Prize for Physics.[20]

IMAGENET

If there was one single event that suddenly brought Hinton's work and the potential of neural networks to the attention of the computer science community, it was the 2012 ImageNet competition organised by Fei-Fei Li, herself often regarded as the 'Godmother of AI'. Although the introduction of GPUs meant that neural networks were finally beginning to work, few were aware of this development. It took a high-profile event such as this to draw it to people's attention. At the time, of course, neural networks were still largely considered to be an obsolete technology. Imagine the shock, then, when Hinton's team from the University of Toronto, including Alex Krizhevsky and Ilya Sutskever, showcased their AlexNet convolutional neural network, and won the event by a huge margin. This is how Li herself describes the event:

> What was most startling about the submission was how it did what it did. Despite the decades of development and widespread interest in the modern algorithms that had won in the previous two years, its authors chose to bring the neural network back from the dead – and were absolutely steamrolling the competition with it. Second place wasn't even close . . . A 10-percentage-point leap? In a single year? And from a neural network? . . . It was like being told that the land speed record had been broken by a margin of a hundred miles per hour in a Honda Civic.[21]

In one single stroke of genius, Hinton and his team had put neural networks on the map.

Hinton was to joke about the AlexNet project, 'Ilya thought that we should do it, Alex made it work, and I got the Nobel Prize'.[22]

DEEPDREAM

This, however, was just the beginning. The holy grail for the computer science community was the capacity not to recognise an image, but to generate one.

Figure 0.8 David Alf, Kyoto House 2, generated using Midjourney, 2025

It soon became clear that it would be possible to 'invert the network'. In other words, instead of a neural network being run from left to right – from image to text – so as to recognise an image, it could be run from right to left – from text to image – so as to generate an image. A version of this technique was developed by Alex Mordvintsev of Google, and became known as

DeepDream.[23] This was the first example of AI being used to generate images, the beginning, in other words, of what we now call 'generative AI'.

The resultant images, however, looked somewhat trippy, in that information on where to position objects in an image had been lost, so that objects in the resultant image were all over the place, or 'pose invariant'. Moreover, the process modified the images somewhat and exaggerated certain features. Think of it like a form of 'AI pareidolia' – the tendency to see faces or objects in random patterns, but from the AI's point of view. DeepDream caused something of a sensation at the time, and an exhibition of DeepDream – the

Figure 0.9 Balaji Bal, An Architecture of Division, generated using Midjourney, 2025

first ever exhibition of AI-generated art – curated by Blaise Agüera y Arcas, was held in San Francisco in 2016.[24]

GANS

An important step forward in terms of generative AI came with the invention of generative adversarial networks (GANs). Originally proposed by Ian Goodfellow in 2014, a GAN is based on two competing neural networks, a 'generator' and a 'discriminator'.[25] The 'generator' generates images from random noise, while the 'discriminator' judges them against a training set, rejecting those of an insufficient standard. This is a bit like an artist being judged by a critic. In the process the 'discriminator' trains the 'generator'. GANs proved to be very popular, and many different versions – a whole 'zoo' of GAN models – were developed. GANs were definitely an improvement on DeepDream, but they were not without their limitations. GANs took a long time to train, required an advanced understanding of computation, and produced outcomes low in resolution. Unsurprisingly, not everyone was convinced by GANs.

Meanwhile, architects found themselves a long way behind. A few pioneers had begun exploring the possibilities of GANs, and with time the number of researchers presenting papers on AI at conferences, such as ACADIA, began to pick up. But the first person to generate a GAN image of an architectural design was most likely the media artist Refik Anadol in 2019, using his version of a StyleGAN.[26] Daniel Bolojan took this further, and started using CycleGANs to effectively 'breed' images, by using two unpaired datasets.[27] Whereas StyleGANs could interpolate images by effectively blending or averaging the data to produce novel images, but ones which were always constrained by their dataset, CycleGANs were able to extrapolate, and introduce totally novel forms. Gradually, architects were beginning to pay attention to AI.

Eventually, the first ever mainstream book on AI and architecture in the English language of the Deep Learning era, *Architecture in the Age of Artificial Intelligence: An Introduction to AI for Architects*, was published at the end of 2021, and was followed by a slew of other books on the topic in early 2022.[28] By mid-2022, however, a very significant technical breakthrough was to happen which would not only fire up interest in AI, but also render these books out of date, at least in terms of their illustrations.

Figure 0.10 Greg Tate, Traffic Jambing, Midjourney, 2025

DIFFUSION MODELS

OpenAI caused something of a sensation when it announced its new diffusion model, DALL-E 2, in April 2022, and released some images that it had generated. One particular image – an astronaut riding a horse – attracted considerable attention. It showed how the model was able to interpolate successfully what an astronaut riding a horse would have looked like, even if there had probably never been an instance of an astronaut riding a horse. By extension, it also served to illustrate that AI does not copy, despite what some architectural historians might think.[29]

The diffusion model was a major breakthrough, and represented a considerable improvement on the GAN model. It is both substantially quicker than a GAN and much easier to use, in that it does not require advanced computational knowledge on the part of the user. In addition, the resolution of the images generated is far superior. As a result, the diffusion model has more or less rendered the GAN obsolete.

A diffusion model operates in a very different way to a GAN model. Rather than using two competing neural networks, it uses two diffusion processes, the first one to disrupt an image using forward diffusion, and the second one to repair the image

Figure 0.11 David Alf, Cozy Terrace, generated using Midjourney, 2025

using backward diffusion. In so doing it generates an entirely novel image, that – by definition – cannot be a copy. Also, unlike a GAN, a diffusion model is pretrained. It is a giant neural network trained on a vast quantity of generic data. Finally, it is a text-to-image model that works through prompts – text descriptions – that generate images, by effectively searching through its vast dataset and matching images with words through captions and other verbal descriptions.

OpenAI announced the first ever commercial diffusion text-to-image model on 6 April 2022. Surprisingly, however, OpenAI did not actually release a Beta version of DALL-E 2 until July 2022, by which time Midjourney had already released a rival version, thus failing to capitalise on its initial role as the market leader. There then followed a host of other models including Stable Diffusion, and other proprietary models, such as LookX, that are themselves based on Stable Diffusion. For the moment at least, Midjourney appears to be the diffusion model of choice among architects, although LookX is also highly popular because it is trained specifically on architectural data.

TEXT TO VIDEO

History appeared to be repeating itself when OpenAI posted a series of remarkable videos in February 2024 generated by its new text-to-video model, Sora, shocking the world with its extraordinary breakthrough.[30] Text-to-video models had been around since late 2022, but had produced nothing anywhere near as impressive as this. Sora appeared to be a game changer. But again – somewhat surprisingly – OpenAI waited over half a year before actually releasing Sora. This delay opened the doors for other text-to-video models, such as Runway Gen-3 and Luma.[31]

When Sora was eventually released on 9 December 2024, it became clear that it was indeed superior to its competitors, but within days Google had released its own highly impressive text-to-video model, Veo 2, leaving Sora on the back foot. Since then, the market has been inundated with new text-to-video models launched on an almost daily basis, not least the far superior second version, Sora 2, and some remarkable Chinese models.[32] So which platform is the best? This is far from clear. What is clear, however, is that competition is becoming intense, and that no text-to-video model remains at the top for long. In March 2026, OpenAI announced that Sora would be withdrawn.

PERFORMANCE-BASED DESIGN

Much of the recent interest in diffusion models, such as Midjourney, has been centred around the generation of images and videos. This overlooks perhaps the most important potential contribution of AI – performance-based design. Performance-based AI design, as Theodoros Galanos notes, refers to a design approach that uses AI to generate, evaluate, and optimise design solutions according to specific, measurable performance criteria, such as structural efficiency, environmental impact, cost, or

Figure 0.12 Robert Cha, Singularity Performing Art Center, digital rendering, generated with Midjourney, Gemini, Magnific, and Photoshop, 2025

user experience.[33] Unlike traditional design driven by aesthetics or intuition alone, performance-based AI design is goal-oriented. Likewise, performance-based AI can also be used to optimise designs. AI models can often work alongside simulation tools, such as energy analysis tools, to assess a building's fitness. These might include 'surrogate models' that can offer approximate but rapid simulations at lower computational cost, to give the designer a 'rough idea' of performance; so too they might include multi-object optimisation to balance conflicting criteria, such as cost versus performance, and machine learning algorithms used to predict performance outcomes.

AI is also poised to automate many aspects of architectural design in the future. It will streamline time-consuming tasks such as code compliance checks, including building regulations and fire safety. It will help to generate layouts, simulate environmental conditions, and keep check of cost. It will also be possible to integrate AI with building information modelling (BIM) and other design tools. In short, AI will find itself embedded in all our design applications.

WHAT DO WE MEAN BY THE AI DESIGN REVOLUTION?

Let's start by defining the term 'revolution'.[34] A revolution refers to an 'overturning' – a radical change that alters the fundamental structure or logic of how things are done. It refers to a disruptive moment that breaks from previous models or norms, and is transformational in that it redefines the possibilities within the field. A revolution constitutes a paradigm shift in a way of operating, acting as a catalyst for further changes.

How, then, might generative AI lead to a revolution in the design process?

Generative AI (text-to-image, text-to-form, text-to-video) radically overhauls the design process from being a human-centred, intuition-driven process, by introducing a new form of computational agency into the design process. AI becomes a form of co-curator, generating endless iterations and options.

Algorithmic design had already set the scene for generative AI. With algorithmic design we began to witness the emergence of a fundamentally different way of designing. When using an algorithmic approach, it is less a question of designers imposing form from above than conducting a bottom-up search for solutions. This challenges many traditional assumptions about the design process:

> If we think through the logic of the search in the context of 'design', what such an approach suggests is that if all possible solutions already exist, it is simply a question of defining a set of constraints and conducting a search, and then selecting one of the many outcomes. The potential implications of this are far reaching. Not only does it challenge the traditional notion of the 'genius' of the architect/designer and the originality of the work of art, but it also suggests that if there is still any creativity in the 'design' process, it should lie, firstly, in defining the constraints that generate the range of possible solutions to a problem, and, secondly, in developing an effective method of filtering or evaluating them.[35]

This echoes, in some sense, the way that photography has shifted from the singular, perfectly planned photograph that was taken in the past with a camera carefully set up on a tripod, to taking a burst of sample photos in the present, from which one outcome is eventually selected and then digitally enhanced. The shift, then, is towards defining a search space, selecting the best outcome, and then carefully editing it. This is a revolutionary new approach that has been consolidated by the emergence of AI.

Generative AI, however, offers significant advantages over algorithmic design, transforming it from rule-based computation into a more open-ended, 'creative', and collaborative process. There are some important distinctions to be made here. Firstly, algorithmic design relies on explicit rules and parameters set by the designer. Generative AI, by contrast, learns patterns from data and introduces probabilistic emergent behaviour – producing results that are not predefined, but inferred, interpolated, or imagined. Secondly, whereas algorithmic design involves coding logic, generative AI uses natural language prompts. These verbal prompts generate images or videos that themselves 'prompt' the designer to imagine a different world. This opens computational design to non-coders. Thirdly, generative AI can explore possibilities that lie beyond human preconceptions, leading to novel geometries and composition. Fourthly, while algorithmic design is often visual-geometric, generative AI is multimodal, making it possible to move fluidly across representations, from words to form, image to structure. Finally, whereas algorithmic design relies on explicit instructions, generative AI learns from data and uses data-driven strategies.

What results is a highly novel approach to design, whereby generative AI helps in brainstorming possibilities that we could otherwise never have imagined. It is also possible to integrate generative AI (in the form of deep learning, diffusion models, and LLMs) with performance-based design, looking at issues such as structural efficiency, energy use, daylighting, and cost). The aim here is to produce designs that are data-informed, goal-directed, and functionally optimised.

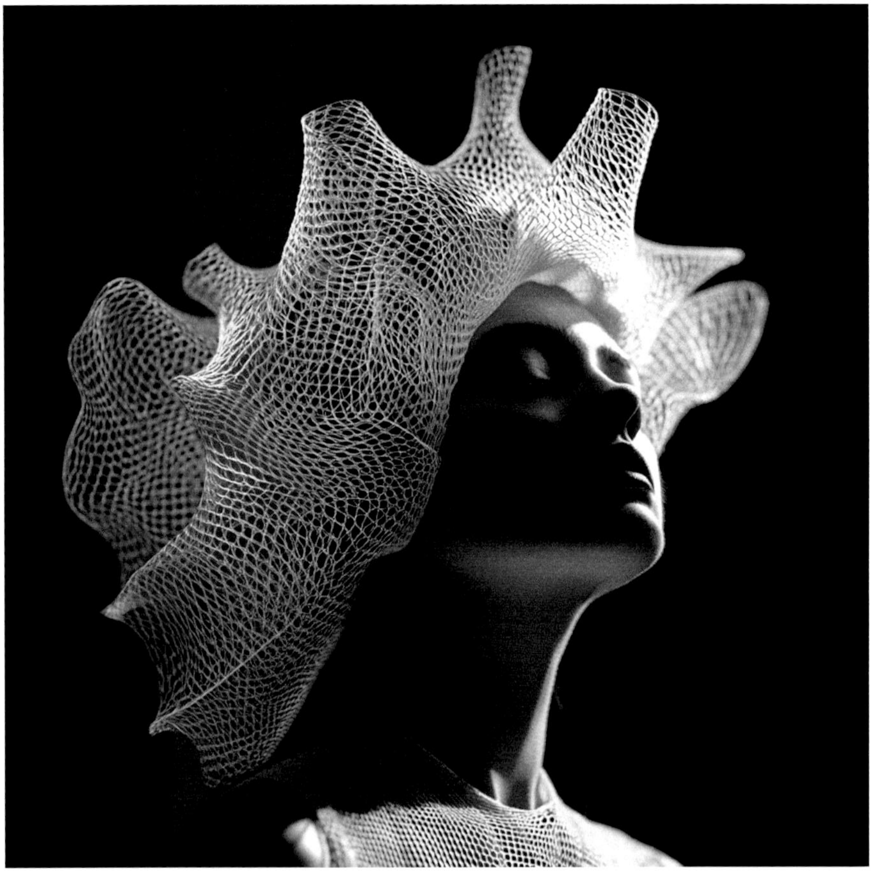

Figure 0.13 Mitra Allahmoradi, Proto Architecture: Tensile Conical Headgear, generated using Midjourney, 2025

FROM CREATOR TO CURATOR: AN INVERTED PROCESS

Generative AI, then, is a revolutionary new process of generating designs. It represents a paradigm shift. The traditional method of operating is inverted. It is no longer a question of the designer sketching out an early concept and then developing it. Rather, the designer writes a prompt, waits to see what outcomes are generated, and then proceeds to iterate from there. Of course, the designer still maintains a limited amount of control, by influencing the way in which the design develops. In the context of diffusion models, such as Midjourney, this means that the designer can select a particular 'seed', and using it to 'breed' different forms – much like a greyhound breeder does by selecting particular 'genes' – and subtly encourage the design to develop in a particular direction. This process is akin to the way in which a professor might attempt to subtly steer a student in the design process, by giving feedback to the student, or indeed how a design principal in an office might offer advice to those working on a project. But with generative AI the designer is never in complete charge, in that the tool itself is difficult to control. At the same time, that very lack of control opens up the door for certain unexpected outcomes. In effect, the designer writes the prompt, but then the outcomes prompt the designer. The process of design has been inverted, opening up a new field of possibilities.

As a result, an important shift also appears to be happening in the nature of design. In effect, the emphasis on judging or 'discriminating' turns us all into 'curators'. No longer is the genius designer – the one with the greatest imagination – the only one to excel. Now the 'curator' – with a refined sense of aesthetic judgment – can also play a role. Indeed, 'a good eye' becomes essential in this new mode of operating. In this context, then, we must all become 'prompt engineers', with a strong command of language. Meanwhile theorists – with their strong command of language – discover a new role for themselves in effectively 'curating' designs. What we see emerging, then, is a new breed of theorist-curators taking on a new 'creative' role within this new landscape of design.

Alongside this – but operating in a radically different way – we find the emerging culture of 'spatially intelligent AI', also referred to as simply 'spatial intelligence'. This is a form of AI operating in 3D that understands physics. Of course, we humans already possess our own sense of 'spatial intelligence'. It's what allows us to operate in the material world. We have been 'trained' – through exposure to countless examples – to understand how that 'real world' operates. We know what it looks like, for example, for someone to climb up a staircase. In this sense, we could also say that we have already developed a form of 'intuitive physics'. In other words, even though we might not be experiencing physics directly, we know what its effects would look like. Now, generative AI has also developed some sense of intuitive physics. For example, it has already begun to generate convincing videos of people climbing a staircase. But 'spatially intelligent AI' goes well beyond this, and, as Neil Leach notes, offers us not an intuitive sense of physics, but a precise simulation of physics.[36] As such, spatially intelligent AI offers architects the chance to model 'worlds' in 3D convincingly during the design process.[37] Unlike generative AI, then, spatially intelligent AI is not a tool for generating designs. Rather, it is a tool which can be used in the design process to help designers understand more precisely their designs in 3D.

FROM GENERATIVE AI TO AGENTIC AI

With the emergence of 'agentic AI', however, there has been a further development – a revolution within the AI design revolution, as it were.[38] With agentic AI, as Daniel Bolojan notes, the logic of 'design' is further reconfigured.[39] The role of the architect shifts from being that of the 'curator' to becoming the 'orchestrator' of a range of agents, each addressing a different concern. With agentic systems, AI becomes an active design participant rather than a passive generative tool, enabling architecture to be approached as an evolving process of negotiation, rather than as a fixed problem that needs to be solved. In this new paradigm, agentic systems do not simply generate forms or optimise predefined parameters; rather these systems are charged with their own modality and logic – with their own 'design intent' – operating within a multimodal scenario. So, for example, a structural agent might be used to simulate structural behaviour, an environmental agent to analyse energy performance, while a spatial agent to optimise circulation patterns, an aesthetic agent to address aesthetic concerns, and so on. With agentic AI, then, AI extends its remit from being a passive generator to an 'active negotiator'. As such, agentic systems help to frame and reframe the design problem itself by proposing options, critiquing outcomes, managing trade-offs between competing criteria such as performance, cost, structure, and cultural intent, and revising strategies as priorities shift. Within this multimodal domain, a distributed network of specialised agents negotiates and opens a 'dialogue of

Figure 0.14 Robert Cha, Mobile Urbanism, digital rendering, generated with Midjourney, Magnific, and Photoshop, 2025

possibilities'. As such, the design emerges not through consensus, but out of the tension between the different, competing agents.

Agentic AI also plays an important role in the context of performance-driven design, as Theodoros Galanos notes.[40] Here agentic AI serves to transform environmental analysis from a late-stage evaluation process into a continuous, goal-oriented design driver. Rather than simply assessing performance after the design process, agentic systems actively steer design exploration by coordinating multiple specialised AI agents – each focusing on different domains, such as energy, daylight, comfort, carbon, microclimate, or code compliance – and orchestrating their interaction with simulation engines, predictive models, and design software. These specialised agents start to work synergistically 'performing multi-objective optimisation across diverse domains simultaneously'.

Design therefore emerges as a form of 'intelligent collaboration'. This allows for more 'intuitive and fluid interfaces' between humans and AI, engendering new forms of collaboration, where AI is seen less as a separate tool, and more as an 'integrated, intelligent collaborator', and a 'partner in the creative and problem-solving context'. Increasingly, we are shifting into a domain that Ethan Mollick calls 'co-intelligence'.[41] Through iterative cycles of generation, evaluation, negotiation, and refinement, agentic AI supports a continuous dialogue between human judgment and machine inference, allowing performance, meaning, and intent to co-evolve while preserving the architect's role as the ultimate curator, ethical guide, and author of design direction. Crucially, then, the architect remains in charge; the architect defines priorities, interprets trade-offs, and makes value-based decisions, while agentic AI handles complexity, speed, and scale. In this way, agentic AI enables performance to become an intrinsic and formative aspect of design, augmenting human judgment rather than replacing it.

A NEW LEXICON?

An important question to be asked, then, is whether or not we might need to adopt a new lexicon of terms to deal with these new conditions.

With traditional design, the designer uses a tool – a pen, pencil, or even computational drafting tools – to produce an authored product – a 'design' – through a linear and iterative series of decisions. Even parametric and algorithmic design methods, despite their sophistication, remain

Figure 0.15 David Alf, Enmeshed in the Treehouse, generated using Midjourney, 2025

procedurally legible: the designer defines the rules, and iteration unfolds within a known logic.

Generative AI, however, challenges traditional approaches to design. With generative AI, it is no longer the case of a designer producing 'designs', so much as AI generating 'outcomes'. These emerge as fully formed objects, often without a traceable lineage. The system does not operate through explicit rules, or deterministic logic. Rather design moves occur in a high dimensional abstract space that cannot be directly observed. In effect, Generative AI operates through neural networks, which, like the brain itself, are black boxes. Generative AI does not compute, it hallucinates; it does not derive, it interpolates; it does not solve, it samples. The 'outcomes' are 'generated', although the underlying logic remains something of a mystery. It is then the role of the 'designer' to evaluate those 'outcomes' and work with the preferred one. As such, we should maybe question whether the verb 'to design' might still be so appropriate with these new ways of operating. Should we not use the verb 'to generate' instead? And, as for the final product of this generative process, does the noun 'design' still make so much sense anymore? Should we not use the noun 'outcome' or 'possibility' instead?

With agentic AI a further shift has occurred. Generative AI systems are primarily concerned with producing artifacts. They do not possess goals of their own, nor do they act autonomously in the world. Agentic AI systems, by contrast, are defined by goal-directed behaviour. They plan, act, evaluate outcomes, and adapt over time. While with generative AI, the designer remains the primary agent, with agentic AI the design process is distributed. It becomes non-linear, adaptive, and open-ended, resembling an ongoing conversation or co-evolution rather than a sequence of iterations. If with generative AI, we sample and curate, with agentic AI, we delegate decisions but maintain control and orchestrate the process. If the terms used for generative AI include 'prompting', 'curating', 'iterating', and 'sampling', the terms used for agentic AI include 'delegation', 'goal-setting', 'orchestration', and 'co-evolution'. There is a clear difference. Generative AI produces 'possibilities'; agentic AI pursues 'objectives'. Because they transform different aspects of design – one reconfiguring the process of design itself, the other one distributing agency in design – a new lexicon would seem to be necessary. Without it, architectural discourse risks describing radically new practices using concepts inherited from a fundamentally different epistemic regime.

Whether we adopt new terms, or simply change the way in which we use existing terms, it is clear that AI has genuinely disrupted traditional methods of design, first by the shift to generative AI, and then with the shift to agentic AI.

CONCLUSION

Ultimately, *The AI Design Revolution: From Representation to Agentic Architecture* is not about faster rendering, richer imagery, or even expanded formal possibilities. It is about a structural shift in the approach to design itself. Where architecture once relied on static representations – drawings, models, and simulations that described a world from the outside – it now confronts systems capable of operating within that world as adaptive, intelligent agents. The revolution lies in this migration from representation to participation, from image to model, from tool to collaborator. In moving into the age of agentic architecture, we are not simply upgrading our instruments; we are redefining what it means to design.

Welcome to the AI Design Revolution!

NOTES

1 Adrian Malleson, 'RIBA AI Survey: Findings', *RIBA AI Report*, 2024. www.riba.org/work/insights-and-resources/ai-report/riba-artificial-intelligence-report-2024/
2 Margaret Boden, *AI: Its Nature and Future*, Oxford: Oxford University Press, 2016, p. 1.
3 Max Tegmark, *Life 3.0: Being Human in the Age of Artificial Intelligence*, New York: Vintage, 2017, p. 314.
4 Yuval Noah Harari, *Homo Deus: A Brief History of Tomorrow*, New York: HarperCollins, 2017, p. 314.
5 Harari, *Homo Deus*, p. 314.
6 Wanyu He, 'From Data to Fabrication', pp. 63–81.
7 Blaise Agüera y Arcas, *Intelligence: Lessons from AI About Evolution, Computing and Minds*, Cambridge, MA: MIT Press, 2025.
8 The term 'cybernetics' was itself coined in 1947 by MIT Mathematician Norbert Wiener and several others. Agüera y Arcas, *Intelligence.*
9 Importantly, Wiener himself was not invited to the workshop in Dartmouth College. Nils J. Nilsson, *The Quest for Artificial Intelligence*, Cambridge: Cambridge University Press, 2009.
10 Margaret Boden, *AI: Its Nature and Future*, Oxford: Oxford University Press, 2016, p. 79.
11 In fact, there were broadly five different approaches to AI – or 'tribes' as Pedro Domingos calls them – in the first 50 years: Symbolists, Connectionists, Evolutionaries, Bayesians, and Analogisers. Pedro Domingos, *The Master Algorithm: Why the Quest for the Ultimate Learning Machine Will Remake the World*, New York: Basic Books, 2018.
12 Warren McCulloch and Walter Pitts, 'A Logical Calculus of the Ideas Immanent in Nervous Activity', *Bulletin of Mathematical Biophysics* 5 (1943): 115–133.
13 Frank Rosenblatt, *Principles of Neurodynamics*, Washington, DC: Spartan Books, 1962.
14 Many have suspected that the death of von Neumann might have been caused through exposure to radiation during the Manhattan Project in which he was involved.
15 Marvin Minsky and Seymour Papert, *Perceptrons: An Introduction to Computational Geometry*, Cambridge, MA: MIT Press, 1969.
16 Blaise Agüera y Arcas and Melanie Mitchell, 'How Close Are We to AI?', Seattle Town Hall, 14 July 2022, www.youtube.com/watch?v=Bi8IIolOq2g
17 This is because whereas CPUs have a few powerful cores, GPUs have thousands of smaller cores, perfect for doing many simple operations in parallel. GPUs can therefore perform certain parallel tasks way faster than CPUs. This has had the effect of significantly improving the capabilities of computers.
18 Hinton comes from a highly distinguished family in the UK. His great-great-grandfather was George Boole, of Boolean geometry fame. Hinton's journey into the world of AI was decidedly circuitous. Unsure of which discipline to pursue at the University of Cambridge, Hinton studied architecture for

two days, until he discovered that it was not for him. He then tried out a range of other disciplines, including natural sciences, history of art, and philosophy, before settling for a degree in experimental psychology, as he was interested in understanding how the brain works.

19 Although Hinton is known more generally as the person who rediscovered neural networks, and popularised deep neural networks, he has been responsible for a number of highly significant innovations, including the development of the backpropagation algorithm. This is a technique that allows a neural network to correct various prediction errors, by adjusting its weights, thereby allowing the system to converge on the correct answer. https://awards.acm.org/about/2018-turing

20 The Nobel Prize was shared with John Hopfield. The prize was awarded for his early work on neural networks in the 1980s, specifically the development of the Bolzmann machine, that utilised principles from statistical physics to enable machines to learn to recognise characteristic elements in a set of data.

21 Fei-Fei Li, *The Worlds I See: Curiosity, Exploration, and Discovery at the Dawn of AI*, New York: Flatiron, 2023, pp. 195–196.

22 Hansen Hsu, 'CHM Releases AlexNet Source Code', Computer History Museum, 20 March 2025. https://computerhistory.org/blog/chm-releases-alexnet-source-code

23 DeepDream was based on earlier research undertaken by others as part of the ImageNet Large-Scale Visual Recognition Challenge (ILSVRC) in 2014. Christian Szegedy, Wei Lu, Yangqing Jia, Pierre Sermanet, Scott Reed, Dragomir Anguelov, Dumitru Erhan, Vincent Vanhoucke, and Andrew Rabinovich, 'Going Deeper with Convolutions', *Computing Research Repository* (2014), https://arxiv.org/abs/1409.4842.

24 www.theverge.com/google/2016/3/1/11140374/google-neural-networks-deepdream-art-exhibition-san-francisco

25 Ian Goodfellow, JeanPouget-Abadie, Mehdi Mirza, Bing Xu, David Warde-Farley, Sherjil Ozair, Aaron Courville', and Yoshua Bengio, *Generative Adversarial Networks. Proceedings of the International Conference on Neural Information Processing Systems*, NIPS 2014, pp. 2672–2680.

26 This image appears on the cover of Neil Leach, *Architecture in the Age of AI: An Introduction to AI for Architects*, London: Bloomsbury, 2021.

27 Leach, *Architecture in the Age of AI*, p. 104.

28 Leach, *Architecture in the Age of AI*; Phil Bernstein, *Machine Learning: Architecture in the Age of Artificial Intelligence*, London: RIBA Publishing, 2022, Neil Leach and Matias del Campo, *Machine Hallucinations: Architecture and Artificial Intelligence*, London: Wiley, 2022; Stanislas Chaillou, *Artificial Intelligence and Architecture: From Research to Practice*, Cham: Birkhäuser, 2022.

29 Mario Carpo, 'Imitation Games', *Art Forum*, Summer 2023.

30 https://openai.com/sora

31 https://runwayml.com; https://lumalabs.ai

32 The Sora web and app experienced were discontinued on 26 April 2026. https://help.openai.com/en/articles/20001152-what-to-know-about-the-sora-discontinuation

33 Theodoros Galanos, 'Introduction', pp. 189–194.

34 As has been noted, 'The term "revolution" is frequently overused, often as a mere marketing strategy to promote the latest trends or fashion. Indeed, "revolution" is often used in many design disciplines, including architecture, to refer to ephemeral changes in aesthetics. In short, the term, "revolution", itself has often been aestheticized'. Neil Leach, *The Anaesthetics of Architecture*, Cambridge, MA: MIT Press, 1999.

35 Neil Leach, 'There Is No Such Thing as Digital Design', in David Gerber and Mariana Ibanez (eds), *Paradigms in Computing: Making, Machines, and Models for Design Agency in Architecture*, Los Angeles: eVolo Press, 2014, pp. 148–158.

36 Neil Leach, 'Predictive Design: AI, Neuroscience, and Architecture', pp. 135–160.

37 See, for example, Marble, a frontier multimodal world model, developed by World Labs. www.worldlabs.ai/blog/marble-world-model

38 We should be cautious, however, and not overstate the agency of AI. Genuine agency would include having a sense of intrinsic goals, possessing intentional beliefs, having the capacity to self-model, possessing normative understanding, and having a sense of counterfactual ownership ('I could have done otherwise') – none of which current AI systems possess.

39 Daniel Bolojan, 'Agentic Creativity: Towards Agentic AI in Design', pp. 107–127.

40 Theodoros Galanos, 'AI, Agentic Automation, and the Future of Design and Engineering', p. 217

41 Ethan Mollick, *Co-Intelligence: Living and Working with AI*, New York: Portfolio, 2024.

PART 1

AI AND THE ARCHITECTURAL OFFICE

WANYU HE

Figure 1.1.1 Longmenshan Biodiversity Museum, China

CHAPTER 1.1
INTRODUCTION

Wanyu He

The architectural profession stands at the precipice of a transformative era, one where AI promises to redefine workflows, enhance creativity, and reshape the very foundations of design practice. While debates persist about whether AI will replace architects or merely augment their capabilities, we can imagine a future where AI serves as a collaborative partner, liberating professionals from repetitive tasks while amplifying their capacity for innovation. This vision hinges on understanding how AI integrates with the core functions of architectural offices – design, project management, compliance, sustainability, and client collaboration – while respecting the irreplaceable human elements of creativity, ethics, and cultural sensitivity.

At its core, the architectural office remains a hub for translating human needs into physical spaces through consultation, design, and technical execution. Key functions include:

- Client-driven design processes requiring nuanced interpretation of preferences and cultural contexts
- Technical workflows spanning 2D drafting (e.g., AutoCAD), 3D modelling (Rhino, Revit), and BIM coordination
- Regulatory navigation through complex zoning laws and sustainability standards
- Cross-disciplinary collaboration with engineers, urban planners, and contractors

While digital tools like BIM software have revolutionised drafting efficiency, they remain constrained by manual input requirements and linear workflows. Even advanced tools like Revit still require architects to manually input and

DOI: 10.4324/9781003347330- 3

manipulate data, leaving the creative ideation process fundamentally human-driven. This sets the stage for AI's disruptive potential – not as a replacement, but as a force multiplier.

The integration of AI introduces paradigm-shifting capabilities across the architectural value chain:

- Generative Design Innovation: AI algorithms can rapidly produce thousands of design variations optimised for parameters like energy efficiency, spatial functionality, and material costs. Tools like XKool's 'AI Creative Library' demonstrate how inputting keywords like 'Zaha Hadid style' generates concept renderings that respect architectural DNA while exploring novel forms. This accelerates early-stage ideation while preserving human oversight for cultural and aesthetic refinement.
- Predictive Project Management: Machine learning models analyse historical project data to forecast timelines, budget risks, and resource allocation needs with 92% greater accuracy than traditional methods in pilot implementations. AI-enhanced platforms like Deltek Ajera now automate progress tracking while flagging potential compliance issues in real time.
- Sustainable Design Optimisation: By simulating microclimate impacts, material lifecycles, and energy flows, AI enables data-driven sustainability decisions. XKool's daylight optimisation algorithms automatically adjust building massing to meet lighting regulations while preserving design intent – a process that previously required weeks of manual analysis.
- Immersive Client Collaboration: AI-powered VR/AR tools like XKool's cloud-based visualisation platform allow clients to interact with photorealistic 3D models, making iterative design changes in real time. This reduces revision cycles by 40% in pilot projects while improving stakeholder alignment.

While AI-generated 2D renderings have achieved professional-grade results, 3D model generation remains challenging. XKool's experiments with point cloud reconstruction and material prediction have revealed persistent issues:

- Data scarcity: Only 12% of architectural firms maintain AI-ready 3D model libraries.
- Material complexity: Algorithms struggle with light-reflective properties and contextual material appropriateness.

- Precision gaps: Current AI-generated models achieve only 78% geometric accuracy versus human-designed equivalents.

Emerging solutions include hybrid workflows where AI handles massing studies and structural optimisation, while architects refine details. The adoption of SMART L5 standards – machine-readable 3D models with embedded regulatory logic – promises to bridge this gap by 2030.

It is clear that the architect remains essential, in that there are four irreplaceably human roles:

- Cultural interpretation: AI lacks contextual understanding of heritage sites or community symbolism.
- Ethical judgment: Algorithms cannot weigh gentrification impacts or social equity concerns.
- Creative intuition: While AI generates options, humans curate designs with emotional resonance.
- Adaptive problem-solving: Unprecedented challenges (e.g., climate-resilient structures) require human ingenuity.

As noted in our analysis, 'AI operates on data patterns, but architecture operates on human stories'. This dichotomy ensures architects will transition from drafters to 'design strategists', focusing on high-level creative direction while AI handles technical execution.

The future office will likely adopt a blended operational model:

- AI copilots: Embedded in tools like Revit plugins for automated code compliance checks.
- Cloud collaboration: XKool's 'ABC' system enables real-time global teamwork on centralised BIM models.
- Specialised AI roles: Prompt engineers tailoring generative algorithms to firm-specific design languages.

Firms embracing this transition report 35% faster project delivery and 20% higher client satisfaction scores. However, success requires reinvesting efficiency gains into creative R&D – training architects in AI literacy, while nurturing the human-centric skills that algorithms cannot replicate.

In conclusion, the architectural office of 2030 will likely resemble a symphony orchestra more than a factory floor – AI instruments amplifying human conductors who blend technical mastery with creative vision. This evolution promises not obsolescence, but renaissance: 'Liberated from documentation drudgery, architects can finally focus on architecture'. The future belongs not to AI alone, nor to humans resisting change, but to those who harness this symbiosis of both AI and human contributions in order to build smarter, more humane environments.

Figure 1.2.1 Ross Lovegrove, LookX rendering on CAD wireframe to building, 2023

CHAPTER 1.2
POWERED BY AI
THE ARCHITECTURAL OFFICE OF THE FUTURE

Wanyu He

FROM DRAFTING BOARDS TO DIGITAL STUDIOS: HOW ARCHITECTURAL OFFICES HAVE EVOLVED

Architectural offices have always been spaces of creativity, collaboration, and meticulous planning. However, with the rapid rise of AI, questions are emerging about the future of the profession. Some envision a future where architects are largely replaced by intelligent machines, while others see AI as a collaborator that amplifies human creativity. Before we can speculate about what lies ahead, we must first step inside the architectural office – examining how architects currently conceive, design, and refine their creations.

By understanding the core functions and roles that define an architectural office, we can better anticipate how AI might transform this landscape. Whether augmenting creativity, streamlining operations, or opening new avenues for innovation, the integration of AI promises to reshape the very foundations of architectural practice.

An architectural office is a professional workspace where architects and related staff carry out the design, planning, and oversight of building projects and other physical structures. Here are the key services that an architectural office offers[1]:

- **Consultation:** Architects often consult with clients to understand their needs, preferences, budget, and any specific requirements for the space or building. This consultation process helps in tailoring designs to meet the exact needs of the clients.

DOI: 10.4324/9781003347330- 4

Figure 1.2.2 Urban Intervention, generated using LookX, 2025

- **Design and Planning:** The primary function of an architectural office is to provide design services for new constructions, renovations, and extensions. This includes the production of detailed drawings, 3D models, and renderings to visualise projects before construction begins.
- **Project Management:** Many architectural offices also handle project management duties, which include coordinating with stakeholders, overseeing construction to ensure it adheres to the design, managing timelines, and staying within budget.
- **Regulatory Compliance:** Architects must ensure that all designs comply with local, state, and federal building codes and regulations. This involves understanding complex zoning laws and environmental restrictions.
- **Collaboration:** Architectural offices often work with other professionals, such as engineers, interior designers, landscape architects, and urban planners, to ensure that all aspects of a project are integrated and fully coordinated.
- **Sustainability and Innovation:** Many architectural offices focus on sustainable design, aiming to minimise environmental impact through energy-efficient buildings, use of sustainable materials, and environmentally friendly practices.
- **Research and Development:** Continual research into new materials, technologies, and methods is common in architectural practices to enable

them to stay at the forefront of the industry and offer innovative solutions to clients.

Traditionally, architectural work has been performed by human architects using software tools like AutoCAD, Rhino, Revit, and others. These tools represent modern equivalents to older, physical tools such as rulers, compasses, tracing paper, and paper documents. The evolution of these tools has significantly transformed architects' workflows. For example, CAD software allows architects the flexibility to revise every detail of a design with options to undo, redo, and replicate repetitive elements, enhancing efficiency not just in architectural practices but across the entire building industry.

The typical workflow with existing software:

- **Conceptualisation and Initial Design**
  a. SketchUp: Ideal for quick 3D modelling and visualisation of initial concepts.
  b. Excel: Useful for early project calculations, such as preliminary budgeting and feasibility studies.
- **Detailed Design and Drafting**
  a. AutoCAD: Provides precision for detailed 2D drafting and initial 3D modelling.
  b. Rhino: Applied for designing complex forms and geometries, often used here for its advanced modelling capabilities.
- **Building Information Modelling (BIM) and Documentation**
  a. Revit: Integrates all building design aspects into a unified BIM model, ideal for detailed 3D modelling and documentation (Monograph).
  b. ArchiCAD: Similar to Revit, used for comprehensive BIM and project documentation.
- **Visualisation and Client Presentations**
  a. V-Ray: Employed for creating high-quality detailed renderings from BIM or 3D models.
  b. Lumion: Used for quick and beautiful real-time visualisations and walkthroughs.
  c. PowerPoint: Commonly used to compile and present project visuals and data to clients or stakeholders.

- **Project Management and Coordination**
    a. Project Management Tools (Deltek Ajera, Smartsheet, Wrike): Facilitate project scheduling, resource allocation, and budget tracking throughout the project lifecycle.
- **Final Documentation and Presentation**
    a. Adobe Suite (Photoshop, InDesign): Used for final touch-ups on visuals and creating professional project documentation and presentation materials.

However, despite the advances in digital tools compared to non-digitalised tools, the core of architectural creativity – how architects conceive and develop ideas, or in another word, 'think' – remains largely unaffected by these tools. Architectural ideation typically follows one of two paths: one driven by poetic imagination and visual renderings, and the other by rational analysis and logical reasoning. Both approaches can lead to the creation of exceptional architectural works, even masterpieces.

AI ENTERS THE SCENE: NEW OPPORTUNITIES

As we look toward the future, however, the integration of AI into architectural practice holds the potential to transform the basis of design practice in unprecedented ways. The merging of AI with architecture is expected not only to assist architects but also to reshape entire methodologies and approaches to design and project management. AI's ability to analyse large datasets quickly and efficiently can be harnessed to optimise the design process, and to enhance both aesthetic appeal and functionality. Moreover, the predictive capabilities of AI can streamline project management processes, forecasting potential delays and recalibrating resources accordingly to maintain project timelines and budgets.

Additionally, AI-driven tools such as virtual reality can revolutionise client interactions by providing more immersive and interactive visualisations of proposed projects, thereby enhancing communication and allowing for real-time feedback and modifications. These enhancements facilitated by AI indicate a significant shift in how architectural projects are conceived, planned, and executed, suggesting a future where technology and creativity converge to redefine the limits of the profession.

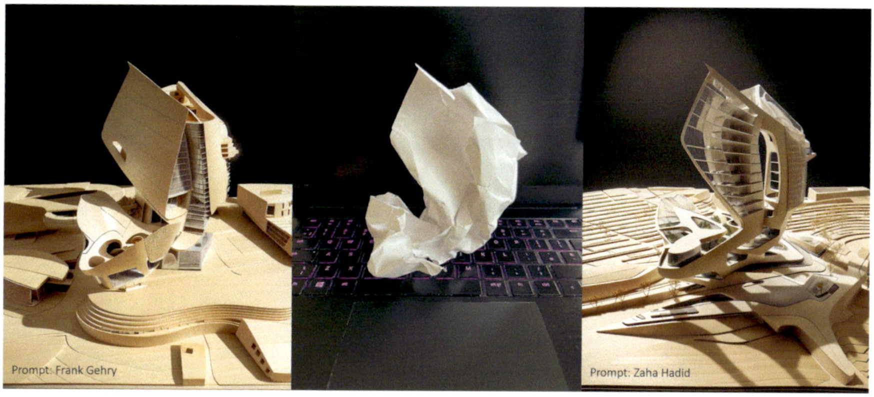

Figure 1.2.3 Tim Fu, Crumpled Paper Renderings, generated using LookX render mode, 2023

Here we can imagine a few exciting possibilities:

- **Design Assistance for Conceptualisation and Initial Design**
  - Generative Design: AI can help create numerous design options based on objectives and constraints set by the architect, allowing for exploration of options that may not have been initially considered.
  - Visualisations and Simulations: AI tools can generate realistic 3D models and simulations to visualise how a building will look and function, considering factors like sunlight, wind patterns, and energy efficiency.
- **Improved Efficiency for Drafting, Visualisation, and Project Management**
  - Automated Drafting: AI can automate routine drafting tasks, such as creating initial site models or adjusting building elements, freeing up architects to focus on more complex design aspects.
  - Project Management: AI can predict project timelines, budget management, and resource allocation, optimising the workflow and reducing overheads.
- **Data Analysis**
  - Building Information Modelling (BIM): AI can enhance BIM systems to analyse vast amounts of data in order to make more informed decisions about materials, structural integrity, and environmental impact.

- Predictive Analytics: AI can use data from previous projects to predict outcomes, identify potential design and construction issues, and suggest mitigations before they become costly.

- **Client Interaction and Customisation**
  - Virtual Reality (VR) and Augmented Reality (AR): AI-powered VR and AR can offer immersive previews of architectural projects, helping clients to make informed decisions and request changes before construction starts.
  - Personalisation Algorithms: AI can tailor designs to individual preferences and needs, enhancing client satisfaction and engagement.

- **Sustainability Optimisation**
  - Energy Efficiency: AI can optimise building designs for energy efficiency by analysing climate data and building orientation, and suggesting materials and technologies that reduce energy consumption.
  - Sustainable Material Selection: AI can help in selecting the most sustainable materials by analysing their lifecycle impacts in real time.

- **Learning and Adaptation**
  - Continuous Learning: AI systems can learn from each project and continually refine and improve design suggestions, leading to ever-more efficient and innovative designs.

- **Documentation and Compliance**
  - Regulatory Compliance: AI can keep track of changes in building regulations and automatically adjust designs to comply with the latest standards.

This highlights two distinct paradigms in architectural technology. The first paradigm is characterised by tools that primarily handle information and graphics – these tools are designed to search, edit, and present data. Such tools require significant human intervention, relying on architects to manually input and manipulate data. The second paradigm, on the other hand, represents a shift towards using patterns and models for analysis, simulation, learning, and generation. This more recent approach leverages advanced algorithms that reduce the necessity for manual operation, enabling the software to independently learn from data patterns and execute complex tasks. This evolution marks a significant departure from traditional practices, paving the way for more automated and sophisticated processes in architectural design.

However, AI has a lot more to offer for the future.

Since 2022, there has been a boom in AI-generated content (AIGC), triggering an explosive growth in the use of AIGC and its applications. For this reason, many people are beginning to think that the era of strong AI is not so far away. However, few applications have been developed during this boom. At present, the most successful applications mainly lie in the field of personal use, while the use of AIGC applications in the building industry is still in the experimental stage.

Sequoia Capital made the following predictions on AIGC in 2022: AI text generation would enter the golden period in 2023, and AI image generation in 2025; AI 3D generation and AI video generation would still be in their early stages in 2023 and would enter their golden period in 2030.[2] It is undeniable that AI text generation and AI image generation have taken an early lead, AI video generation and AI game generation are also developing, but AI 3D generation is still in its research and development stage.

In terms of AIGC's industrial applications in the manufacturing industry, when it comes to the construction industry and companies or organisations

Figure 1.2.4 Longmenshan Biodiversity Museum

further up the supply chain, AIGC's content will not only focus on images and text, but also evolve towards 3D once more data is available.

The following sections will go into further detail about the applications of AI across three phases: evaluation, design, and optimisation. The final section will then look forward to the age of AI-assisted architecture.

AI IN THE EVALUATION PHASE: COMPUTATIONAL SITE ANALYSIS

This process begins with the systematic collection of environmental and contextual information such as site conditions, climate data, spatial constraints, and user requirements that form the foundation of any architectural concept. These datasets are then structured and translated into digital form, enabling their integration within computational design tools. Through simulation and parametric modelling, the gathered information is analysed to evaluate factors such as daylight performance, energy efficiency, spatial flow, and material impact. The outcomes of these simulations not only provide designers with evidence-based insights, but also supply computational design algorithms with data-driven feedback to iteratively guide and refine their architectural proposals. In doing so, the process transforms raw environmental data into both human and machine-readable design intelligence.

In Chapter 1.3, 'From Data to Fabrication', we offer a more detailed discussion about the flow of data, and about how data is gathered and used in the supply chain in the construction industry. In this chapter, we will focus on how machine-readable site information and intelligent evaluation outcomes can help with the later design phase.

Up until now, site-related data required for architectural design has been stored in various fragmented forms – on paper or across different digital systems – without being integrated into a systematic data flow that can interface with intelligent algorithms. Before we move on to this question, we should first distinguish the types of data involved. According to SMART (Standards, Machine, Applicable, Readable, and Transferable), a digital standard definition of content given by ISO[3]:

- Level 1 refers to paper-only documents, with no possibility of machine readability.

- Level 2 refers to machine-accessible structure in PDF format (e.g., headings, bookmarks), but not fully smart.
- Level 3 refers to documents in XML format where a machine can identity clauses, and can parse sections but not meaning.
- Level 4 refers to documents where there is semantic tagging, so that a machine can identify clauses, comprehend structure, and link content.
- Level 5 refers to documents that a machine can interpret, reason with the content, map to ontologies, and reuse clauses intelligently.

In industry, Level 3 information content is now widely used, and Level 4 digital content is developing. Level 5 intelligence is the core foundation of Industry 4.0 and intelligent manufacturing. The future aim of AIGC, then, is to generate machine readable content above Level 4, and especially Level 5 intelligent content.

In the construction industry, the underlying data standard is progressing from the Level 3 CAD era of machine-readable documents to the Level 4 BIM era of machine-readable content. The requirement for 3D models in the construction industry is that the content objects come with accurate full three-dimensional information. If this information is included, then the models can be equipped with intelligent capabilities such as self-sensing, self-learning, and self-iteration. At present, the application of Level 3 CAD and Level 4 BIM software has already been monopolised, so the space and potential of our development is inevitably centred on Level 5 operating at a basic level.

This insight into the digital revolution within the construction industry has led us to realise that the underlying data of the entire industry must be redefined. Since XKool's foundation in 2016, we have been dedicated to the research and development of the underlying technology for Level 5 3D modelling AIGC and its application in the construction industry. Based on a set of AI systems that include business flow logic, interactive contents such as building information and multi-dimensional data, 3D massing models can be generated, leading to the generation of actual architectural design projects.

We call such underlying data, 'AI-driven building information model on Cloud' (ABC for short) and break down intelligent generation into four practical steps:

1. AI identification of existing contents for training or structured data reconstruction
2. Data evaluation and analogue simulation

3. Optimisation of preliminary data results
4. Generation of outcomes in the form of a series of AI models

In terms of Level 5 goals, we can now implement a simulated analysis of a physical environment, simulate data and forecast human behaviour, as well as undertake project-related analyses and simulations of common building types such as residences and shopping malls. In terms of applications, it can assist customers in analysing project proposals. As a result, XKool was chosen as the first AI judge for a housing design competition organised by China Real Estate Association. This capability has also been used in the development and operation of a dozen shopping malls in Hong Kong and on the Chinese mainland.

In a further example, we used AI-empowered data evaluation to generate our conceptual design of our Longmenshan Biodiversity Museum project. Through a wind environment analysis model, using computational fluid dynamics simulations, we conducted a systematic study of the site's prevailing

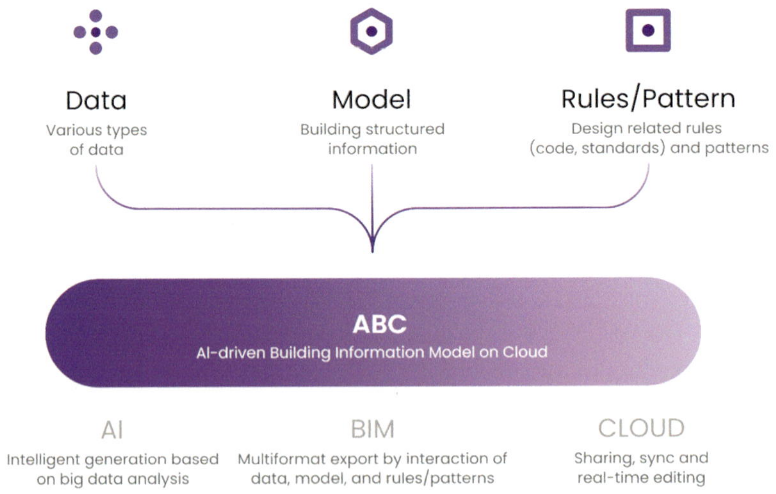

Figure 1.2.5 Schematic diagram of ABC intelligent cloud model in L5 building intelligent format

wind directions and airflow patterns. The analysis revealed that a centralised layout aligned with the site's geometry would cause wind resistance and heat retention, which would have a negative impact on outdoor thermal comfort and the ecological microenvironment. By contrast, a decentralised layout could effectively guide airflow through the site, establish ventilation corridors, and foster a more natural interaction between architecture and landscape. The design therefore adopts a layout strategy combining curvilinear and decentralised forms, allowing air to flow and converge naturally between the volumes, creating a continuous micro-climate circulation system.

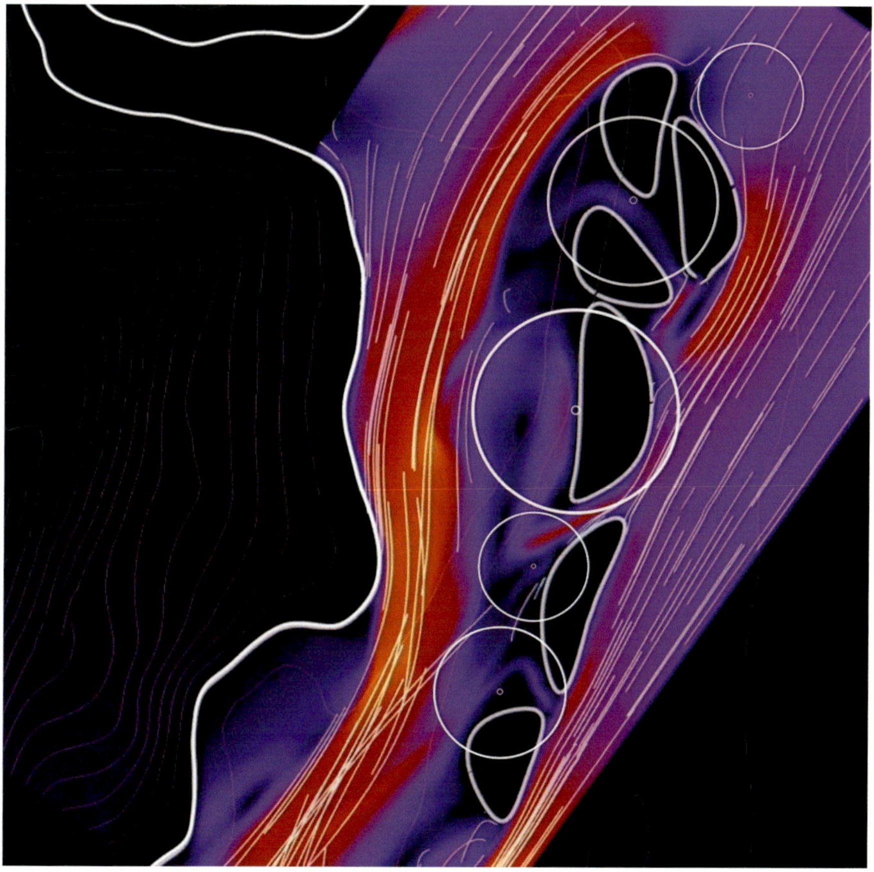

Figure 1.2.6 Computational fluid dynamics simulations for the Longmenshan Biodiversity Museum

AI IN THE DESIGN PHASE: GENERATING CREATIVE AND FUNCTIONAL SCHEMES

The design phase has always been the most creative yet uncertain stage of architectural practice. Today, with the rise of AIGC, architects are witnessing a shift from intuition-driven sketching to data-informed ideation. AI tools can now translate simple text prompts or hand-drawn shapes into conceptual and comprehensive design schemes that capture spatial intent and aesthetic tone, helping designers rapidly explore possibilities that once took days or weeks to develop.

Since 2019, we have led this transformation by developing systems such as *Kool Sketch*, the *AI Creative Library*, and later the *XKool AI Cloud*. These platforms combine generative models, fine-tuned on architecture-specific data, with real-time visualisation, enabling the creation of expressive 2D concepts and even preliminary 3D forms. While technical challenges remain – especially in reconstructing geometry and materials – AI is increasingly becoming a co-creator in design, bridging imagination and computation to produce both creative and functional architectural schemes.

2D Design Ideation

At the beginning of 2019, a series generated by GANs, 'This Building Does Not Exist', attracted considerable attention overseas. We released the series in April and subsequently set up the 'Kool Sketch' series, enabling the generation of corresponding conceptual designs from 2D hand-drawn sketches.

We then launched our 'AI Creative Library' for mobile phones in August 2022. With a single sentence prompt, the model could quickly understand the semantics and generate multiple conceptual designs that look very realistic. On this basis, designers could input an existing image and modify the keywords in the prompt, and the model would generate a series of derivative further images as a form of ideation.

We then undertook further research to improve our 'AI Creative Library'. Since the existing algorithms and generative models were based mainly on generic internet material, there was insufficient data for architecture-related images, descriptions, and styles. We therefore developed a special identification system for construction-related data so as to compile a fine-tuned dataset. This new model was trained specifically on architectural images. This led to an AI creative library for the construction industry that proved to be 13.6% better than the original model.

Figure 1.2.7 Optimised curtain wall of the Longmenshan Biodiversity Museum

On May 7, 2023, we then launched our 'XKool AI Cloud' (cloud.xkool.ai), a 'one-stop AIGC creation platform' that integrated 'image generation', 'model training', and 'shared community'. We updated the underlying large model by incorporating the vast existing database, leading to significant improvements in terms of the imaging effect and precise control of volumetric space.

Generation of 3D Models

Although AI can generate some remarkable images, for now these can still only be used for brainstorming ideas early on in the project. If we want to generate a result that can be developed into a design idea, we need to move towards 3D and a higher level of information.

In 2020, when AIGC was not as mature as it is now, we were exploring how to use AI to generate 3D models and released an algorithm for turning 2D images into 3D models. Although the results at that time were far from ideal, the exercise was still valuable in helping us understand the link between 2D images and 3D models.

We subsequently released a further algorithm to turn satellite images into 3D forms by using GANs to understand the relationship between satellite images and 3D form. The algorithm is able to approximate the main 3D forms in the satellite images, and to predict their heights by learning the features of different layered elements in the satellite images. Of course, this method still has some defects. It can only be used in satellite image scenarios, and the relationship between similar images and 3D shapes is difficult to clarify; likewise, although the heights of the 3D forms can be predicted with some degree of accuracy, the algorithm is often very inaccurate when generating other details. It can therefore only be used in early research and for evaluating the project, and has limited applications.

With the boom of AIGC algorithms and increasingly mature 3D algorithms, it is noticeable that the top AI companies have begun to take on more advanced technologies with a view to improving their models in order to tackle 3D-AIGC. For example, OpenAI have launched their Point-E system, which uses an algorithm to interpret any 2D image as a point cloud and then predict 3D objects through the point cloud.

We immediately tested the model and found some limitations in terms of the quality of the forms generated. The shortcomings of the model are reflected in the following three aspects:

1. Difficulty in generating 3D forms: 2D image data is more plentiful and accessible than 3D model data. While 2D image data can be used for a number of applications, 3D model data has limited applications and does not help much in generating 3D forms.
2. Lack of materials as a whole: The prediction of materials is very important for 3D models. However, for AI generation, techniques for predicting materials directly from the image are still insufficiently advanced, in that the appearance of materials differs depending on their form, environmental conditions, and light sources. When we encounter each of these variables in a single image, material reconstruction is almost impossible.
3. Substandard accuracy of the generated model: A model defined by a point cloud usually depends on the density of the point cloud to reconstruct the object surface mesh. If the point cloud is not dense enough, the object will appear severely distorted, and the 3D form cannot be reconstructed.

Understandably, there are a few technical bottlenecks. If we set a lower goal, choose a simple shape generated using 3D modelling software, make a 2D screenshot and reconstruct it in Point-E model, we will find that the outcome is better than the above tests, but it is still at the preliminary stage. Much depends on the training set. One of the easiest ways to obtain training data for this model is to generate 2D views from various angles using 3D modelling software.

To sum up, the technical route of text, images, point clouds, and 3D objects has great potential, but we need greater input from AI scientists to apply it in industry. However, the question that needs to be asked is whether this is the only technical way to generate 3D models.

AI IN THE OPTIMISATION PHASE: TOWARD 'PERFECT' CONSTRUCTION SOLUTIONS

If the design phase represents the birth of ideas, the optimisation phase is where those ideas are refined toward perfection. In architecture, optimisation means more than aesthetic refinement – it involves achieving the best balance between performance, cost, and constructability. Building upon earlier advances in AI-based identification and analysis, we then introduced 'intelligent optimisation' systems capable of automatically improving designs based on performance criteria.

One of the outstanding examples of the use of AI for optimisation was the design of the curtain wall system for the free-form architectural surfaces of the

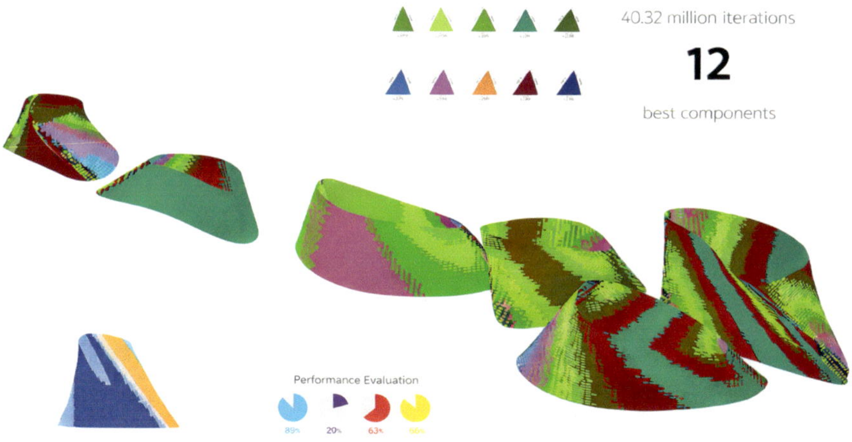

Figure 1.2.8 XKool AI algorithm for curtain wall optimisation

Longmenshan Biodiversity Museum. The key challenge in terms of both design development and cost control was to maintain the complex geometries, while using the minimum number of standardised units. We employed a clustering algorithm to perform geometric similarity analysis on more than 30,000 non-standard units, automatically grouping and optimising them based on parameters such as area, edge length, angle, and vertex distance. After multiple rounds of machine learning computation and dynamic simulation, 30,000 irregular panels were reduced down to 12 standardised module units, thereby cutting material and manufacturing costs by nearly 90%, while maintaining geometric continuity.

In addition, we developed a comprehensive optimisation system powered by both traditional and AI algorithms, addressing seven concerns related to the physical environment: sunlight, thermal radiation, view of landscape, quietness, ventilation, layout quality, and human behaviour.

Sunlight Module

The daylight optimisation tool can iteratively adjust a scheme until it meets solar exposure standards while preserving the original spatial layout. The tool iteratively adjusts distances between buildings and their layouts to ensure compliance with solar exposure standards, while preserving the original spatial concept and preferred economic indicators. The system first identifies areas receiving insufficient or excessive sunlight, then proposes subtle modifications in building placement or spacing to improve light distribution. After each adjustment, it reevaluates solar exposure, repeating the process until the scheme meets the required criteria. By combining performance-driven computation with designer intent and cost constraints, the tool enables architects to optimise daylight conditions efficiently, without compromising functional layout or economic feasibility.

Thermal Radiation Module

The thermal radiation optimisation tool iteratively adjusts the layout and orientation of buildings to achieve optimal solar heat gain and thermal comfort, while maintaining the original spatial arrangement and economic parameters. This approach enhances occupant comfort and energy efficiency without compromising functionality or budget.

Landscape View Module

The landscape view optimisation tool evaluates the landscape quality of different building floors based on factors such as proximity to water features, mountain views, city parks, and visual distance, and uses intelligent algorithms to adjust the layout of the scheme in order to enhance the overall landscape quality score.

Quietness Module

The quietness optimisation tool integrates data on surrounding road types, public building functions, and noise propagation patterns to intelligently evaluate noise levels in a design proposal. Based on user-defined adjustment parameters, it can automatically optimise the spatial layout to enhance overall quietness and environmental tranquillity.

Ventilation Module

The ventilation optimisation tool conducts both outdoor and indoor ventilation simulations under specific wind conditions. For outdoor environments, it models airflow patterns considering seasonal variations in wind direction, speed, and pressure, allowing designers to assess and enhance natural ventilation at the site scale. For indoor environments, it focuses on the rate of air changes per hour to evaluate ventilation efficiency and thermal comfort. Through iterative simulation and parameter adjustment, the tool optimises building form and spatial organisation to achieve a balanced microclimate and improve overall air circulation performance.

Layout Quality Module

The layout quality optimisation tool evaluates living quality at both the building and unit levels. At the building level, it considers factors such as inter-building distance, public space utilisation, and overall spatial efficiency. At the unit level, it analyses elevator efficiency, balcony views, and movement routes within residential layouts. By quantifying these parameters, the tool assists architects in prioritising and optimising key design objectives, helping them achieve a balanced and high-quality living environment.

Human Behaviour Module

The human behaviour optimisation tool simulates occupant movement and interaction patterns across different spatial scales to enhance spatial efficiency and user experience. Through behavioural simulations on different floors it assesses the rationality and accessibility of public spaces, optimising the functional layout through a balance between high- and low-accessibility zones. For instance, although a compact ground floor plan might improve spatial efficiency, excessive corners can reduce accessibility – an issue that can be mitigated through visual guidance strategies. Even at the scale of an individual

Figure 1.2.9 Longmenshan Biodiversity Museum

unit, the tool can model natural movement patterns formed by residents' daily activities, using these behavioural traces to refine room organisation, circulation routes, and spatial usability.

All these breakthroughs illustrate how generative AI has evolved from creating designs to perfecting them. By integrating data from multiple disciplines – architecture, structure, landscape and mechanical, electrical, and plumbing systems – AI can now simulate, verify, and enhance construction proposals in ways that ensure both efficiency and feasibility. The future of optimisation lies in intelligent collaboration: cloud-based systems that connect designers, engineers, and algorithms through iterative feedback loops. In this phase, AI is no longer merely a design assistant but a strategic partner, steering architecture toward more economical, sustainable, and precisely engineered solutions.

FROM CONCEPT TO CONSTRUCTION: HOW AI UNIFIES THE ARCHITECTURAL DESIGN PROCESS

Generative AI technology is the key for the three phases discussed above. Multiple professionals must collaborate in the construction industry to select economical, applicable, and aesthetically pleasing design proposals and deliver safe, efficient, and high-quality construction drawings. In addition, all aspects of the design must be considered step by step – whether at the macro, medium, or micro scale – in terms of the architecture, structure, electromechanics, water heating, landscape, and so on. Likewise, the different types of buildings, be they residences, apartments, industrials spaces, offices, or commercial buildings, should be taken into account. As such, professional plans satisfying different requirements of companies or organisations further up the supply chain cannot be generated by a single specific model algorithm with a precise set of data. Rather, they need to be generated by the organic integration of many factors, according to the individual scenario, and through continuous iteration based on user feedback.

Based on this business logic, we have established a new set of AIGC business processes for architectural design with AI systems and cloud architecture at their core, by taking the key contents from 24 business production steps required for traditional architectural design, and reconstructing them into six business modules:

1. Retrieval (information retrieval and AI identification)
2. Design (full generative AI and man–machine collaboration)
3. Modification (manual modification and AI optimisation)
4. Verification (data verification and AI review)
5. Collaboration (cloud multi-person collaboration and business management)
6. Output (auto-output of multiple formats – 3D model / 2D drawing / image / PowerPoint / Excel, etc.)

Based on a deep understanding of business workflows, the six core modules are tightly integrated with advanced technologies such as AI-based recognition, generative AI, big data, and cloud collaboration. Together, they address business needs at multiple levels of the construction process – from planning and design to component generation. Over time, the system supports both horizontal workflows (analysis, design, review, coordination, and delivery) and vertical integration across the residential development lifecycle.

LOOKING AHEAD: THE HUMAN TOUCH IN THE AGE OF AI-ASSISTED ARCHITECTURE

So far, we have seen that AI has significantly enhanced various aspects of the software tools used in architectural workflows, bringing about improvements in efficiency, creativity, and data management. Here's a comparison of how AI has contributed to enhancing traditional architectural software:

- **Design and Modelling**
  - Traditional Tools (e.g., AutoCAD, SketchUp, Rhino): These tools primarily rely on manual input for design and modelling, requiring extensive user intervention to create and modify designs.
  - AI-Enhanced (e.g., AI plugins for Rhino, generative design in Revit): AI facilitates generative design, where architects input design goals and parameters, and the software generates multiple design alternatives. This not only speeds up the initial design process but also offers innovative solutions that might not be immediately evident through manual processes.
- **Visualisation and Rendering**
  - Traditional Tools (e.g., V-Ray, Lumion): While highly effective, the rendering process traditionally requires setting up scenes manually, tweaking lighting, textures, and materials to achieve desired results.
  - AI-Enhanced (e.g., AI-based rendering enhancements): AI accelerates rendering times and improves the realism of simulations by automatically adjusting lighting and materials based on the environment. AI can also predict and execute high quality renders faster by learning from previous renderings.
- **Project Management and Operations**
  - Traditional Tools (e.g., Microsoft Project, Smartsheet): These tools require manual setup and updating, relying on the project manager to input and adjust data as the project progresses.
  - AI-Enhanced (e.g., AI integrations in project management software): AI can predict project timelines and potential delays by analysing past project data. It also optimises resource allocation and budget management, offering real-time adjustments as project dynamics change.
- **Data Analysis and Decision-Making**
  - Traditional Tools (e.g., Excel for data analysis): Traditionally, data analysis in architecture involves manual data entry and analysis, which can be time-consuming and prone to human error.
  - AI-Enhanced (e.g., BIM software with AI analytics): AI enhances BIM analytics by providing deeper insights into the building performance,

environmental impact, and life-cycle costs. It can also automatically suggest improvements or highlight areas of concern.

- **Client Interactions and Customisations**
  - Traditional Tools (PowerPoint for presentations): Client interactions typically involve static presentations and manually created visuals.
  - AI-Enhanced (e.g., AI-driven VR/AR tools): AI can generate interactive 3D models and virtual walkthroughs that clients can interact with, providing a more immersive and customisable presentation experience.

In summary, AI introduces a level of automation, prediction, and personalisation that significantly transcends the limitations of traditional software, offering not just efficiency but also enabling creative and innovative architectural solutions that were previously thought challenging or impossible to achieve manually.

However, while AI has greatly enhanced the capabilities in architectural work, there are several areas where it still falls short or cannot fully replace human architects:

- **Creative Intuition and Originality:** AI can generate design alternatives and optimise solutions based on specific parameters, but it lacks the ability to intuitively understand context or cultural significance in the way human architects can. The unique creative vision, especially when it involves integrating new designs into sensitive historical or cultural contexts, often requires a human touch.
- **Ethical and Social Considerations:** AI operates based on data and algorithms, and does not inherently consider ethical implications or social impacts of architectural projects. Decisions that affect community well-being or involve ethical considerations still heavily rely on human judgment.
- **Complex Client Interactions:** While AI can assist in presenting and explaining design concepts through simulations and virtual reality, the nuanced communication required in client interactions – such as negotiating design changes or understanding client aspirations beyond what is explicitly stated – requires human skills.
- **Adaptability in Unpredictable Scenarios:** AI systems are typically designed to operate within the scope of their programming and available data. They may not be able to handle unexpected changes in a project or unusual design challenges as flexibly as a human architect who can draw on a broader range of experiences and creative problem-solving skills.

Figure 1.2.10 Jennifer Haider Chowdury, Urban Design Proposal, generated from sketch using LookX render mode, 2024

- **Oversight and Ethical Deployment of AI:** As AI tools become more integrated into architectural practices, there remains a need for oversight to ensure these tools are used responsibly and do not inadvertently lead to uniformity in design or ignore local nuances. The responsibility to oversee AI, ensure it is used ethically, and integrate its use effectively into the broader goals of projects remains a fundamentally human task.

These limitations highlight the complementary role AI is likely to continue playing in architecture, enhancing human capabilities rather than replacing them.

Although AI is poised to take over many of the labour-intensive tasks traditionally handled by architects and designers, the essence of design remains inherently human. Design is fundamentally an operational research endeavour that involves investigating a project, analysing data, and creatively synthesising information to develop innovative solutions. This process involves articulating positions, exploring various scenarios and hypotheses, and ultimately strategising solutions that culminate in schematic designs expressed through graphical and architectural language. The core of design will continue to revolve around this intellectual process, encompassing critical thinking, reasoning, and multiple decision-making stages throughout the workflow.

Today's AI applications are heavily reliant on human input and decision-making, augmenting rather than replacing the human element in architectural design. Therefore, fears of architects and designers being rendered obsolete by AI are unfounded. Instead, AI will liberate them from mundane, documentary tasks, allowing them to concentrate more on the crux of design work – the thoughtful, reasoned processes and decision-making that define their professions.

As we move forward, the role of architects and designers is not diminishing but evolving, enhanced by AI tools that support and amplify their creativity and efficiency. This symbiotic relationship promises a new era where technology and human ingenuity combine to push the boundaries of what is possible in architecture and design.

NOTES

1 Jason Winters, *The Basic Architectural Services Project Delivery CACE 2017*, AIA. https://content.aia.org/sites/default/files/2017-09/The_Basic_Architectural_Services_Project_Delivery_CACE_2017.pdf
2 Sequioia Capital, 'Generative AI: A Creative New World', 2026. www.sequoiacap.com/article/generative-ai-a-creative-new-world
3 Strategic Advisory Group on Machine-Readable Standards, www.iso.org/smart

Figure 1.3.1 XKool, Bi-Tech City, Shenzhen, 2018 – an early project designed using AI

CHAPTER 1.3

FROM DATA TO FABRICATION

Wanyu He

When discussing architectural fabrication, a critical question arises: should the design prioritise functionality, user flow, aesthetic qualities, or perhaps something else entirely? Traditionally, architects have embraced a holistic approach, considering all aspects pertinent to a project – paying close attention to the context, the client's needs, and the logical arrangement of functional spaces. This method typically follows a step-by-step approach that begins with inspiration and progresses through ideation, concept development, and initial sketches, before moving on to the detailed design phases.

However, this traditional approach often prioritises a specific aesthetics or narrative theme, potentially leading to inefficiencies in the use of space, lower levels of performance, or increased construction costs. Architects have traditionally focused on their strength in modelling form using novel visuals and geometries. Yet, this approach frequently overlooks crucial metrics such as potential environmental impacts, financial implications, ease of manufacture, and complexities associated with construction.

While architects are adept at creating compelling spatial and material experiences, they are less equipped for tasks that require intricate calculations related to mechanics, estimating cost, or evaluating performance. For decades, this focus on the creative aspects of architecture has fostered a generation of 'star architects' – or 'starchitects' – whose work is celebrated for its visionary and aesthetic qualities. Nonetheless, as we advance into an increasingly technological society – marked by the rise of the internet, big data, cloud computing, and AI – the architectural landscape is becoming increasingly complex.

DOI: 10.4324/9781003347330-5

Figure 1.3.2 XKool, Bi-Tech City, Shenzhen, 2018 – an early project designed using AI

LEARNING FROM THE AUTOMOTIVE INDUSTRY

The increasing complexity of the construction industry demands a more integrated approach, one that does not merely focus on the traditional strengths of architectural design but also embraces the rigorous data analytics necessary for the challenges of today. The shift towards design for manufacturing and assembly (DFMA) and modular production is indicative of this new approach.[1] These methods not only streamline the construction process but also ensure more sustainable and cost-effective building practices.

DFMA is a design approach that focuses on simplifying the manufacturing and assembly processes of various components. In architecture, this approach is particularly significant as it aims to reduce costs, minimise waste, and streamline the construction process by designing buildings with ease of manufacture and assembly in mind.[2]

Incorporating DFMA into modern architectural processes represents a critical evolution in design methodology, departing from traditional paradigms. Traditionally, architectural designs often emphasise aesthetic and functional concerns without fully considering the complexities and costs of construction and assembly. This could lead to designs that, while impressive visually, are inefficient and costly to construct.

DFMA challenges this by foregrounding efficiency and simplicity from the outset, ensuring that the design integrates easily with manufacturing and assembly processes. By planning with the end construction in mind, architects and engineers can streamline projects, reduce material waste, and lower labour costs, speeding up project completion times significantly.

For example, Tesla's implementation of DFMA principles in the design of the Model 3 and Model Y showcases the profound impact of this approach.[3] The Model 3 was initially designed with a rear frame that included 70 separate components, necessitating extensive assembly and complex fixtures. However, with the Model Y, Tesla reevaluated and streamlined the design using DFMA principles, resulting in a rear frame that consists of only two pieces. This not only simplified the production process but also reduced costs and improved maintainability, illustrating the substantial benefits that can be realised through thoughtful DFMA application.

To further enhance the effectiveness of DFMA in architectural design, architects may adopt Elon Musk's five-step working method, which offers a systematic approach to refining production processes[4]:

1. **Make requirements less dumb:** Question and reassess existing requirements to ensure they are necessary and optimised for current needs.
2. **Delete parts or processes:** Identify and remove unnecessary components or steps in the design and construction process.
3. **Simplify or optimise:** Streamline designs to be more efficient, using fewer materials and simpler assemblies where possible.
4. **Accelerate fabrication times:** Find ways to reduce the time it takes to move from design to finished product.
5. **Automate:** Implement automation in the manufacturing and assembly processes to increase speed and reduce errors.

These steps encourage a mindset of continuous improvement and efficiency, urging architects to rethink traditional practices and embrace innovations that can significantly enhance both the creative and practical aspects of their work. This method not only supports sustainability but also aligns with the modern demand for faster, more cost-effective building practices. By integrating these principles, the architectural field can produce designs that are not only beautiful and functional but also strategically optimised for today's fast-paced, efficiency-driven construction environments.

Some might be wondering why we are comparing architectural design to the design of a product, such as a car? But why not? Maybe we can think about the two by using the analogy of LEGO.

DFMA IN CONSTRUCTION

LEGO, the iconic toy brand known for its interlocking plastic bricks, exemplifies the power of standardised components and their vast potential for creativity.[5] Each LEGO piece is manufactured to exact specifications, ensuring that it can be combined with other pieces in countless ways while maintaining a secure fit. This standardisation is key to LEGO's universal system. Every brick, regardless of its shape or size, can connect with any other brick in the same system, allowing for a vast range of possible combinations.

The genius of LEGO lies in how these standardised bricks can be assembled to create an astonishing variety of structures, from simple models for young children to complex replicas of iconic buildings for adults. This adaptability reflects DFMA principles where standardisation leads to an efficient and versatile assembly process. Just as in modern DFMA practices in architecture and manufacturing, LEGO's approach minimises waste by ensuring that even the smallest piece can be integrated in multiple configurations and reused in different models.

By maintaining a consistent manufacturing process, LEGO not only upholds high quality and durability across its products but also encourages creative problem-solving and innovation. Builders are not limited by the constraints of their components; instead, they are empowered by the potential to recombine them in novel ways. This model of creative flexibility underpinned by rigorous standardisation has made LEGO a beloved and enduring presence in the world of play and education, illustrating the practical and imaginative benefits of modular construction and design.

The ideology behind LEGO's system of standardised, interlocking components finds a direct parallel in the field of modular construction. Much like LEGO bricks, modular building systems rely on the precision and compatibility of individual units that can be prefabricated, transported, and assembled into larger structures on site. This shared principle of interoperability allows for scalability and flexibility in design. In both cases, the focus lies not on the uniqueness of each piece, but on the seamless integration of parts within a coherent system, which itself is unique and values adaptability, efficiency, and reuse.

The International Space Station (ISS) stands as a remarkable real-world manifestation of this modular philosophy. Constructed from 43 prefabricated modules designed by seven international commercial partners, the ISS was assembled piece by piece in orbit, much like connecting LEGO blocks.[6] Each module, whether a laboratory, living quarter, or docking port, had to conform to strict dimensional and interface standards to ensure compatibility and functionality once assembled in space. This standardisation mirrors LEGO's design ideology, where precision enables creativity: through its modular framework, the ISS fosters continual innovation, as engineers design and attach new modules to meet emerging scientific and operational needs.

In essence, both LEGO and the ISS demonstrate how standardisation can coexist with innovation. By adhering to common design rules, they unlock a remarkable degree of flexibility and longevity. Just as LEGO encourages endless recombination and reinvention within a stable system, the ISS exemplifies how modular construction can support continuous evolution – adapting to new scientific missions and technological upgrades without rebuilding from scratch. This synergy between constraint and creativity underscores a fundamental truth: that modular design, whether in play or

Figure 1.3.3 XKool, Bi-Tech City, Shenzhen, 2018 – an early project designed using AI

in space engineering, transforms uniformity into a platform for expansive possibility.

The construction of LEGO models and the assembly of the ISS both embody the methodology of DFMA. The success of DFMA in these two fields, as well as in automobile manufacturing, vividly demonstrates its potential in the realm of architectural construction, which involves, essentially, larger and more complex versions of a LEGO project or the ISS project.

The ideology of DFMA is especially relevant today as we integrate more advanced technologies like AI into architectural design. When coupled with AI, DFMA opens an entirely new paradigm for architectural design and production. Standardised building components can be treated as datasets within a digital design ecosystem, allowing AI algorithms to analyse, optimise, and generate architectural schemes that balance cost, performance, and aesthetics. This approach is incredibly beneficial for shaping the urban fabric, i.e., building functional, economical, and non-iconic buildings such as residential flats, hotels, and office buildings. By empowering design with AI and modular logic, architects can achieve greater design diversity and responsiveness without sacrificing efficiency or affordability, bringing a new level of creativity and precision to the construction industry.

DFMA has the potential to fundamentally reshape the construction industry by shifting it from a craft-based and site-dependent process to one rooted in precision manufacturing and systemised assembly. By applying DFMA principles, buildings can be conceived as modular systems composed of standardised components that are prefabricated under controlled factory conditions and assembled efficiently on-site. This transition not only improves quality control and reduces waste but also accelerates project timelines and minimises labour-intensive work in unpredictable environments. Much like the precision required in LEGO construction or the modular docking of the ISS, DFMA ensures that each element is designed for compatibility and ease of integration, enabling scalable, repeatable, and sustainable building processes.

FRAME, PANEL, AND INTEGRATED BOX

In contemporary construction, the column and beam system, often implemented as a pre-cast frame system, allows for about 10% of the total manufacturing to be prefabricated in a factory setting, as opposed to being constructed on-site. This system focuses on the essential vertical and horizontal supports, facilitating quicker assembly on the building site but leaving a significant portion of construction activities such as building walls, installing plumbing system, and setting interior finishes to be completed on-site. By concentrating on the primary structural framework, this approach provides a foundation for more advanced off-site construction methods while still relying heavily on traditional on-site labour.

The pre-cast panel system takes this a step further, by increasing off-site work to 20–30%. This approach involves manufacturing large, flat panels which are often made of concrete under controlled conditions in a factory. These panels are then transported to the site and assembled, enhancing the speed of construction and ensuring better quality control. This method not only accelerates the construction process but also improves quality control, as the prefabricated panels are manufactured in a stable environment, increasing construction speed as well as reducing variations and defects compared to fully on-site production.

The most comprehensive application of off-site construction is realised by a prefabricated modular system, in which entire volumetric modules, essentially self-contained 'boxes', are prefabricated in a factory. In particular, by using

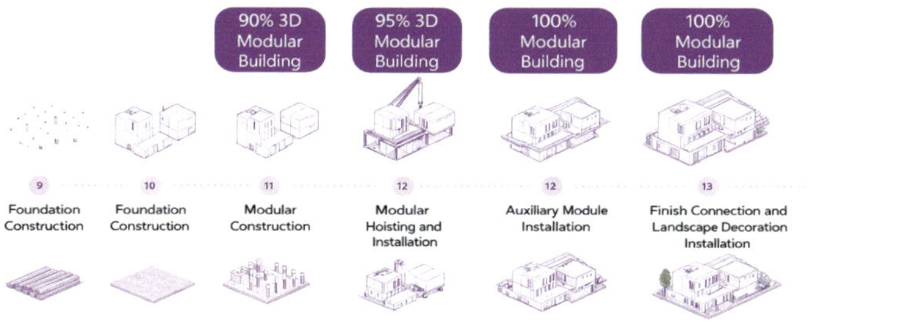

Figure 1.3.4 Typical modular construction process

steel column modules, up to 90% of the building can be prefabricated. Within an integrated box, entire sections of a building, including plumbing, electrical installations, and interior finishes, are completed off-site. These modules are then transported to the building site and assembled like giant LEGO bricks, drastically reducing on-site construction time, minimising environmental disruption, and significantly cutting down the amount of construction labour needed.

By maximising factory-based production, these modern prefabrication techniques offer various benefits to the construction industry, such as ensuring precision, reducing waste, and enhancing overall efficiency. This is especially the case with steel modular systems, which can be considered very close to automobile or aircraft manufacturing systems.

The first obvious benefit is that modular systems provide exceptional scalability and flexibility. Buildings can be easily enlarged or reduced by adding or removing modules based on evolving needs, offering architects and developers significant versatility in design and functionality. This adaptability is particularly valuable in environments where space requirements can change rapidly, such as in developing urban areas or temporary event spaces.

The speed of construction is the major benefit of modular architecture. Since the modules are produced in a controlled factory setting, many of the common delays associated with traditional construction, such as adverse weather conditions or scheduling conflicts, are avoided. Not only does this ensure a higher quality of workmanship and materials consistency, but it also accelerates the overall construction timeline significantly.

Prefabricated construction also offers notable environmental benefits. By shifting a significant portion of work to controlled factory environments, material waste is minimised through precise cutting, standardisation, and reuse of off-cuts. Additionally, on-site construction activities such as noise, dust, and debris generation are greatly reduced, mitigating the ecological footprint of the building process. The reduced on-site labour and shorter construction timelines also translate into lower energy consumption and fewer transportation emissions during the assembly phase. Consequently, prefabrication aligns closely with sustainable building practices and the growing emphasis on green construction standards.

Beyond speed and sustainability, prefabrication enhances cost efficiency across the building's lifecycle. Factory production allows bulk purchasing of standardised materials and reduces labour costs associated with on-site work. Furthermore, the precision inherent in prefabricated components reduces maintenance needs and the risk of defects over time, improving durability and long-term performance. These economic advantages make prefabrication particularly attractive for large-scale residential, commercial, and institutional projects, where both upfront construction costs and long-term operational expenses are critical considerations.

In summary, prefabricated construction – from pre-cast frames to panels and fully integrated modular boxes – transforms the traditional building process by emphasising off-site production, precision, and standardisation. However, DFMA cannot be realised in architecture without a deep understanding of the entire building industry workflow and value chain. Essentially, DFMA requires the integration and leveraging of data across all stages of the construction process.

FLOW OF DATA

In modern architecture, the role of data has evolved to become a central aspect of the design process, reflecting a significant shift from traditional methodologies. Traditionally, data was used primarily at the beginning of a project to inform early design ideas and scheme development. However, data is now more comprehensively integrated throughout the architectural process.

Pre-Design Data

The data required includes all initial conditions necessary for conceptualising a design, such as the context of the built environment, client demands, and specific requirements. The data is gathered from various sources, such as real estate consultants, city municipalities, and specialised platforms, which collate and visualise information from multiple providers. Access to this kind of detailed, organised data often incurs a cost, but it forms the foundation of an informed approach to architectural planning and design.

Post-Design Data

After the initial design phase, a range of data emerges from the design itself, including detailed drawing parameters, performance simulations, and cost estimates. It is straightforward to gather parameters from architectural drawings, but costing requires intricate calculations involving procurement engineers, often consuming considerable time and being susceptible to human error. Performance data, which assess things like fire safety, solar angles, and structural integrity, is critical yet complex to generate as it involves modelling and simulating various scenarios. Energy consumption, thermal radiation, and noise are less frequently simulated but equally important factors that are critical for optimising the design but are all too often relegated to later stages where they have little impact on the final design.

Manufacturing and Construction Data

This includes comprehensive details about components, material specifications, and construction methods. Traditionally, this type of data has been somewhat detached from the early stages of design, and normally only used by technical architects and engineers during the later phases of detailing and construction. However, this disconnect can lead to inefficiencies and complications in realising the design, as modifications at the manufacturing or construction stage can be costly and complex.

The challenge of effectively implementing DFMA in architecture today often revolves around the construction of a robust manufacturing database. This database is crucial as it enables architects to integrate manufacturing considerations early into the design process. The automotive industry offers a valuable model for how such databases can be utilised in architecture. In car manufacturing, the component libraries are not merely collections of parts; they are dynamic databases that include 3D models of components along with detailed specifications and embedded composition rules or methods.

This comprehensive approach ensures that designers have access to not only the physical properties of each component but also the knowledge of how these parts can be combined and assembled. For architects to apply a similar strategy, their databases would need to extend beyond lists of simple parts. They would require detailed, actionable information on the design and assembly implications of each component, including compatibility with other elements, structural considerations, and material specifications.

To make these databases work for DFMA, they must be integrated with the software tools that support the design process. These tools should allow architects to access the database's data in real time, facilitating a seamless flow from design conception through to detailed planning and execution. Such integration would enable architects to design with an acute awareness of manufacturing and assembly processes, much like automotive engineers design with a clear understanding of how each component fits into a vehicle.

By learning from the automotive industry's approach to component databases, architecture can significantly enhance efficiency and efficacy by incorporating DFMA principles into building design, leading to approaches to construction that are not only innovative and aesthetically pleasing but also optimised for cost-effectiveness and sustainability.

The principles of DFMA advocate for a holistic approach where all these types of data are integrated seamlessly throughout the architectural design process. DFMA emphasises the importance of incorporating manufacturing and construction considerations early in the design phase, allowing for a design that aligns more closely with practical, manufacturable, and assembly-friendly criteria. This approach not only streamlines the entire building process but also minimises potential losses and complications during manufacturing and construction, ensuring that the transition from design to physical structure is as smooth and efficient as possible.

The integration of DFMA in modern architectural practices necessitates a more collaborative approach to data usage, bridging the gap between initial design and final construction, and ensuring that all stages of the architectural process are informed by comprehensive, actionable data. This integrated data strategy fosters better alignment between design intentions and practical realisation, ultimately leading to more successful architectural outcomes. Additionally, the integration of DFMA principles into architecture drawing upon a vast database of components constitutes a profound challenge computationally. Consider a scenario where there are ten components; the combinations of these can generate over 10 billion possibilities. As the number of components increases, say to 100, the number of potential combinations becomes astronomically large, far beyond what human designers can effectively manage or analyse.

This is where AI can play a transformative role. AI can handle and analyse massive datasets and complex variables much more efficiently than humans. By employing machine learning algorithms, AI can quickly sift through millions of design possibilities, optimising for factors such as cost, material efficiency, structural integrity, and aesthetic value.

AI can also learn from each project, improving its algorithms over time to make better predictions and propose the most efficient and effective designs. This capability would enable architects and engineers to explore a broader range of design solutions more quickly, ensuring that every project can be tailored to the best possible specifications with respect to DFMA principles.

Moreover, AI can help in the embedding of composition rules and methods into the database, allowing for a more integrated and intelligent system. This system would not only suggest components based on the design requirements but also provide guidance on how these components should be assembled to optimise the entire structure's functionality and efficiency.

In conclusion, the utilisation of AI in applying DFMA principles in architecture represents a powerful solution to the challenge of managing and exploiting vast component databases. AI can dramatically enhance the design process, making it faster, more cost-effective, and more adaptable to the complex needs of modern construction projects. By harnessing the capabilities of AI, the architecture industry can step into a new era of design precision and efficiency.

The transition from data-driven design to physical fabrication represents a pivotal phase in modern architectural processes, heavily reliant on advanced digital fabrication techniques such as 3D printing and robotic assembly. These technologies enable the direct creation of complex architectural components from digital models, offering unprecedented precision and efficiency.

3D printing, for instance, allows for layer-by-layer construction of components, enabling the production of geometrically complex structures that would be difficult or impossible to achieve with traditional manufacturing methods. This technique not only speeds up the production process but also significantly reduces waste, as materials are added incrementally and only where necessary. Similarly, robotic assembly systems can perform highly precise and repetitive tasks with greater speed and accuracy than human workers, further streamlining the fabrication process.

These techniques are integrated into the construction workflow through sophisticated software that translates architectural designs into machine-readable instructions. This seamless flow from digital to physical realms embodies the core of DFMA principles, where designs optimised for manufacturing lead directly to their physical realisation.

Challenge of Digitalisation

However, there are several challenges in integrating digital design with physical fabrication processes. One of the primary issues is ensuring that the digital data accurately translates into physical materials and components. Discrepancies between digital models and their physical outputs can occur due to material inconsistencies, fabrication errors, or limitations in the precision of the manufacturing equipment.

Another significant challenge is the compatibility of digital design software with fabrication machinery. Ensuring that these systems can communicate effectively requires standardised file formats and protocols, which are still being developed and refined across the industry. Additionally, there's the need for ongoing adjustments and calibrations during the fabrication process to align with the specified design parameters meticulously.

Despite these challenges, the benefits of digital fabrication technologies in architecture, such as increased efficiency, reduced costs, and enhanced capabilities in building complex structures, far outweigh the difficulties. As the industry continues to advance, further innovations and improvements in software and hardware integration are expected, making the digital-to-physical fabrication process even more seamless and effective. By embracing these technologies, the field of architecture is set to revolutionise the way buildings are designed and constructed, making the leap from digital models to physical structures smoother and more reliable.

TURNING A CRISIS INTO AN OPPORTUNITY

Prefabricated modular construction, empowered by digital and intelligent manufacturing technologies, can cover the entire process from conceptual

Figure 1.3.5 Prefabrication allowed this hotel complex to be designed and constructed in 16 weeks

design to production and construction with a high level of quality, greater efficiency, low pollution, and low carbon emissions. These advantages will play a huge role in projects with special requirements. For example, in response to an emergency during the pandemic, this technological approach was used in China to quickly build a series of isolation hotels in only 16 weeks. After the pandemic, these hotels were converted into high-end hotels, such that their construction specifications are no different from regular hotels.

Design Generation

This project benefited from the support of Xtect, an AI-integrated design platform tailored for modular construction. During the initial stage of module configuration, this platform identifies and categorises uploaded elements, including structural components, interior features, and engineering systems. Once recognised, these elements can be dynamically regenerated in response to manual adjustments to the modules. The system also allows for the storage of these newly generated modules in its library for future applications.

The platform's high level of detail, equivalent to LOD400, enables precise construction spreadsheet calculations. This feature significantly enhances the coordination between designers, suppliers, and manufacturers, leading to a more streamlined process. As a result, the accuracy of cost estimates is greatly improved, minimising uncertainties in budgeting.

During the early design phase, the system generates layouts by considering the site boundaries and utilising modules from a pre-established library. The resulting designs adhere to local regulations, including required setbacks and building separations. Real-time data for multiple design options is displayed in a side panel, allowing users to compare and select the most suitable design options based on various parameters such as plot ratio, building density, and quantity of units.

As a result of options generated based on the library of modules, the basic information associated with the model is exported to the list of components required for the prefabricated hotel, and a direct data interchange is established between design and production. In addition, each component is assigned a unique ID, making it possible to inspect the model in a comprehensive manner and identify any problems in a timely manner. This ensures consistency in information for the site, building, module, and components, as well as future links to production.

The integration of DFMA with digital technologies introduces a new paradigm in prefabricated construction – one that is fundamentally data-driven and algorithmically assisted. The process begins with the establishment of a comprehensive components database, in which all standardised building elements such as structural frames, façade panels, HVAC modules, and interior systems are digitally catalogued with detailed information on dimensions, materials, performance metrics, and costs. This database serves as the foundation of a digital design ecosystem, enabling seamless interoperability between design, engineering, and manufacturing processes. It transforms the traditional supply chain into a dynamic, data-rich environment where every component can be instantly accessed, compared, and assembled through computational methods.

Building upon this foundation, AI-driven algorithms can rapidly generate and optimise prefabricated building layouts by combining these standardised components according to predefined design and performance objectives. The system can simultaneously produce various design schemes, automatically evaluating each one against a range of economic, environmental, and regulatory indicators – including construction costs, selling price, sunshine duration, and code compliance. Designers and engineers can then interact with a visualised dashboard that presents these alternative schemes, allowing data-informed decisions at every stage of design development. This closed-loop system, from data to design to evaluation, streamlines the entire construction workflow, making architectural production more efficient, sustainable, and transparent while preserving opportunities for creative differentiation within a standardised framework.

With this approach, the aforesaid project achieved remarkable speed of design and construction. From the client's perspective, every day that can be saved in this process amounts to an extra day of potential revenue from the hotel rooms. This focus on using AI to improve the speed of production is in line with the approach taken by leading international architectural firms, such as Foster + Partners.[7]

Prefabricated Production

The integration of this platform with production line management systems enables ordering, tracking, and manufacturing of components specified for the chosen design. To construct the modules, the manufacturer has to implement an advanced production line. This module assembly system employs non-standard automation engineering equipment, utilising high-precision mechanisms. Coupled with an automated control system, it boosts overall efficiency by over 50%. The modules produced are adaptable in all dimensions, accommodating more than 85% of commercial requirements.

Figure 1.3.6 Interior of hotel room, Shenzhen, China

The majority of the work is completed in the factory, leaving just the module assembly and joint finishing for on-site execution. The precision of the manufacturing process allows for a total tolerance of just 0–2 mm, with on-site module installation taking less than an hour. As production scales up, the cost per modular unit typically decreases, and construction timelines are significantly reduced.

RESHAPING THE FUTURE OF CONSTRUCTION

As we look to the future, the integration of AI and DFMA in architecture promises to reshape the industry with groundbreaking innovations and improved efficiencies. Emerging trends such as the use of augmented reality (AR) for assembly guidance highlight the dynamic potential of further technological integration.[8] AR can superimpose a digital overlay on the physical world, providing real-time, step-by-step visual guidance to workers during the assembly process. This not only helps in reducing errors and increasing precision but also significantly speeds up the construction process by simplifying complex tasks.

The potential impacts of AI and DFMA on the construction industry are profound. One of the most significant changes is likely to be observed in the labour market. Automation could lead to a shift in the roles and skills required on construction sites, emphasising more technologically advanced jobs and potentially reducing the demand for traditional unskilled labour. This shift will necessitate retraining and upskilling programs to prepare the workforce for new types of jobs that focus more on monitoring and optimising AI and robotic operations.

Site management is another area where AI and DFMA will have a considerable impact. With smarter planning tools and algorithms, project managers can optimise workflows and resource allocation more effectively. The ability of AI to analyse large sets of data in real time will support better decision-making, minimising delays and reducing costs by predicting potential issues before they arise.

Overall, the future of AI and DFMA in architecture is geared towards creating more efficient, sustainable, and cost-effective construction practices. These technologies will enable architects and builders to not only design and build more innovative structures but also transform the very nature of the

Figure 1.3.7 The sooner a hotel can be constructed, the sooner the rooms can be rented out. This is where the advantages of prefabrication play out in hotel construction

construction process, ushering in an era of increased automation and precision that will fundamentally change the landscape of the industry.

We have delved into the integration of AI and DFMA within the field of modern architecture, and it is evident that these technologies hold the transformative potential to reshape industry standards and practices. This approach marks a pivotal shift from traditional design methodologies towards more efficient, precise, and sustainable construction practices. Technologies like AR are revolutionising assembly processes by providing real-time, immersive guidance, which helps in minimising errors and enhancing the speed of construction. Simultaneously, AI-driven tools are optimising project management and labour operations, fundamentally altering how tasks are approached and executed on construction sites.

These advances herald a new era of construction that prioritises efficiency, accuracy, and environmental sustainability. The shift from labour-intensive techniques to automated, data-driven approaches is reflective of a broader industry trend towards innovation and sustainability. This evolution in architectural practices is not just about integrating new technologies but about fundamentally rethinking the approach to design and construction to meet the demands of the 21st century.

As we anticipate the future, the introduction of AI and DFMA in architecture promises not only to streamline and enhance the construction process but also to drive the creation of smarter, faster, and greener building practices. The integration of such technologies is poised to redefine the construction landscape, offering a blueprint for a future where technology and traditional expertise converge to foster a more sustainable, efficient, and innovative architectural practice.

In conclusion, the ongoing evolution driven by AI and DFMA is transforming architectural methodologies, merging cutting-edge technology with age-old wisdom to revolutionise the way buildings are designed and constructed. As the industry continues to evolve, embracing these changes will be crucial for architects seeking to remain at the forefront of design and innovation, ensuring that their practices are not only current but also aligned with the future trajectories of the global construction industry.

NOTES

1 G. Boothroyd, P. Dewhurst, and W. Knight, *Product Design for Manufacture and Assembly*, 2nd edition, New York: Marcel Dekker, 2002.

2 Weisheng Lu, Tan Tan, Jinying Xu, Jing Wang, Ke Chen, Gao Shang, and Fan Xue, 'Design for Manufacture and Assembly (DfMA) in Construction: The Old and the New', *Architectural Engineering and Design Management* (2020), https://doi.org/10.1080/17452007.2020.1768505.
3 Austin Weber, 'Tesla Rethinks the Assembly Line', *Assembly*, 2023, www.assemblymag.com/articles/97788-tesla-rethinks-the-assembly-line
4 Zbigniew Huber, 'Five-step design method by Elon Musk', *Super Engineer*, 2024, www.superengineer.net/blog/dfx-elon-musk-design-method
5 www.lego.com
6 NASA, 'Station Assembly Elements', 2026, www.nasa.gov/international-space-station/international-space-station-assembly-elements
7 Leach, *Architecture in the Age of AI*, pp. 158–159.
8 Molly Hayes and Amanda Downie. 'What Is Augmented Reality?' *IBM Think*, IBM Corporation, 2024. www.ibm.com/topics/augmented-reality

PART 2

AI AND EXPERIMENTAL DESIGN

DANIEL BOLOJAN

Figure 2.1.1 Versur AI – Agentic workflow with specialised agents reasoning over sectional massing, spatial hierarchy, and aesthetic continuity

CHAPTER 2.1
INTRODUCTION

Daniel Bolojan

What happens when computation moves beyond predefined rules and begins to participate in the evolving logic of design – reorganising constraints, negotiating intent, and contributing as a creative agent? In recent years, we have witnessed a fundamental reconfiguration in how we conceive, model, and engage with computation. No longer confined to deterministic, rule-based systems, AI is entering a new phase, defined not merely by *generativity*, but by *agency*. This is not an incremental evolution but a transformation in kind – it signals a deeper transformation in the architecture of thought itself: from command-driven systems to adaptive intelligences capable of inference, collaboration, and situated response.

But what does this mean for architecture and design?

Design, by its nature, resists closure. It thrives in ambiguity, contradiction, and negotiation – between form and performance, constraint and intuition, memory and projection. Can generative AI models, trained on statistical priors, meaningfully participate in such a process? Or do they merely interpolate what already exists, unable to see beyond the dataset's edge?

What if creativity is no longer exclusively human? What if intelligence, distributed across neural layers and agentic systems, begins to act – proposing, critiquing, refining – not as a mirror of human intention, but as something other, something parallel, expanding what architecture could become?

The emergence of transformer architecture, diffusion models, and multimodal neural networks has extended the computational frontier. Yet what remains unresolved is not merely a technical challenge – it is a cognitive and creative one. Can these systems reason across modalities, *learn* to *learn*, and construct internal models of the world? Can they move from producing outputs to offering situated, context-aware interpretations?

The first chapter, 'Towards a New Computational Paradigm', traces this transformation – from symbolic expert systems to neural learning models,

DOI: 10.4324/9781003347330-7

from retrieval-based computing to generative paradigms. What emerges is not simply a story of technological progress, but one of conceptual rupture: where software becomes less a set of instructions and more a field of latent potential, activated through prompts, context, and learned representations.

This is not simply a shift in tools, but in the ontology. Where once we encoded logic, we now cultivate behaviours; where we defined rules, we now train systems to infer them. The implications for design are profound: what does it mean to work with a system that infers design intent, rather than merely executes instruction?

We are learning to brief machines, not to command them.

In doing so, we begin to recognise that this transformation is not only technical but epistemological, ethical, and pedagogical – changing how we understand computation, how we collaborate with it, and how we learn to design alongside intelligent systems.

If the first chapter maps this evolution, the second, 'Agentic Creativity: Towards Agentic AI in Design', explores how machines might begin to *negotiate*. It introduces the notion of agentic AI – a framework where machines do not merely generate outputs but participate in redefining the problems themselves. Here, agency is understood not as autonomy in the abstract, but as the capacity to pursue goals, evaluate outcomes, and revise strategies within an evolving design process. Architecture, inherently multimodal, offers fertile terrain for such inquiry: from sketches to simulations, from text to spatial form, it operates across multiple representations and scales. As design becomes increasingly entangled with data, what forms of intelligence are needed to interpret, synthesise, and orchestrate across scales and modalities?

In this vision, agentic AI operates through a network of specialised agents – each with its own modality and logic – collaborating to negotiate the evolving nature of design. One may optimise structure, another assesses aesthetics, a third interprets cultural or semantic cues. Together, they produce not a single output but a dialogue of possibilities. Authorship becomes distributed. Design unfolds through feedback, friction, and iteration, where novelty arises not from consensus but from the productive tension between competing ideas.

In this ecology, the designer's role also transforms – from originator to orchestrator of agentic processes. The designer curates intentions across modalities, shaping the interplay between human intuition and machine inference. Here, the next frontier is not interpolation but extrapolation: generating what lies beyond the edge of the dataset – speculative, unfamiliar, and open-ended. For this to happen, AI must evolve from passive generator to active negotiator.

This evolution raises not only technical but philosophical questions. What counts as creativity in such a system? Where is intent located? How do we critique or collaborate with these intelligences? And how might they not only reflect but also challenge our assumptions?

These two chapters trace an evolving topology rather than a fixed map – marking a shift from systems that passively generate to those that reason, interact, and negotiate; from tools that extend the designer's will to intelligences that expand and redefine it.

Could we be moving toward a future where intelligence is ecological – emergent from the interplay of many agents, modalities, and minds? And if so, what kind of architecture, and what kind of designer will be required to orchestrate a symphony of intelligences?

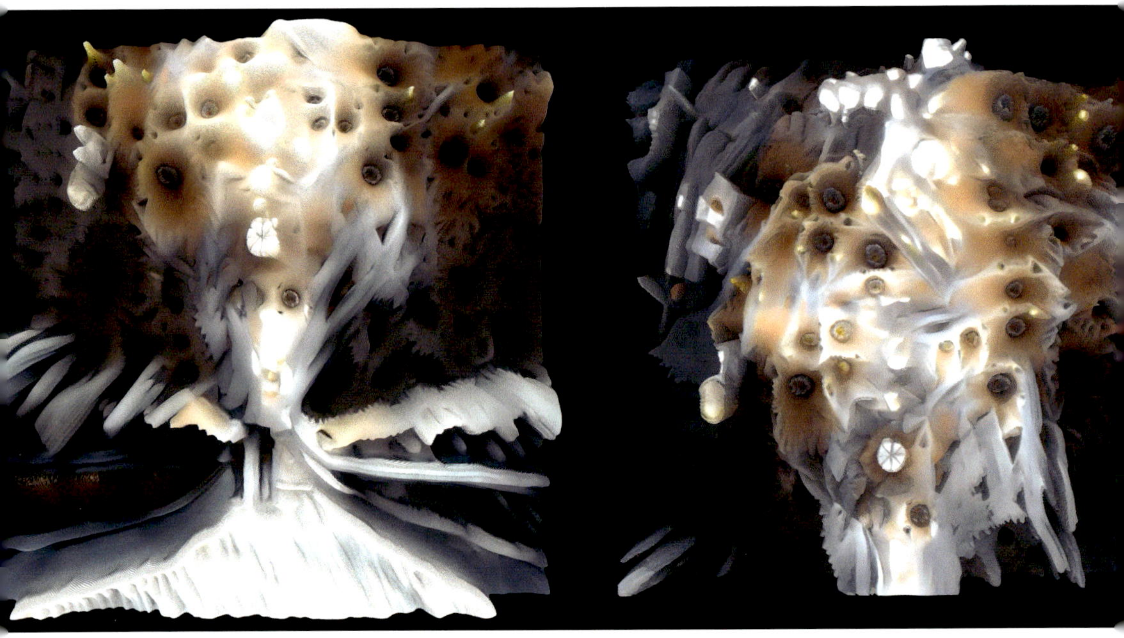

Figure 2.2.1 Gaudí + Neural Networks – The system allows design intention to be encoded at various design levels. Methods such as cross-network feature blending enable the designer to emphasise or de-emphasise desired semantic features

CHAPTER 2.2
TOWARDS A NEW COMPUTATIONAL PARADIGM

Daniel Bolojan

The creative industries are undergoing a profound transformation, driven by advances in computational intelligence. These shifts are not merely incremental improvements but a redefinition of the boundaries of creativity and problem-solving. At the core of these transformations are breakthroughs in neural network architectures – such as transformers – supported by availability of large datasets and powerful hardware.[1] Together, these developments have catalysed the rise of generative models, including generative adversarial networks (GANs), diffusion models, and large language models (LLMs), which are reshaping how we conceive and produce across art, design, architecture, and beyond.

Models such as DALL-E 2, Midjourney, and Stable Diffusion generate high-quality images from textual prompts, while multimodal and LLMs such as CLIP, BERT, GPT, LLaMA, and Claude enhance natural language processing capabilities, enabling machines to understand, generate, and interact with humans at a completely unprecedented level.[2] These tools are not only transforming existing creative practices but also unlocking new forms of expression. They challenge conventional notions of authorship, raise questions about the future of human–machine collaboration, and prompt us to reconsider what computational models of creativity might become.

DOI: 10.4324/9781003347330-8

THE REAL HURDLE: A COMPUTING PROBLEM

For decades, the limits of intelligent systems stemmed from hardware – particularly chip design. Yet the real constraint proved computational. The breakthrough came in 2017 with the introduction of the transformer architecture, revealing that the limitations of earlier models – such as recurrent neural networks (RNNs) and long short-term memory (LSTM) models – were bottlenecked not by hardware but by how they processed data.[3] The transformer's *self-attention* mechanism enabled parallel processing and long-range relationships, transforming sequence modelling and becoming the foundation for systems like GPT, DALL-E 2, Midjourney, Flux, and Stable Diffusion.

Earlier advances paved the way. In 1997, Sepp Hochreiter and Jürgen Schmidhuber's LSTM addressed the *vanishing-gradient* problem that plagued RNNs,[4] much like how a message gets lost in the game of telephone. By the mid-2010s, Ilya Sutskever and Dzmitry Bahdanau introduced *attention mechanisms* that allowed models to focus on relevant data within large sequences.[5] Aäron van den Oord's WaveNet (2016) further proved that recurrence wasn't essential, using masked convolutions to enable partial parallelisation. Vaswani *et al.* then unified these insights with the transformer, dispensing with recurrence entirely in favour of attention-based computation.[6]

These innovations reveal a deeper story: that progress in AI has been driven less by faster hardware than by a reimagining of computation itself. They signal two interrelated shifts: from expert systems to learning systems, and from retrieval-based to generative computing. These shifts have profound implications for many fields, including architecture. This evolution is not merely a technological transformation; it represents a fundamental rethinking of how we design computational systems and approach problem-solving.[7]

FROM EXPERT SYSTEMS TO LEARNING SYSTEMS

Expert and learning systems embody two fundamentally different conceptions of intelligence. Expert systems, grounded in *symbolic AI*, rely on explicit, human-written rules to represent knowledge.[8] Their logic is sequential and deterministic: reasoning unfolds step by step through predefined inferences.[9] Learning systems, by contrast, are adaptive and *data-driven*. Inspired by the brain, they learn patterns and relationships from examples rather than from hand-crafted rules.[10]

The Era of Expert Systems

From the 1970s to the early 2000s, expert systems dominated AI. They embodied the belief that intelligence could be formalised: if human expertise were fully described, machines could reason like experts. Each system consisted of a *knowledge base* – a codified set of facts and rules – and an *inference engine* that applied those rules to specific cases.[11] They excelled in structured domains where all possibilities could be anticipated, but their dependence on fixed rules made them rigid and unable to adapt to novel situations.

John Gero's *Design Prototypes* exemplified this paradigm. His system encoded expert knowledge about design elements, their relationships, and constraints, allowing computers to infer new design solutions much like human designers.[12] Similarly, SEED (Software Environment to Support Early Phases in Building Design) used rule-based reasoning to guide architects in complying with building codes and design standards.[13] Both systems demonstrated the potential of encoded expertise but also its limits: once rules were defined, the systems could not evolve beyond them.

As computational power and programming methodologies evolved, languages such as, C++, VB, C#, and Python enabled the development of more versatile design tools. This progression led to the emergence of comprehensive CAD systems like AutoCAD, Rhino, and Maya, which offer robust 2D drafting, 3D modelling, and parametric capabilities. However, these tools remained within the paradigm of Software 1.0, as defined by Andrew Karpathy, where human programmers write explicit instructions in programming languages, defining specific behaviours line by line.[14]

The Rise of Learning Systems

A major breakthrough came in 2012 with AlexNet, a deep neural network that transformed image recognition by learning patterns directly from data rather than relying on hand-crafted rules. This success marked the beginning of the modern *deep learning* era and showed that machines could outperform traditional AI systems across a wide range of tasks, including design and architecture.[15]

AlexNet's impact signalled a decisive shift from expert systems, which depended on fixed, human-written rules, to learning systems, where models acquire knowledge from examples.[16] In this new paradigm, programmers no longer define every step explicitly; instead, they create algorithms capable of improving through experience. The system learns the underlying structure of the data, developing its own internal representations to make predictions or decisions.

At the core of these learning systems are neural networks, computational models inspired by the brain's structure. They consist of layers of interconnected nodes – or *neurons* – that adjust their internal connections through training. This ability to learn from data allows neural networks to handle complex, unstructured problems that are difficult or impossible to solve with traditional rule-based systems.[17] Learning systems can generalise and offer solutions to new conditions, making them effective for discovering insights that may not be apparent.

In the traditional paradigm, what Andrej Karpathy calls *Software 1.0*,[18] a computer follows explicit, deterministic code: every operation was predefined by the programmer. Neural networks introduced *Software 2.0*, where the 'code' is learned through data. Programmers now design neural network architectures and supply training examples that shape how systems learn. This shift redefines computation itself – from rule-based execution to adaptive inference, from deterministic logic to probabilistic generation – establishing the foundation for creative and agentic AI.

Figure 2.2.2 Semantic Universes – Sequential studies illustrating how a personalised semantic universe materialises as multi-agent grammars negotiate texture, curvature, and compositional logic

FROM RETRIEVAL TO GENERATIVE COMPUTING

Building on the transition from expert to learning systems, computing has entered a new paradigm: the shift from *retrieval* to *generative* methods. While retrieval systems respond to queries by locating existing information, generative systems respond to *prompts* by creating new content.

Today's computing paradigm predominantly centres around data retrieval. Whenever you use your smartphone, tablet, or computer, it sends a request across a network. In response, a distant data centre retrieves the files and sends them back to your device. However, retrieval computing is inherently limited by the scope of the available data. It can only provide answers based on existing information, making it less effective for tasks that require creativity.[19]

Generative computing moves beyond retrieval. Instead of retrieving, it *creates* new content. These systems generate text, images, audio, and other media by learning patterns and relationships from vast datasets. Rather than retrieving stored results, they synthesise novel outputs that reflect the structures they have learned.[20]

GANs made it possible to synthesise realistic images, sounds, and text by learning to imitate real data.[21] Variational autoencoders[22] and later diffusion models[23] expanded this capability, enabling more diverse and detailed content generation, including today's text-to-image systems.

The introduction of the transformer architecture marked a decisive leap, allowing models to capture long-range relationships and process information in parallel.[24] This innovation paved the way for large-scale language models such as GPT-3, which can generate coherent, contextually rich text, compose code, and engage in dialogue.[25] Together, these advances established the foundation of generative computing – a paradigm where machines no longer retrieve information but produce new content that mirrors human creativity and reasoning.

Imagine a world where computers don't just fetch pre-existing data but generate new, real-time, personalised information on the fly. Could the future of computing shift from a retrieval-only paradigm to one that combines retrieval and generation with a focus on real-time generative computing?

In such a paradigm, we could envision exploring a virtual world that does not exist until you enter it. As you turn left, a forest materialises – not retrieved from a preloaded map but generated in real time by a local model. Each tree, sound, and beam of light is synthesised based on the system's learned understanding of ecosystems, physics, and aesthetics.

If you turn right, an entirely different landscape emerges, perhaps a desert at dusk or a futuristic city, shaped by the same generative principles, not by stored assets. The world is *computed as experience unfolds*, rather than rendered from predesigned data.

In this paradigm, there is no 'server' sending files or 'database' of scenes to retrieve. The model running locally on your device generates every texture, every interaction, every possible narrative in real time. The computer becomes a generative system, one capable of producing its own logic, space, and meaning. Computation is no longer predefined execution but adaptive inferences: a continuous negotiation between intent, context, and learned representation.

This shift redefines what we mean by computing itself, transforming it from a process of retrieval to one of creation, and preparing the ground for new kinds of interfaces, such as LLMs, which can mediate between human intention and generative computation.

LEARNING WORLD MODELS

Today's generative AI systems exhibit remarkable capabilities in producing realistic images, text, and motion, yet they still lack understanding. As Yann LeCun argues, their limitation is not capacity but scope – they remain confined to the modalities on which they are trained. Their understanding remains superficial: they can make accurate predictions without grasping the underlying reasons for their accuracy.[26] A model may output a convincing render, but it does not understand what a building *is* – its structure, purpose, or cultural meaning.[27] The distinction between output and understanding remains essential. Generative models may simulate intelligence, but comprehension – the ability to reason about causes, intentions, and contexts – is still emerging.

World models are internal representations that simulate and predict outcomes based on environmental interaction. Unlike single-modality systems confined to text or image, they integrate multiple sensory and spatial channels – language, vision, audio, motion, and 3D geometry – into a unified representation. This allows them to infer relationships and anticipate consequences.[28] For instance, a model trained on architectural data might not only generate an image of a building but also infer its structural logic, function, and environmental logic. This capacity extends well beyond generative synthesis – it moves toward *computational inference*.

Figure 2.2.3 Gaudí + Neural Networks – Interpolative vs. Extrapolative – The extrapolative capability of the system enables the generation of novel compositions that retain the semantics of the underlying architectural domain

Recent advances in text-to-video models such as Runway Gen-3, Luma Dream Machine, and Kling, or world builders Google Genie, WorldLabs illustrate this transition. OpenAI described Sora as a 'general-purpose world simulator', trained on vast image and video datasets through diffusion-transformer architectures. It demonstrated emergent properties such as spatial coherence, intuitive physics, and 3D consistency – signalling an evolution from mere image synthesis toward dynamic environmental simulation. In effect, Sora performed a kind of *soft simulation*: it modelled causal processes rather than simply rendering appearances.[29]

Yet these models remained fragile. Their grasp of physics and causality was often inconsistent, producing artifacts or impossibilities that betrayed their lack of embodied understanding. They occasionally hallucinated scenarios that were incompatible with our physical common sense and lacked a comprehensive grasp of object interactions, as evidenced by some uncanny mistakes in the generated videos.

THE IMPORTANCE OF MULTIMODALITY

Among all modalities, vision holds a unique role in understanding the world: humans learn more through sight than through language. As John Berger observed, we first comprehend the world visually, and this perceptual foundation shapes how we think, speak, and design.[30] This reliance on vision suggests that AI models, too, may derive more fundamental insights from visual data than from any other modality. Yet, just as human understanding is enriched by integrating multiple senses, an *architectural world model* cannot rely on vision alone. It must weave together multiple modalities to achieve a comprehensive grasp of complex environments.

When large neural networks are trained on vast multimodal datasets, they move beyond simple correlations and patterns in the dataset. They begin to form abstracted representations of the world – compressed models of the underlying processes that generate reality itself. In this sense, text and images and other modalities function as *projections of the world*, and learning to map between them gives rise to a primitive form of world understanding within the network.

The role of vision in learning physical laws offers a powerful example. Humans do not understand gravity by memorising Newton's equations but by observing countless visual interactions: apples falling, liquids spilling, objects colliding. Similarly, as Ilya Sutskever has noted, a neural network could learn biomechanics such as how an arm connects to a shoulder simply by analysing large collections of videos. Through exposure alone, the network infers the dynamics of movement, an implicit, emergent understanding rather than one explicitly programmed.[31]

Visual learning has also demonstrated surprising generalisation. Discrete diffusion models can, for instance, solve algorithmic problems like finding the shortest path through a maze using pixel data alone.[32] Likewise, research such as *The Sound of Pixels* shows that auditory information can be reconstructed from visual cues, revealing how one sensory domain can implicitly encode another.[33] These examples highlight how perception across modalities can produce forms of computational reasoning.

In architectural contexts, this insight carries profound implications. An Architectural World Model could be trained not through explicit environment 3D data but through the interplay of multiple 2D and 3D modalities: drawings, renderings, photographs, and textual descriptions combined with information about materials, structure, acoustics, climate, and human behaviour. Each modality contributes a distinct perspective, and their convergence enables a model to infer not only appearance but performance, use, and atmosphere. Multimodality thus becomes indispensable, allowing AI to construct a holistic representation of the built environment, one that mirrors the richness of human perception and cognition.

FROM ONE TO MANY – A THOUSAND BRAIN THEORY

The exploration of multimodal learning naturally aligns with Jeff Hawkins' *'A Thousand Brains'* theory, which proposes a fundamental shift in how we understand cognition.[34] Rather than conceiving intelligence as a single, centralised process, Hawkins suggests that it emerges from a multitude of semi-independent *mini-brains* – cortical columns distributed across the neocortex. Each column constructs its own model of the world from sensory input – visual, auditory, tactile, and beyond – encoding partial perspectives of reality.

These local models communicate and converge through intricate neural connections, forming the unified perception we experience.[35] The theory emphasises that understanding arises not from a single representation but from the *integration of many*, each offering distinct sensory and spatial insights. For example, vision provides a cup's shape and colour, while touch conveys its texture and weight. Over time, the brain merges these perspectives, yielding a coherent and nuanced model of the object.

In this view, the brain is not a singular computational entity but a distributed ecosystem of models, each contributing to our collective intelligence. Cognition, then, is emergent, born from the coordination of many partial understandings into one coherent world model.

Figure 2.2.4 DeepHimmelblau – combining the massing with gestalt nodes

NODE-BASED SYSTEMS

Expanding on Jeff Hawkins theory, the evolution of AI appears poised to follow a similar logic: not toward a single, all-encompassing intelligence, but toward a decentralised ecology of collaborating models – from an all-powerful AI to an ecology of AI systems. Just as the brain relies on the coordination of thousands of cortical columns – each constructing its own partial model of the world – the future of AI, particularly in design and creative domains, will depend on the interaction of many specialised systems.

These models will operate as interconnected nodes within a broader network,[36] combining distinct forms of expertise: functional, structural, and fluid-dynamics models alongside broader cultural or contextual models. The challenge will not lie in building one universal model, but in developing frameworks that enable these diverse agents to communicate, influence one another, and converge on complex tasks.[37]

Task-specific AI models, analogous to specialists, 'zoom in' on particular tasks with high precision, delivering high accuracy within their narrow scope. Conversely, domain-general AI models, akin to generalists, 'zoom out' to manage a wide array of tasks, offering flexibility across various domains, though potentially with reduced accuracy in specialised areas. This diverse composition allows the AI ecosystem to capitalise on the strengths of each model type, creating a more resilient and comprehensive approach to problem-solving.

In architecture, the necessity for such a node-based, multimodal approach becomes especially clear. As John Gero notes, design is one of the most sophisticated forms of human behaviour[38] – an inherently multimodal process involving sketches, text, diagrams, renderings, and models at varying levels of abstraction. Christopher Alexander similarly emphasised that architecture is not a closed system but a vast network of interdependent systems.[39] Following this logic, AI integration in design must mirror architecture's own systemic complexity.

By leveraging a network of specialised AI models, each contributing its expertise to different aspects of the design process, we can begin to address the multi-faceted challenges of architectural design. This approach not only enhances the accuracy and creativity of AI-generated designs but also fosters a more holistic understanding of the built environment, in line with the principles of multimodal cognition and distributed intelligence.

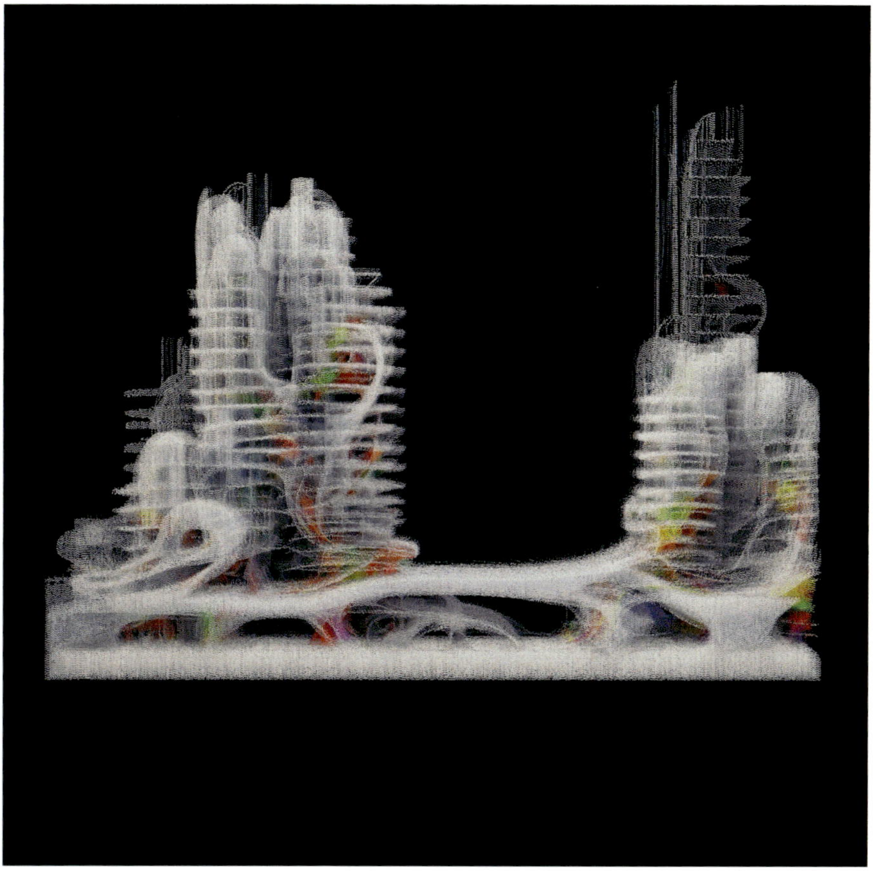

Figure 2.2.5 Deep Semantics – Point cloud explorations of design domains encoded in city sequences

LARGE LANGUAGE MODELS AS COMPUTING INTERFACES

Integrating multiple specialised and general AI models into a cohesive system requires an interface capable of interpreting intent, selecting models, and coordinating their interaction. In many ways, this mirrors Jeff Hawkins' *A Thousand Brains* theory.[40] Likewise, an effective AI ecosystem will depend on a network of interconnected models – functional, structural, and contextual – whose combined intelligence exceeds that of any single component.[41]

Most generative systems today, however, operate primarily within what Daniel Kahneman calls System 1 thinking: fast, intuitive, and associative.[42] They generate fluent, contextually relevant outputs but lack genuine understanding, imitating relationships in data rather than reasoning about underlying principles.[43] A model like Midjourney can render a convincing façade without grasping structure, purpose, or meaning. Its creativity is associative rather than reflective.

Still, these systems display remarkable *intuitive* fluency. Their behaviour parallels the way an architect sketches early concepts – working from intuition, habit, and visual experience rather than analytical deliberation. Likewise, in a fast-paced game like Go, where time is limited, a player must make swift decisions. Rather than meticulously analysing every move, the player relies on their intuition and pattern recognition developed through extensive practice, much like how an AI model draws on its training data. In both cases, expertise manifests as *learned pattern recognition*, an emergent intelligence grounded in experience rather than explicit reasoning. These are habitual patterns, which allow us to react quickly and efficiently in familiar situations, relying on patterns, instincts, and learned behaviours.

Here, *intuition* refers to the model's ability to generate outputs that align with expected patterns and aesthetics, derived from vast exposure to data – even without explicit reasoning or understanding. In this sense, what we describe as *intuition* may be the surface expression of what researchers call emergent capabilities: novel behaviours that arise spontaneously as models scale in complexity and internal coherence.[44]

Once trained, generative AI models operate in inference mode – much like intuitive systems, or what Daniel Kahneman describes as System 1 in *Thinking, Fast and Slow*. To address more complex tasks requiring nuanced understanding, however, these systems must move beyond intuition and engage System 2 processes: slower, more deliberate, and analytical forms of reasoning essential for navigating unfamiliar or ambiguous situations.[45]

Deeper intelligence requires the integration of System 2 *reasoning*.[46] AI must evolve from generation to self-improvement. Without mechanisms for evaluation and refinement, models remain confined to the boundaries of their datasets – mirroring human intuition without achieving reflective thought.[47] In architecture, this means moving from systems that simply generate design representations to those that can iterate, critique, and refine them through feedback, optimisation, and simulation. Quantitative criteria – such as structure, performance, or energy use – could anchor such iterative learning, while qualitative dimensions – like spatial experience or cultural expression – could be explored through human–AI dialogue.

To achieve this synthesis, AI must combine intuitive and analytical reasoning within a coordinated framework of interconnected models, each contributing specialised insight. LLMs are central to this paradigm, acting not merely as conversational agents but as *computational interfaces* that mediate between diverse systems – translating human intent into computational action, coordinating multimodal inputs, and synthesising results across domains. In cognitive terms, they could embody both the fast, associative fluency of System 1 and the deliberate, reflective reasoning of System 2, enabling a continuum between intuitive generation and analytical problem-solving within a single framework.

In architectural contexts, an LLM serving as the interface for an Architectural World Model would transcend image generation or simulation. It would engage in multimodal reasoning – linking text, geometry, material properties, environmental data, and structural performance into a unified design process. Such a system could generate novel solutions and adapt to new design challenges in ways that traditional expert systems cannot. More than a tool for task execution, the language model becomes an adaptive collaborator in the design process – capable of both intuitive and analytical reasoning, and adept at negotiating the complexities inherent in architectural thought.

Figure 2.2.6 Versur AI – Agentic design workflow where specialised agents iteratively reason from massing to section, structure, and facade

A NEW COMPUTATIONAL PARADIGM

The transition from expert systems to learning systems, and from retrieval-based to generative computing, signals the emergence of a new computational paradigm – one defined by multimodal intelligence. By integrating textual, visual, and spatial reasoning, AI systems now achieve a context-aware understanding of complex design environments.

At the centre of this shift are LLMs, which serve as mediators among diverse, specialised AIs. They combine intuitive generation with analytical reasoning, transforming computation from passive execution into active collaboration. Through them, the computer evolves from a passive instrument into an active collaborator – capable not only of generating output but of reasoning, reflecting, and adapting within context.

This transformation echoes a longer trajectory in the history of design tools. Each new medium – from pencil to computer – has expanded our expressive capacity while simultaneously shifting, and at times diminishing, older forms of proficiency. As design practice evolved from solitary authorship to collaborative teamwork, we learned to prompt and coordinate not just tools but people – guiding colleagues to explore alternative directions within a shared project. Today, that same logic extends to AI: we are learning to brief and orchestrate multiple intelligences, each capable of generating, evaluating, and refining design possibilities. The question is no longer how we use a single tool, but how do we orchestrate a network of intelligent agents, each contributing a distinct perspective within a shared creative ecology.

Viewed across this continuum, computation evolves from retrieval to generation, from reasoning to orchestration, and finally toward collaboration. Each stage deepens the relationship between human and machine, transforming computation from a closed mechanism of execution into an open ecology of interacting intelligences. This marks a significant advance in our approach to computational problem-solving and design, opening new opportunities for innovation as we move toward a more integrated understanding of AI's potential in creative domains.

NOTES

1 Ian Goodfellow, Yoshua Bengio, and Aaron Courville, *Deep Learning*, Cambridge, MA: MIT Press, 2016.
2 Devlin, J., et al. 'BERT: Pre-Training of Deep Bidirectional Transformers for Language Understanding', in *Proceedings of the 2019 Conference of the North American Chapter of the Association for Computational Linguistics: Human Language Technologies*, 2019.

Tom Brown, Benjamin Mann, Nick Ryder, Melanie Subbiah, Jared D. Kaplan, Prafulla Dhariwal, Arvind Neelakantan et al. 'Language Models Are Few-Shot Learners', *Advances in Neural Information Processing Systems* 33 (2020): 1877–1901.

Ashish Vaswani, Noam Shazeer, Niki Parmar, Jakob Uszkoreit, Llion Jones, Aidan N. Gomez, Łukasz Kaiser, and Illia Polosukhin, 'Attention Is All You Need', Advances in Neural Information Processing Systems 30 (2017).

3 David E. Rumelhart, Geoffrey E. Hinton, and Ronald J. Williams, 'Learning Representations by Back-Propagating Errors', *Nature* 323, no. 6088(1986): 533–536.

4 Sepp Hochreiter and Jürgen Schmidhuber, 'Long Short-Term Memory', *Neural Computation* 9, no. 8 (1997): 1735–1780.

5 Ilya Sutskever, Oriol Vinyals, and Quoc V. Le, 'Sequence to Sequence Learning with Neural Networks', Advances in Neural Information Processing Systems 27 (2014).

Dzmitry Bahdanau, Kyunghyun Cho, and Yoshua Bengio, 'Neural Machine Translation by Jointly Learning to Align and Translate', *arXiv preprint*, arXiv:1409.0473 (2014).

6 Ashish Vaswani, Noam Shazeer, Niki Parmar, Jakob Uszkoreit, Llion Jones, Aidan N. Gomez, Łukasz Kaiser, and Illia Polosukhin, 'Attention Is All You Need', Advances in Neural Information Processing Systems 30 (2017).

7 Goodfellow, Bengio, and Courville', *Deep Learning*.

8 Stuart J. Russell and Peter Norvig, *Artificial Intelligence: A Modern Approach*, Harlow: Pearson, 2016.

9 Frederick Hayes-Roth, Donald A. Waterman, and Douglas B. Lenat, *Building Expert Systems*, Boston, MA: Addison-Wesley, 1983.

10 Yoshua Bengio, Yann LeCun, and Geoffrey Hinton, 'Deep Learning for AI', *Communications of the ACM* 64, no. 7 (July 2021): 58–65. https://doi.org/10.1145/3448250

11 Edward A. Feigenbaum, Bruce G. Buchanan, and Joshua Lederberg, 'On Generality and Problem Solving: A Case Study Using the DENDRAL Program'. No. NASA-CR-123182 (1970).

12 John S. Gero, 'Design Prototypes: A Knowledge Representation Schema for Design', *AI Magazine* 11, no. 4 (1990): 26.

13 Ulrich Flemming and Robert Woodbury, 'Software Environment to Support Early Phases in Building Design (SEED): Overview', *Journal of Architectural Engineering* 1, no. 4 (1995): 147–152.

14 Andrej Karpathy, 'Software 2.0', *Medium*, November 11, 2017, https://karpathy.medium.com/software-2-0-a64152b37c35

15 Alex Krizhevsky, Ilya Sutskever, and Geoffrey E. Hinton, 'Imagenet Classification with Deep Convolutional Neural Networks', Advances in Neural Information Processing Systems 25 (2012).

16 Goodfellow, Bengio, and Courville, *Deep Learning*.

17 Yann LeCun, Yoshua Bengio, and Geoffrey Hinton, 'Deep Learning', *Nature* 521, no. 7553 (2015): 436–444.

18 Andrej Karpathy, 'Software 2.0'.

19 Yao Lu, Song Bian, Lequn Chen, Yongjun He, Yulong Hui, Matthew Lentz, Beibin Li et al., 'Computing in the Era of Large Generative Models: From Cloud-Native to AI-Native', *arXiv preprint*, arXiv:2401.12230 (2024).

20 Alec Radford, Jeffrey Wu, Rewon Child, David Luan, Dario Amodei, and Ilya Sutskever, 'Language Models Are Unsupervised Multitask Learners', *OpenAI Blog* 1, no. 8 (2019): 9.

21 Ian Goodfellow, Jean Pouget-Abadie, Mehdi Mirza, Bing Xu, David Warde-Farley, Sherjil Ozair, Aaron Courville, and Yoshua Bengio, 'Generative Adversarial Nets', Advances in Neural Information Processing Systems 27 (2014).

22 Diederik P. Kingma and Max Welling, 'Auto-Encoding Variational Bayes', *arXiv preprint*, arXiv:1312.6114 (2013).

23 Jascha Sohl-Dickstein, Eric Weiss, Niru Maheswaranathan, and Surya Ganguli, 'Deep Unsupervised Learning Using Nonequilibrium Thermodynamics', *International Conference on Machine Learning*, pp. 2256–2265, PMLR (2015).

24 David E. Rumelhart, Geoffrey E. Hinton, and Ronald J. Williams, 'Learning Representations by Back-Propagating Errors', *Nature* 323, no. 6088 (1986): 533–536.

25 Tom Brown, Benjamin Mann, Nick Ryder, Melanie Subbiah, Jared D. Kaplan, Prafulla Dhariwal, Arvind Neelakantan et al., 'Language Models Are Few-Shot Learners', *Advances in Neural Information Processing Systems* 33 (2020): 1877–1901.

26 Jacob Browning and Yann LeCun, 'AI and the Limits of Language', *Noema Magazine*, August 23, 2022, www.noemamag.com/ai-and-the-limits-of-language

27 Daniel Bolojan, 'Creative AI in Architecture: How AI is Shaping the Future of Design', in James F. Kerestes, Ebrahim Poustinchi, and Vahid Vahdat (eds), *A Purple Architecture: Design in the Age of the Physical-Virtual Continuum*, Pittsburgh, PA: ETC Press, 2024, pp. 76–104.

28 David Ha and Jürgen Schmidhuber, 'World Models', *arXiv preprint*, arXiv:1803.10122 (2018). Yann LeCun, 'A Path Towards Autonomous Machine Intelligence Version 0.9. 2, 2022-06-27', *Open Review* 62, no. 1 (2022): 1–62.
29 OpenAI, *Video Generation Models as World Simulators*, https://openai.com/index/video-generation-models-as-world-simulators
30 John Berger, *Ways of Seeing*, London: British Broadcasting Corporation and Penguin Books, 1972.
31 Ilya Sutskever and Jensen Huang, 'Ilya Sutskever (OpenAI) and Jensen Huang (NVIDIA CEO): AI Today and Vision of the Future', Uploaded by UC Berkeley Computer Science, April 20, 2023, www.youtube.com/watch?v=Ckz8XA2hW84.
32 Jacob Austin, Daniel D. Johnson, Jonathan Ho, Daniel Tarlow, and Rianne Van Den Berg, 'Structured Denoising Diffusion Models in Discrete State-Spaces', *Advances in Neural Information Processing Systems* 34 (2021): 17981–17993.
33 Hang Zhao, Chuang Gan, Andrew Rouditchenko, Carl Vondrick, Josh McDermott, and Antonio Torralba, 'The Sound of Pixels', in *Proceedings of the European Conference on Computer Vision (ECCV)*, pp. 570–586 (2018).
34 Jeff Hawkins, *A Thousand Brains: A New Theory of Intelligence*, New York: Basic Books, 2021.
35 Hawkins, *A Thousand Brains.*
36 Wolf dPrix, Karolin Schmidbaur, Daniel Bolojan, and Efilena Baseta, 'The Legacy Sketch Machine: From Artificial to Architectural Intelligence', *Architectural Design* 92, no. 3 (2022): 14–21.
37 Daniel Bolojan, Shermeen Yousif, and Emmanouil Vermisso, 'Latent Design Spaces: Interconnected Deep Learning Models for Expanding the Architectural Search Space', in *Architecture and Design for Industry 4.0: Theory and Practice*, Cham: Springer International Publishing, 2023, pp. 201–223.
38 John S. Gero, 'Ten Problems for AI in Design', Workshop on AI in Design, IJCAI-91 (1991).
39 Christopher Alexander, 'Systems Generating Systems', *Architectural Design* 38 (1968): 605–610.
40 Hawkins, *A Thousand Brains.*
41 dPrix, Schmidbaur, Bolojan, and Baseta, 'The Legacy Sketch Machine'.
42 Daniel Kahneman, *'Thinking, Fast and Slow'*, New York: Farrar, Straus and Giroux, 2017.
43 Andrej Karpathy, 'Intro to Large Language Models'. www.youtube.com/watch?v=zjkBMFhNj_g
44 Jason Wei et al., 'Emergent Abilities of Large Language Models', *arXiv preprint*, arXiv:2206.07682 [cs.CL] (2022).
45 Karpathy, 'Intro to Large Language Models'.
46 This distinction is exemplified by DeepMind's AlphaGo, which evolved from imitation to insight. In its first phase, AlphaGo relied on a *Policy Network* trained on human games, emulating expert intuition to select moves – a System 1-like process. Later, it incorporated a *Value Network* to evaluate board positions and a *Monte Carlo Tree Search* to explore possible future sequences of play. Through *reinforcement learning*, it then played millions of games against itself, iteratively refining its strategies. This self-training allowed AlphaGo to discover tactics no human had taught it, surpassing its own initial models and moving from pattern recognition to genuine strategic reasoning. The system thus illustrates how AI can evolve from fast, associative intuition toward more reflective, self-correcting forms of understanding. For further discussion of AlphaGo, see 3.3: 'The Dark Side of AI'.
47 Karpathy. 'Intro to Large Language Models'.

Figure 2.3.1 DeepHimmelblau – Combined massing and gestalt nodes generating unified spatial–formal resolutions

CHAPTER 2.3
AGENTIC CREATIVITY
TOWARDS AGENTIC AI IN DESIGN

Daniel Bolojan

Architectural design is entering a profound transformation driven by generative AI, multimodal intelligence, and emerging agentic frameworks. Building on the historical progression from expert systems to learning systems – and from retrieval-based to generative computing – agentic AI marks the next stage: one where machines move beyond augmentation to act as co-creators within design.

For decades, computation in architecture has functioned as a tool of augmentation – a means to extend human capability through automation, optimisation, and generative exploration.[1] This paradigm enabled architects to offload repetitive tasks and systematically vary parameters. Yet as artificial intelligence grows increasingly capable, a critical question arises: Can AI move beyond augmentation to participate meaningfully in the creative act itself?

BEYOND AUGMENTATION

This shift from augmentation to agency is not without precedent. In the late 1960s, Nicholas Negroponte's Architectural Machine envisioned a dialogue between 'two intelligent systems – the man and the machine' (1969). Unlike early CAD systems that codified geometry, Negroponte imagined computational agents that evolve through interaction, anticipate design needs, and reshape problem spaces – a vision of computation as a partner, not a servant. His model suggested that computational agents should not merely automate tasks but dynamically evolve alongside human designers, anticipating needs and reshaping problem spaces.[2]

DOI: 10.4324/9781003347330-9

Today's generative AI systems, diffusion models like Midjourney or Stable Diffusion and transformer models such as GPT, Claude, or Llama, demonstrate extraordinary expressive range. Yet they remain fundamentally reactive: producing variations within learned distributions rather than redefining the design problem itself. Architecture, by contrast, operates within ill-defined or 'wicked' problems,[3] where the task is not only to generate forms but to reorganise constraints and reinterpret goals as the process unfolds.

Negroponte's foundational ideas anticipated precisely this king of shift: a computational partner that does not merely optimise existing parameters but actively participates in the evolving complexity of design.[4] Recent advancements signal a shift, one where AI moves beyond simple generation to incorporate visual reasoning[5] and strategic reasoning[6] as seen in the DeepSeek, xAI Grok3, and Open AI o1 and o2 models.

This evolution defines the premise of agentic AI[7]: systems that pursue goals, critique results, and adjust their reasoning through feedback. Within my research, Creative AI emerges as an agentic framework integrating generative intuition (Kahneman's System 1) with analytical reflection (System 2).[8] By combining rapid ideation with structured evaluation across multiple agents, Creative AI seeks to establish co-creative workflows where humans and machines negotiate intent, restructure constraints, and propose new design directions. Rather than producing static alternatives, such systems participate in the evolving dialogue of architecture – engaging the discipline's open-ended and multi-dimensional nature as active collaborators.

FROM COMPUTATIONAL DESIGN TO AGENTIC AI

Computational design transformed architectural practice by shifting attention from direct form-making to the creation of generative rules. Instead of shaping final geometries, designers began encoding the DNA of systems capable of producing multiple outcomes in response to variable parameters. This approach expanded the horizon of formal exploration but remained tethered to human-defined goals; algorithms or parametric models could vary results endlessly yet still operated within fixed, *a priori* pre-specified boundaries.[9]

A similar limitation defines today's generative AI models. While they have advanced far beyond expert systems'[10] rule-based logic toward learning systems[11] that derive patterns from data, their creativity remains statistical rather than conceptual. Diffusion models such as Midjourney, DALL-E, or

Stable Diffusion generate images by reconstructing statistical patterns from vast datasets, while transformer-based models like GPT, Claude, or Llama assemble outputs through probabilistic predictions. A transformer model, for instance, predicts the next word, or *token*, based on likelihoods learned from past data, while diffusion models estimate pixel distributions or latent-space patterns derived from training images. These learned distributions define the scope of their generative capacity: they synthesise within existing structures rather than fundamentally rethinking them.

When prompted to 'design a radical new museum', for instance, such systems may generate striking formal variations yet still default to familiar typologies, central atriums, linear circulation, enclosed exhibition halls, because these structures dominate their training data. They interpolate within precedent rather than extrapolate beyond it. As Demis Hassabis observes, current AI models demonstrate *interpolative creativity*, combining what it already knows, rather than *extrapolative creativity*, which creates ideas outside the learned domain.[12]

This is the challenge that the Creative AI framework seeks to address. By structuring intelligence as a node-based, agentic system, it integrates multimodal inputs – text, imagery, parameters, and simulation – into a collaborative network capable of dynamically reshaping constraints. Rather than reproducing statistical priors, Creative AI aspires to enable adaptive, extrapolative creativity, enabling machines to generate novel architectural strategies that extend beyond the limits of their training data and co-evolve with human intent.

NEGOTIATION VS. GENERATION: A CRITICAL DISTINCTION

Creative AI, as proposed, moves beyond conventional generative models by envisioning a system that not only generates but also negotiates, moving from passive synthesis to active reasoning. Diffusion and transformer models excel at producing variations within the statistical priors of their training data, yet they remain bound by predefined objectives. In contrast, a node-based agentic framework integrates multimodal intelligence, to dynamically rethink problem spaces rather than merely populate them with options.

Architectural design rarely presents well-defined problems. It involves reconciling competing demands, form, function, cost, context, and culture, each introducing friction that fuels creativity. Creative AI seeks to emulate this complexity, merging rapid generation with constraint negotiation to foster what Demis Hassabis calls *extrapolative creativity*[13]: the ability to move beyond precedent and propose genuinely new design logics. In doing so, it mirrors the architect's iterative process, balancing tensions, exposing trade-offs, and discovering unforeseen possibilities.

Early agentic AI points toward systems capable of continuous self-refinement, echoing AlphaGo's evolution from human imitation to self-play.[14] These systems could function akin to a human design team, continuously debating trade-offs between form, performance, and cultural context, realigning priorities as needed. They could reweigh priorities – favouring, for instance, timber over steel when environmental imperatives surpass economic ones – and orchestrate a dialogue among agents evaluating performance, aesthetics, and cultural resonance. By iteratively renegotiating constraints across scales, from high-level concepts to tectonic detail,[15] it could cultivate a multi-perspective design process that mirrors architectural practice itself.

While it is too early to know whether agentic AI will serve as a stepping stone toward artificial general intelligence (AGI), researchers suggest that systems capable of *renegotiating constraints*, rather than optimising a single goal, may signal an early form of generality.[16] David Deutsch observes that current AI are 'almost exact opposites': today's systems excel at obedient execution, analysing billions of chess moves within fixed parameters, while human creativity depends on *reflective disobedience*, exploring fewer paths but with intention and insight.[17] Most AI remains narrowly specialised, confined to tasks like diagnosis, chess, image generation etc. Humans, by contrast, transcend optimisation itself, a chess grandmaster might abandon the game to pursue philosophy, just as an architect might rethink a project entirely when confronted with new constraints. This ability to *step outside the frame*, to reflect and reorganise the problem itself, is regarded as central to genuine creativity.[18]

MULTI-AGENT SYSTEMS: THE NEXT STEP TOWARD AGENTIC AI

The shifts from (1) augmentation to agency, from (2) interpolative to extrapolative generation, and from (3) passive generation to active negotiation could redefine AI's role in architectural design. These transitions enable dynamic constraint-reshaping, transforming rigid grids into fluid spatial flows or balancing functional clarity with expressive form. Yet negotiation alone captures only one dimension of agentic AI. Equally important is the emergence of multi-agent systems, where diverse intelligences – specialised, generalist, domain-specific, or supportive – interact through cooperative, adversarial, or parallel exchanges.

In such systems, multiple agents collaborate across distinct facets of design – structure, environment, circulation, cost, or aesthetics – each contributing specialised insight while continuously exchanging information. This approach bridges a crucial divide: specialist models offer precision and domain-specific accuracy but lack adaptability, whereas generalist models provide flexibility

Figure 2.3.2 DeepHimmelblau – Diagram of a multi-node framework, illustrating how specialised and generalist nodes negotiate, exchange information, and co-evolve design intent, generating unified spatial–formal resolution

across broader contexts at the cost of depth and precision. Through coordinated interaction, a multi-agent framework can leverage both, achieving depth and adaptability simultaneously. It also balances deterministic reliability – ensuring structural safety or compliance – with predictive exploration, generating speculative or unconventional solutions. Rather than following a fixed top-down hierarchy, these agents could dynamically critique and refine each other's outputs and negotiate across multiple layers of complexity.

Within this node-based framework, each agent addresses a distinct layer of the design ecology. A budgeting agent negotiates costs and material availability; a structural agent runs load simulations; an aesthetic agent generates formal or spatial rhythms. Coordinated through well-designed communication protocols, these agents could collectively reshape constraints and realign priorities as design goals evolve. LLMs could function as mediators in this ecology – interpreting intent, translating briefs into computational directives, orchestrating multimodal interactions, and integrating intuitive generation with structured reasoning.

AlphaGo's self-play model illustrates this paradigm: two instances of the same AI competed continuously, discovering strategies that surpassed centuries of human expertise. By training against its evolving counterpart, the system moved beyond mere interpolation, developing genuinely novel tactics through a self-reinforcing feedback loop.[19]

Translated into architecture, multi-agent systems could function similarly – with generalist and specialised networks challenging and refining one another to generate insights beyond the reach of human teams or an AI model alone. This iterative, negotiated intelligence underpins my Creative AI vision for architectural design, explored through projects such as Gaudí + Neural Networks,[20] DeepHimmelblau,[21] and Deep Semantics,[22] as well as through Versur.[23] These projects blend generative intuition with structured reasoning to enable human–machine co-creation.

AGENTIC AI AND AUTHORSHIP

Building on the collaborative potential of multi-agent systems, the evolution of computation in architecture – from parametric design to agentic frameworks – has continually reshaped the designer's role. Early parametric tools initially raised fears that automation might erode authorship, yet they ultimately redefined it. Rather than shaping final forms, architects began scripting the generative logics that produce them,[24] granting agency through the structuring of dependencies, relationships, and constraints rather than direct geometric manipulation. While parametric systems enable design variation, they remain contingent on predefined constraints – the architect still establishes parameters, runs simulations, and interprets results.[25]

Generative design extended this agency by introducing adaptive, rule-based systems such as genetic algorithms, swarm intelligence, and cellular automata. Here, architects encoded behaviours instead of fixed geometries, establishing conditions from which solutions could emerge. This shift redefined authorship once again: from defining relationships to defining system rules and interactions. Yet even these systems remain bound by their initial premises – capable of optimisation and exploration, but not of questioning or reformulating their own rules.

With recent advances in generative AI, designers now engage across multiple levels of agency – balancing structured logic with intuitive prompt-based exploration. Techniques such as prompt engineering, latent vector interpolation, and cross-network blending fuse conceptual guidance and computational emergence. Through prompt engineering, designers steer model outputs via carefully constructed textual instructions; latent vector interpolation offers finer control, enabling transitions between design states or stylistic variations; and blending latent spaces across networks – merging sparse, high-level features with more detailed layers – can synthesise distinct stylistic traits into coherent new compositions, as demonstrated in the DeepHimmelblau project.[26] Conditioning inputs further allows architects to guide the generative process while preserving AI-driven variation. This marks a new mode of authorship that extends the lineage from parametric and generative design toward the strategic navigation and curation of a model's latent space.[27] The architect now shapes design through feedback and negotiation, guiding the model's creative trajectory rather than prescribing its form.

Agentic AI could intensify this evolution by introducing systems capable of redefining the problem itself. Moving beyond fixed boundaries, it may function as a co-designer – identifying latent opportunities, proposing alternative workflows, reorganising constraints, and prompting designers to reconsider assumptions. This could represent a shift from directive to co-creative agency: a reciprocal dialogue in which AI actively reshapes design intent.

Such an expansion of agency raises profound questions of authorship and creativity. If a system can reformulate its problem space, can it also explain its reasoning or justify its decisions? Agency here could extend beyond generation

Figure 2.3.3 A composite study illustrating how prompt-encoded design intentions, structural logics, and biomorphic grammar converge within a shared latent space, allowing human and AI models to co-evolve sectional, tectonic, and volumetric possibilities

to include critique, reflection, and self-improvement. As David Deutsch observes, the challenge lies in constructing machines that not only perform tasks but *reflect* on them – adapting their strategies as contexts evolve and perhaps even redefining the nature of the design inquiry itself.[28]

If realised, this transformation could recast architecture from a discipline structured around sequential workflows into a dynamic negotiation between human and artificial intelligences. Design would no longer unfold through linear, human-defined iterations but through a continuous exchange in which multiple intelligences – human and artificial – propose, critique, and refine each other's contributions. The architect's role would move from defining static systems to orchestrating an evolving ensemble of specialised and generalist intelligences, cultivating adaptive, open-ended design ecologies.

THE COMPLEXITY OF ARCHITECTURAL DESIGN: A MULTIMODAL, MULTI-LAYERED PROCESS

Architectural design, with its inherent complexity, demands a framework capable of negotiating competing constraints and balancing intuitive exploration with analytical rigor. A node-based, agentic AI system offers such a structure – coordinating specialised and generalist models that collaboratively generate, critique, and refine design solutions across modalities, integrating rapid, generative intuition with structured reasoning at multiple levels of abstraction. Within this framework, architectural design emerges as a multimodal, multi-layered process[29] that weaves sketches, drawings, parametric models, environmental data, material constraints, and cultural narratives into a single evolving synthesis.[30]

Unlike disciplines with well-defined problem sets, architecture engages 'wicked' problems that resist singular solutions and demand continuous negotiation across competing priorities.[31] An agentic AI framework could mirror this complexity by distributing intelligence across a network of specialised agents, each with its own modality, logic, and domain of expertise.

Within such a system, a structural agent might simulate load paths, an environmental agent analyse performance and site conditions, a spatial agent optimise circulation, and an aesthetic agent evaluate form. These agents interact through continuous feedback – exchanging data, critiquing outputs, and renegotiating constraints as new priorities emerge. Much like a human design team, they collectively debate trade-offs between form, function, and context.

Architecture's multimodal nature amplifies the need for such distributed intelligence. Design operates across multiple scales – from concept to tectonics – where no single model can span the entire spectrum. Text-to-image generators may excel at visual fluency while neglecting structural logic; optimisation algorithms may solve narrow problems while ignoring contextual nuance.[32] An agentic system, by contrast, orchestrates collaboration among specialised agents, each contributing through parametric, semantic, or visual modes toward a negotiated solution. Echoing Jeff Hawkins' insight that intelligence arises from the coordination of many partial models,[33] such a framework could integrate structural, spatial, and cultural relations into a dynamic, adaptive representation.

Ultimately, architecture's complexity calls for an adaptive design ecology capable of navigating vast design spaces while reconciling diverse constraints. Creative AI, structured through multi-agent and multimodal processes, offers such a framework: design becomes a cyclical dialogue where each proposal triggers new refinements in real time. The architect's role shifts from problem-solver to orchestrator of intelligences, curating agent interactions and aligning their evolving outputs.

To ground these ideas, projects such as Semantic Universes, Machine Perceptions: Gaudí + Neural Networks, and DeepHimmelblau demonstrate components of agentic AI in architectural design. Semantic Universes explores multimodal agent collaboration to construct new semantic design spaces[34]; Gaudí + Neural Networks extrapolates historical context into speculative reimagining[35]; and DeepHimmelblau investigates how these systems can be deployed in practice within Coop Himmelb(l)au's architectural workflow.[36] Together with Versur.ai – a workflow-based agentic AI platform – these projects test how agentic frameworks can mediate between intuition and computation, contributing to a foundation for adaptive, co-creative design systems. Their aim is to define distinct modes of agent interaction and examine the implications of these strategies for a dynamic interplay between human and artificial intelligence.

This trajectory echoes Nicholas Negroponte's early vision of interactive computational agents – systems that evolve through dialogue rather than execution.[37] Today, that vision finds renewed form in agentic AI frameworks where intelligence emerges not from a singular model but from the interplay of multiple specialised, generalist, and task-specific agents. This shift – from isolated computational tools to adaptive, networked intelligence – marks a profound transformation in architectural thinking: from designing *within* constraints to designing *through* their continuous renegotiation.

APPLICATION OF CREATIVE AI FRAMEWORK IN DESIGN

To develop the Creative AI framework – a node-based, multi-agent, multimodal system for architectural design – my research began by dissecting and mapping existing design workflows. This process involved breaking complex design tasks into discrete steps, identifying relationships among components, and iteratively testing adaptive strategies. The goal was twofold: first, to distil these processes into rules and interactions that would enable an agentic system to operate autonomously; and second, to define the optimal balance between deterministic and predictive methods, as well as between specialised and generalist agents, suited to different levels of architectural abstraction. Ultimately, the aim is to construct a system that, once prompted, can decompose a design problem into actionable steps and generate solutions independently – embodying the cyclical dialogue between human and artificial intelligence envisioned at the outset.

Figure 2.3.4 DeepHimmelblau – Combined massing and gestalt nodes generating unified spatial–formal resolution

SEMANTIC UNIVERSES

Extending the multimodal and multi-agent framework outlined earlier, the Semantic Universes project presents a focused application of Creative AI – one that constructs personalised creative ecosystems, or 'semantic universes'. These universes emerge from the synthesis of multiple data types – text, images, and parameters – into expressive frameworks where designers define their own formal languages, syntaxes, and conceptual spaces. At the core lies the construction of an *expressive grammar*: a set of rules and relationships through which form, texture, and composition reflect a designer's philosophy. Designers begin by articulating aesthetic intent – perhaps favouring fluid transitions or fractured silhouettes – and translate these into structured syntaxes that AI can interpret and refine. Leveraging a multi-agent architecture, this approach moves beyond the stylistic limitations of public generative AI models, enabling adaptive systems that evolve in dialogue with a designer's unique sensibility.

This marks a shift from prompt-based image generation toward the creation of fully embedded, multi-agent design ecosystems. Rather than adopting predefined styles, designers can train AI systems to internalise the specific formal and semantic logic of their own design philosophy. Each designer weaves a distinct tapestry of references, fragments, and principles – a *semantic universe* that encodes personal semantic universe.[38] To integrate AI meaningfully, models must not only recognise these semantic structures but also learn to encode the subtle formal distinctions that define an individual's work. For example, generative models often default to generic curvilinear archetypes, failing to distinguish between Baroque, Renaissance, or Art Nouveau forms. Even within the Baroque, Borromini's dynamic spatial undulations differ radically from Bernini's theatrical compositions. Because of such variation, encoding a designer's specific features into AI models is crucial to ensuring that their distinct vision – rather than a generic approximation – defines their semantic universe. Once encoded, AI becomes not a tool of replication but a medium for externalising imagination, transforming a designer's latent world into a dynamic, living realm of creative exploration.

Figure 2.3.5 Deep Semantics – Features encoding results from nine design fields

The Semantic Universes – Deep Semantics project embodies this vision through a distributed network of specialised and generalist agents, each addressing a distinct stage of semantic and aesthetic synthesis. Developed through collaborative research at the FAU School of Architecture's Design 10 Studio with Arie Chocron, Alysa Scherger, and Thomas Tucker, the project employs a trifold strategy: extracting contextual sections, encoding semantics from nine non-architectural domains, and synthesising them into cohesive design universes.[39]

Within this architecture, a *semantic cross-examiner* (1) analyses and merges semantics from various non-architectural design domains, identifying relationships that form the backbone of a new syntax. An *aesthetic evaluator* (2) assesses visual quality, composition, and coherence, aiming to align the output with the designer's intent. A *visual attributor* (3) examines the influence of textural descriptors on generated outputs, e.g., how 'soft' or 'rigid' alters form, while an *image generator* (4) produces visuals from input prompts, creating the initial expressions of the syntax. A *sentiment analysis agent* (5) evaluates the emotional tone of these outputs, aiming to align them with the designer's expressive goals, while a *context evaluator* (6) interprets contextual data to ground the universe in relevant influences. A *descriptor agent* (7) interprets visuals as semantic markers, extracting potential meanings from form, while a *semantic encoder* (8) curates and evaluates these descriptors for precision. A *domain synthesiser* (9) integrates features across domains, blending aesthetics, while a *spatial synthesiser* (10) predicts sectional relationships to ensure spatial coherence. A *feature transmuter* (11) transfers traits between domains, e.g., from texture to rhythm, while a *descriptors curator* (12) filters and refines semantics, and a *sample selector* (13) sorts input data for relevance, curating the foundation. Together, these 13 agents form a system that collaboratively constructs semantic universes, extending the multi-agent dynamics essential for a Creative AI agentic framework.[40]

GAUDÍ + NEURAL NETWORKS

Machine Perception: Gaudí + Neural Networks – presented at the 17th Venice Architecture Biennale's Italian Pavilion – explores Antoni Gaudí's Sagrada Família through a network of neural networks. Conventional generative models remain confined to statistical priors, interpolating within learned distributions; this project instead introduces multi-node negotiation to enable extrapolative generation that pushes beyond dataset boundaries. Rather than replicating historical artifacts, it examines how a node-based system of AI models can move beyond augmentation, dynamically reshaping constraints and expanding architectural creativity.

This shift parallels the evolution of strategic reasoning in AI systems such as AlphaGo: early versions recombined human strategies, while later iterations, through self-play, discovered moves that transcended human intuition. Likewise, Gaudí + Neural Networks establishes adversarial and collaborative exchanges between nodes, unlocking novel spatial logics that extend beyond the interpolative reach of precedent. Machines interpolate derivatives with ease, but genuine creativity demands extrapolation[41] – a system capable of redefining its design space through continuous negotiation.

To achieve this, the project implements three core strategies. First, it refines machine perception through feature maps prioritising architectural characteristics. Second, it employs progressive training to disentangle curvature, seriality, and branching logic so each can be manipulated independently. Third, it deploys a node-based framework of interacting nodes operating at different compositional scales, each critiquing and refining the others' outputs within a feedback loop. Unlike goal-driven parametric systems, this network evolves adaptively, treating design as an ongoing negotiation among form, structure, and context.

In the context of Sagrada Família, one node might generate variations of Gaudí's vaulted forms, say, extending the nave's branching columns into new spatial configurations, while another assesses their tectonic detail. These nodes continuously exchange data, refining column curvature, aperture geometry, and tectonic rhythm. The process yields a dynamic design ecology, in which local decisions by individual nodes collectively produce coherent architectural order.

The system's six agents each target a layer of design abstraction. One decodes low-level tectonics – parabolic arches, helical columns, textured surfaces – capturing Gaudí's structural logic. Another navigates latent space through text queries such as '*enhance organic continuity*' or '*amplify vertical thrust*', embedding strategic intent into generation. A third extracts high-level principles from natural formations like tree canopies, where branching and layered growth inform spatial articulation. A complementary node encodes Gaudí's compositional logic, mapping relationships among nave symmetry, column placement, and spire articulation. Two synthesising nodes merge these insights – one integrating low-level tectonics with external influences,

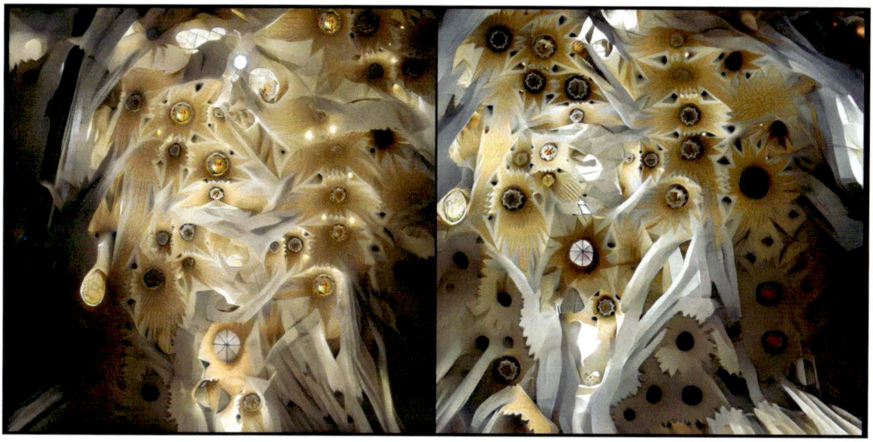

Figure 2.3.6 Gaudí + Neural Networks – Vaulted configurations generated through interacting nodes that disentangle curvature, seriality, and structural branching

the other facilitating cross-domain translation of structural patterns into new configurations.

Through this multimodal interplay of visual, textual, and structural data, the project moves beyond stylistic replication toward an extrapolative design process. It establishes a continuous negotiation between competing constraints, where solutions emerge from structured dialogue rather than isolated computation. As generative AI advances from System 1-style intuition to System 2-style deliberation, Gaudí + Neural Networks explores a shift from augmentation to agency. By transforming constraints into dynamic variables that evolve through interaction, it suggests how agentic AI might surpass the limits of precedent – not by discarding history but by critically reinterpreting it.

DEEPHIMMELBLAU: POTENTIAL OF AGENTIC AI IN ARCHITECTURAL PRACTICE

DeepHimmelblau advances Creative AI beyond project-based experimentation toward a systemic integration within architectural practice. Building on Semantic Universes and Gaudí + Neural Networks, it explores how a node-based framework can operate as a co-creative system – augmenting design processes, interpreting multimodal data, and redefining architectural authorship within the workflow of Coop Himmelb(l)au.

Since joining the practice in 2014 as head of the Chbl|Code team, my focus has been on developing tools that streamline workflows, enhance creative methodologies, and establish frameworks that integrate computation directly into design thinking. These efforts laid the groundwork for DeepHimmelblau, formally launched in 2017 under the leadership of Wolf D. Prix, Karolin Schmidbaur, and myself as Creative AI & Computational Design Specialist. Conceived as an exploration into the potential of artificial intelligence within architectural practice, the project was recognised in 2021 with the DigitalFUTURES Project Award as one of the most exemplary applications of AI in architectural design. Drawing from Coop Himmelb(l)au's 50-year multimodal archive, DeepHimmelblau 'explores the possibility – in connection with human beings – of teaching machines to be creative, to interpret, perceive, propose new designs, augment design processes, and enhance design creativity'.[42]

At the foundation of Coop Himmelb(l)au's design philosophy lies the concept of the 'open process' – a non-deterministic, continuously negotiated framework that enables design to evolve through interaction between human agents, tools, and modalities across multiple scales and abstraction levels. The central question driving DeepHimmelblau is whether such an open process could be mirrored and extended through AI: could a node-based system act as its computational counterpart, engaging in negotiation rather than rigid optimisation?[43]

This inquiry is situated within a broader lineage in which tools have continuously reshaped architectural thought – from the chisel and perspective drawing to algorithmic design. As John Culkin observed, 'We shape our tools, and thereafter our tools shape us'. Today, AI introduces a new complexity, expanding beyond automation toward systems capable of multimodal reasoning and early forms of agency. In this context, architects may evolve from singular decision-makers to curators of intelligence, orchestrating dynamic exchanges between human insight and machine cognition.

To support this transformation, the DeepHimmelblau architecture was conceived as a node-based, reconfigurable framework in which diverse AI models interact – some cooperatively, others adversarially – across image, language, parametric, and three-dimensional modalities. This reflects the fluid workflows of the practice, where a design might evolve from sketch to model to simulation and back again. The system accommodates both generative exploration and technical precision, privileging adaptability over linear sequencing.

The framework addresses the persistent tension between deterministic reliability and predictive exploration. Here, negotiation occurs among nodes themselves: between practical constraints, structural analysis, and aesthetic emergence, between optimisation and speculation. The system's nodes are organised into three principal categories. Organisational nodes handle large-scale architectural decisions such as massing, circulation, and functional logic. Technical nodes focus on performance-driven processes like surface rationalisation or structural optimisation. Gestalt nodes engage with the perceptual, spatial, and aesthetic dimensions of architecture, capturing emergent qualities that cannot be reduced to purely technical parameters.

Each node is defined not only by its disciplinary scope but also by its operational logic – deterministic, generative, domain-specific, or generalist – allowing the network to reconfigure dynamically according to design intent.[44] Some nodes negotiate adversarially, testing and refining competing configurations, while others cooperate, merging multimodal data into cohesive architectural responses. At its core, the system positions AI models as specialised agents negotiating across multiple levels of abstraction. Intelligence emerges not from a single model but from distributed interaction, echoing Jeff Hawkins' *Thousand Brains Theory*, where cognition arises through the coordination of many semi-independent entities.[45]

Ultimately, DeepHimmelblau aspires to evolve into a self-organising design ecology – a system that can deconstruct a design task into actionable steps, activate relevant nodes, and autonomously establish meaningful connections. Rather than operating as a directive tool, it acts as a co-creative partner, engaging designers through dialogue, critique, and adaptation. A system capable of '*thinking through*' the design problem, determining which nodes must be activated, and autonomously establishing meaningful connections. This reciprocal relationship redefines authorship: AI becomes a participant in an open, non-linear process where intuition and computation continually recalibrate one another.

The framework draws on the duality of System 1 and System 2 thinking.[46] The AI's capacity for rapid, generative variation mirrors the intuitive, exploratory mode of System 1, while its analytical negotiation and refinement correspond to the reflective deliberation of System 2. Within this structure,

Figure 2.3.7 DeepHimmelblau – Gestalt nodes generating spatial–formal resolution

design unfolds as a continuous feedback loop across three levels – 1) Iterative Design Exploration – where AI generates a diverse array of formal, material, and organisational possibilities, providing a foundation for designers to curate, modify, and refine through direct and indirect interventions; 2) Cooperative and Adversarial Interactions – AI systems could function as both collaborators and disruptors, encouraging designers to explore alternative spatial hierarchies, tectonic articulations, and structural logics; 3) Agentic Learning Mechanisms – AI models could refine their generative capabilities through iterative feedback, incorporating human input, contextual constraints, and emergent formal tendencies.

Ultimately, this exploration raises a fundamental question: can designers and AI grow together, enabling a co-creative paradigm that advances both human intuition and machine intelligence?

A NEW PARADIGM: AGENTIC AI AS CO-CREATOR

The emergence of agentic AI could signal a fundamental shift in architectural practice from execution to authorship. No longer confined to fixed parameters, these systems could negotiate constraints in real time – testing alternatives, reframing briefs, and proposing pivots – thereby forcing a reconsideration of the architect's role. If AI can critique its outputs, reinterpret goals, and surface unexpected directions, does it remain a tool, or does it become a collaborator?

Generative models synthesise within statistical priors; they are powerful at variation yet limited at rethinking the problem itself. Agentic systems, by contrast, distribute intelligence across specialised and generalist agents that deliberate across scales and modalities. Instead of passively responding to prompts, they could participate in the creative act – questioning assumptions, trading off criteria, and mediating between intuition and analysis. In such a setting, the architect's authorship shifts from direct command to orchestration: defining a search space, curating signals, and steering a conversation among human and non-human contributors.

If AI can analyse spatial hierarchies, refine materials, and optimise structures, the architect's role may shift from directing outcomes to orchestrating intelligence, defining a search space within which human and machine agents negotiate and refine solutions. This evolution introduces a paradox: as AI improves through cooperative and adversarial feedback, could it begin proposing strategies that exceed human comprehension, echoing the self-taught reasoning seen in AlphaGo? Architecture may soon face a similar condition, where AI-generated design logics extend beyond familiar heuristics.

Such developments inevitably challenge traditional notions of authorship. When design emerges through negotiation among human and non-human intelligences, authorship becomes distributed, shared across a network of agents rather than contained within an individual. The architect's role thus transforms from singular author to curator and orchestrator of emergent intelligence, steering and interpreting rather than prescribing.

In this context, architectural workflow itself could evolve from linear iteration to dynamic co-evolution. Human and AI agents might operate in a recursive feedback loop, continuously exchanging insight and intent, a shift from the master–apprentice paradigm to one of peer collaboration. While the implications for agency, creativity, and authorship remain open, one point is certain: AI is no longer a passive tool. Its integration compels a redefinition of how design intelligence is structured, distributed, and evaluated, signalling not just a technological shift but a transformation in what it means to design.

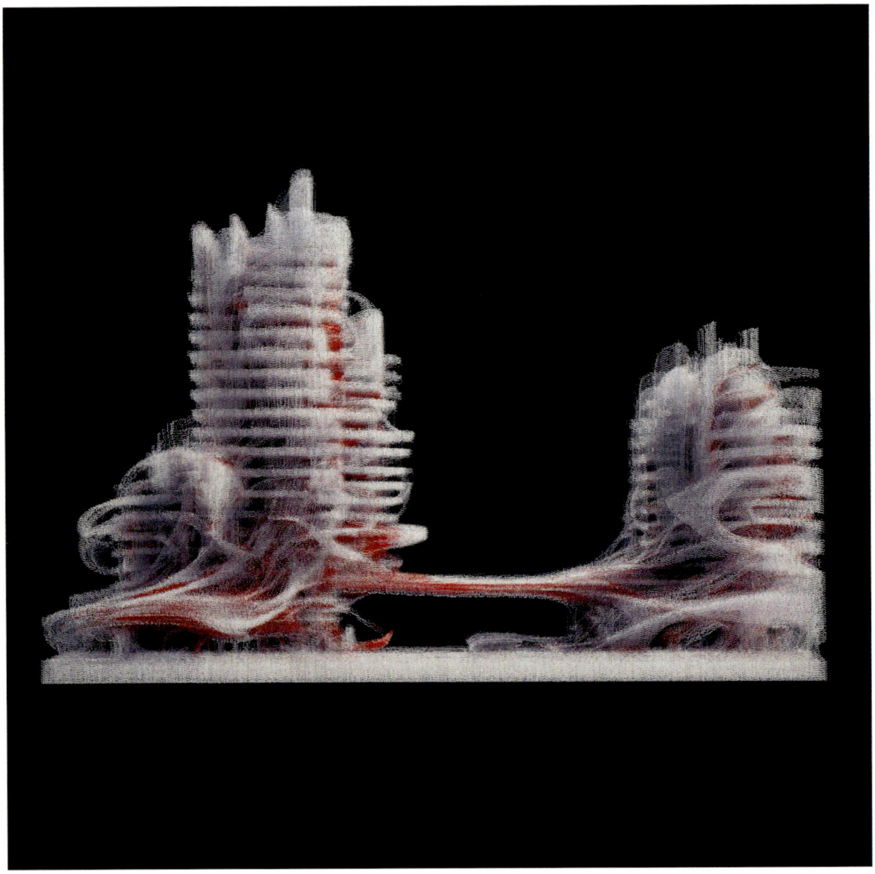

Figure 2.3.8 Deep Semantics – Point cloud explorations of design domains encoded in city sequences

NOTES

1 Achim Menges and Sean Ahlquist, eds., *Computational Design Thinking*, Chichester: Wiley, 2011.
2 Nicholas Negroponte, *The Architecture Machine: Toward a More Human Environment*, Cambridge, MA: MIT Press, 1970.
3 Horst W. J. Rittel and Melvin M. Webber, 'Planning Problems Are Wicked Problems', in Nigel Cross (ed.), *Developments in Design Methodology*, New York: John Wiley & Sons, 1984, pp. 135–144.
4 Nicholas Negroponte, *The Architecture Machine*.
5 Justin Johnson, Bharath Hariharan, Laurens van der Maaten, Judy Hoffman, Li Fei-Fei, C. Lawrence Zitnick, and Ross B. Girshick, 'Inferring and Executing Programs for Visual Reasoning', IEEE International Conference on Computer Vision (ICCV) (2017): 3008–3017.
6 Melody Y. Guan, Manas R. Joglekar, Eric Wallace, Saachi Jain, Boaz Barak, Alec Helyar, Rachel Dias, Andrea Vallone, Hongyu Ren, Jason Wei, Hyung Won Chung, Sam Toyer, Johannes Heidecke, Alex Beutel, and Amelia Glaese, 'Deliberative Alignment: Reasoning Enables Safer Language Models', *ArXiv* abs/2412.16339 (2024).

7 Jue Wang, Anne Hoecker, and Chuck Whitten, 'What Is Agentic AI?' Bain & Company, January 23, 2025, www.bain.com/insights/what-is-agentic-ai
8 Kahneman, *Thinking, Fast and Slow.*
9 Menges and Ahlquist, *Computational Design Thinking.*
10 Hayes-Roth, Waterman, and Lenat, *Building Expert Systems.*
11 Goodfellow, Bengio, and Courville, *Deep Learning.*
12 D. Hassabis, *Creativity and AI,* The Rothschild Foundation Lecture: The Royal Academy of Arts; 2018. www.youtube.com/watch?v=d-bvsJWmqlc
13 Hassabis, *Creativity and AI.*
14 David Silver, Julian Schrittwieser, Karen Simonyan, Ioannis Antonoglou, Aja Huang, Arthur Guez, Thomas Hubert, et al. 'Mastering the Game of Go Without Human Knowledge', *Nature* 550, no. 7676 (2017): 354–359. https://doi.org/10.1038/nature24270
15 Daniel Bolojan, 'Creative AI: Augmenting Design Potency', *Architectural Design* 92, no. 3 (2022): 22–27. https://doi.org/10.1002/ad.2809
16 Ben Goertzel and Cassio Pennachin, eds, *'Artificial General Intelligence,'* Berlin: Springer, 2007.
17 TNO, *Peter Werkhoven Joins David Deutsch Digitally to Talk About Quantum Computing,* September 20, 2022. www.youtube.com/watch?v=C3XP0CAARU4&list=PL4cl2VeMbE30Q3oZcU7w_DtkIPQVybHSj&index=34
18 David Deutsch, *The Beginning of Infinity: Explanations That Transform the World,* New York: Viking, 2011.
Jürgen Schmidhuber, 'A Formal Theory of Creativity, Fun, and Intrinsic Motivation (1990–2010)', *IEEE Transactions on Autonomous Mental Development* 2, no. 3 (2010): 230–247.
19 Silver, Schrittwieser, Simonyan, Antonoglou, Huang, Guez, Hubert, et al. 'Mastering the Game of Go Without Human Knowledge'.
20 Bolojan, 'Creative AI'.
21 dPrix, Schmidbaur, Bolojan, and Baseta, 'The Legacy Sketch Machine'.
22 D. Bolojan, A. Chocron, A. Scherger, and T. Tucker, 'Deep Semantics: Crafting Design Semantic Universes', CDRF 2024, Symbiotic Intelligence, 2024.
23 Versur is one of the early software products that explore the potential of agentic AI in architectural design; a workflow-based agentic AI platform that lets users design dynamic, multi-step AI workflows and orchestrate collaborations between autonomous agents. Built as a *creative engine* for design professionals, it emphasises co-creation with agentic systems that think, iterate, and act as part of the design process rather than merely responding to prompts – extending beyond simple automation toward human–machine collaborative reasoning and adaptive workflows (versur.ai).
24 R. Snooks, *Behavioral Formation: Multi-Agent Algorithmic Design Strategies,* Melbourne: RMIT University, 2014.
25 Menges and Ahlquist, *Computational Design Thinking.*
26 dPrix, Schmidbaur, Bolojan, and Baseta, 'The Legacy Sketch Machine'.
27 Bolojan, 'Creative AI'.
28 TNO, *Peter Werkhoven Joins David Deutsch Digitally to Talk About Quantum Computing.*
29 John S. Gero, 'Ten Problems for AI in Design'.
30 Daniel Bolojan, Emmanouil Verimsso, and Shermeen Yousif, 'Is Language All We Need? A Query into Architectural Semantics Using a Multimodal Generative Workflow', CAADRIA (2022): 353–363.
31 Daniel Bolojan, 'Are we the last creatives?' TEDxDelrayBeach. YouTube video, 18:00. Posted by TEDx Talks, November 28, 2023. www.youtube.com/watch?v=nnCWuVvVuYs.
32 Bolojan, Verimsso, and Yousif, 'Is Language All We Need?'
33 Hawkins, *A Thousand Brains.*
34 Bolojan, Chocron, Scherger, and Tucker, 'Deep Semantics'.
35 Bolojan, 'Creative AI'.
36 dPrix, Schmidbaur, Bolojan, and Baseta, 'The Legacy Sketch Machine'.
37 Nicholas Negroponte, *The Architecture Machine: Toward a More Human Environment,* Cambridge, MA: MIT Press, 1970.
38 Daniel Bolojan, 'Are We the Last Creatives?' TEDxDelrayBeach. Posted by TEDx Talks, November 28, 2023. www.youtube.com/watch?v=nnCWuVvVuYs
39 Bolojan, Chocron, Scherger, and Tucker, 'Deep Semantics'.
40 Bolojan, Chocron, Scherger, and Tucker, 'Deep Semantics'.
41 Hassabis, *Creativity and AI.*
42 dPrix, Schmidbaur, Bolojan, and Baseta, 'The Legacy Sketch Machine'.
43 dPrix, Schmidbaur, Bolojan, and Baseta, 'The Legacy Sketch Machine'.
44 dPrix, Schmidbaur, Bolojan, and Baseta, 'The Legacy Sketch Machine'.
45 Hawkins, *A Thousand Brains.*
46 Kahneman, *Thinking, Fast and Slow.*

PART 3

AI AND ARCHITECTURAL THEORY

NEIL LEACH

Figure 3.1.1 Neil Leach, Miami Swiss, generated using Midjourney, 2025

CHAPTER 3.1
INTRODUCTION

Neil Leach

It is easy enough to imagine the impact of the AI revolution on architectural design. But what about its impact on architectural theory?

If the role of AI is to enhance the human mind, then any discipline involving the human mind will benefit from it. Back in 2023, research showed that the use of AI can enhance the quality of any output by up to 40%.[1] As AI continues to advance, we can only expect that percentage to increase. Nor will architectural theory be any exception. Of course, we can just switch off our critical thinking, and just use ChatGPT uncritically, but if we use AI as a way of augmenting our critical thinking, it will sharpen our critical faculties and enhance the quality of our writing. Moreover, since architectural theory itself could be argued to be an application of intelligence to the domain of architecture, could we not also argue that in the age of AI this intelligence – this theoretical inquiry – is going to be 'supercharged' by AI?

We can expect AI to have a major impact on every single discipline. Indeed, we might even be surprised by how many disciplines will benefit from AI. For example, some might imagine that historical disciplines, such as the history of art, history of architecture, archaeology, museum studies, or history itself, are less likely to profit from the introduction of AI. But why would this be the case? Indeed, the historian Yuval Noah Harari has already carved out a role for himself as a public intellectual addressing AI. But more importantly, AI could potentially serve as a tool to revolutionise the very discipline of history. Imagine, for example, how AI systems might be used to detect patterns in historical data that have so far escaped our attention. Would AI not be able to seek out new histories and alternative historical narratives? Just as carbon dating and other contemporary technological techniques have helped us to understand the past, could we not assume that AI might become another powerful tool in the hands of the historian?

As yet there is no Nobel Prize in AI. But in 2024, DeepMind AI specialists Demis Hassabis and John Jumper were awarded a share of the Nobel Prize in

DOI: 10.4324/9781003347330-11

Chemistry for developing their AI system, AlphaFold, that is able to predict the structures of proteins. This is surely going to set a pattern for the future. Indeed, the chances are that many Nobel Prizes will be awarded for work that has benefitted from the application of AI. Likewise, we might expect many Pritzker Prize winners in architecture to have benefitted from the assistance of AI.

Another way in which AI will likely revolutionise theory – and especially architectural theory – will be through the introduction of a new AI-related theoretical paradigm – computational neuroscience. There are obvious connections between neuroscience and AI. It is as though neuroscientists and AI specialists are both interested in the same thing – not *artificial* intelligence, so much as intelligence itself. Moreover, artificial neural networks are themselves modelled loosely on the neural networks of the brain. Clearly, AI has benefitted enormously from insights in neuroscience. But could not the corollary also hold true? Might AI also help us to understand how the brain works? Just as neural networks have been modelled on the brain, so too we can surely begin to glimpse many insights about how the mind works in the mirror of AI.

This connection is explored in Chapter 3.2, Predictive Design. This chapter draws heavily on the ideas of neuroscientists who stress the importance of prediction in intelligence, and explores how prediction also informs architectural design. How might architectural design be seen as a form of 'prediction'? If our perception of the world is itself predictive and based on a form of 'hallucination', as Seth argues, does this not suggest that the way in which we imagine possible future buildings is also a form of hallucination? And if, as Seth argues, perception is grounded in previous experiences and prior expectations, might we not expect these to also condition the architectural expressions that we 'hallucinate'?

Turning to philosophy itself, it is clear that this new theoretical paradigm steps beyond the limits of simple pragmatic discussions about the use of technology to engage with issues that are themselves deeply philosophical. For what else are debates about consciousness but philosophical concerns? So too, the dawning realisation that there might be a mechanical intelligence that overshadows natural (human) intelligence raises a series of deeply existential concerns that are also deeply philosophical.

We could even perhaps argue that more traditional approaches to philosophy – including the approaches to continental philosophy found in the works of even the most radical thinkers like Michel Foucault, Gilles Deleuze, and Judith Butler – have been supplanted as the master narrative by cognitive science in general, and neuroscience in particular. This is not to say that these older philosophical debates have been rendered completely obsolete. Rather, cognitive science is now providing us with a new theoretical framework more in tune with the highly advanced technologies of today. For the problem with philosophy, as Stephen Hawking once noted, is that it fails to keep pace with science.

One could even argue that this new theoretical discourse – emerging out of debates about theory of mind, neuroscience, and AI – is itself a new branch of philosophy, echoing the way in which thinkers like Ludwig Wittgenstein or David Chalmers – emerging out of engineering and mathematics respectively – became central to philosophy. Whether or not we refer to this new paradigm as a form of philosophy, clearly there is a new set of theoretical debates that deserve our attention.

Yet AI also poses a threat to architectural theory. This applies not only to those working in the field of architectural theory itself – the academics, researchers, and authors – but also to those studying the subject. As LLMs continue to improve, we have to question how much longer any architectural writer can continue to survive, before being eclipsed by machines. So too the growth of AI poses serious problems for academia. In the age of AI, we need to ask what role is left for the professor? We already know that there is more information on the internet that any professor can offer you. Meanwhile ChatGPT, we are told, knows 10,000 times more that any one human being. We see many consulting ChatGPT over health questions, instead of going to their doctor. Will the same happen in architectural education? In the age of AI, will we still need professors in the traditional sense? And what assignments should these professors set, now that generative AI can write essays and generate designs for every student? Is AI not going to cause a crisis that will completely disrupt architectural education?

As ever, AI shows itself to be full of opportunities and challenges – the central thesis behind the chapter, 'The Dark Side of AI' is that AI can be both amazing and also somewhat terrifying. The chapter tracks the 'dark side' of AI through a series of events in history that began to give us some clue of AI's astonishing potential. While AI will bring significant advantages – especially in the realm of science and medicine, it will also bring certain disadvantages, such as job loss. Nonetheless, the article concludes, these will become our new normal and we will get used to them. 'Keep calm, and carry on'.

NOTE

1 Ethan Mollick, 'Centaurs and Cyborgs on the Jagged Frontier', *One Useful Thing*, September 16, 2023.

Figure 3.2.1 Neil Leach, Alpine Weather Station 1, generated using Midjourney, 2025

CHAPTER 3.2

PREDICTIVE DESIGN

AI, NEUROSCIENCE, AND ARCHITECTURE

Neil Leach

INTRODUCTION

Prediction is central to artificial intelligence (AI). Most AI systems, especially large language models (LLMs), can be described as prediction engines.[1] An LLM predicts the next token in a sequence given its context. Surprising as it may seem, this is exactly how ChatGPT works. It predicts the next token – a word or part of a word – and out of this incremental process it can generate comprehensive sentences.

But what if prediction were to be even more important than this? What if prediction were to be the very basis not only of artificial intelligence, but also of human intelligence itself?

Indeed, the brain is already recognised as a prediction engine. According to Ray Kurzweil, the reason why we have a brain in the first place is to predict the future:

> As one of our ancestors walked through the savannas thousands of years ago, she might have noticed that an animal was progressing towards a route that she was taking. She would predict that if she stayed on course, their paths would intersect. Based on this, she decided to head in another direction, and her foresight proved valuable to survival.[2]

And, if so, what would be the consequences of this for architecture?

DOI: 10.4324/9781003347330-12

INTELLIGENCE

Is it any coincidence that Nobel Laureate and AI expert Demis Hassabis undertook a PhD in neuroscience, and Anil Seth, one of the world's leading figures in the field of neuroscience, undertook a PhD in AI? Likewise, another Nobel Laureate, Geoffrey Hinton, studied physiology before getting into AI: 'I wanted to know how the brain worked'.[3] What is the connection between neuroscience and AI? How can these two ostensibly different disciplines – one dealing with biological systems, and the other dealing with a mechanical system – have anything in common? And what can architects learn from these two different but related disciplines about the architectural design process itself?

It is as though neuroscientists and AI specialists are interested not in *artificial* intelligence, but intelligence itself. Indeed, Hassabis often refers simply to '*intelligent* systems': 'Our ambition in DeepMind is to build *intelligent* systems to help find solutions that can learn to solve any complex problem . . . Put another way, we want to use it to solve everything else'.[4]

The interface between neuroscience and AI becomes most intriguing when we can detect similarities or overlaps between these two fields of enquiry, especially in relation to *prediction*. Intriguingly various researchers in both fields are now focusing on *prediction* as the basis of both intelligence and perception. On the one hand, researchers in the field of neuroscience are developing a theory that perception – and hence also intelligence – might be based on prediction. On the other hand, researchers in the field of AI are also developing various theories of intelligence as being based on prediction. Despite their obvious differences, both are based on the notion that prediction is the key to understanding intelligence.

Here I want to trace out the curious parallels between neuroscience and AI, and argue that 'prediction' can be seen to underpin intelligence in both domains.

KARL FRISTON AND PREDICTION

The neuroscientist Karl Friston has become famous in recent years for the notion that perception – and hence intelligence – is based on prediction. But Friston was not the first. We could perhaps trace the theory back to Hermann von Helmholtz, who in his 19th century work, *Treatise on Physiological Optics*, sowed the seeds of the notion that perception is a form of unconscious inference – a concept deeply influential in modern neuroscience and theories of predictive processing.[5] Helmholtz believed that what we perceive is not a direct imprint of the external world, but rather the brain's best guess or unconscious inference about what might be 'out there', based on noisy and ambiguous incoming sensory data and prior experiences. In other words, perception is not determined simply by the sensory signals received, but rather by an *unconscious inference* made by the brain based on previous experiences. This 'unconscious inference' is essentially an early understanding of a Bayesian process. This is perhaps the earliest formulation of what we now understand as predictive coding or predictive processing – the idea that the brain continuously generates predictions about incoming sensory inputs and adjusts those predictions based on prediction errors.

However, Friston takes this further, and develops it into a comprehensive theory, where prediction goes beyond mere perception and also engages with intelligence. He takes Helmholtz's notion of a form of *passive* unconscious inference – our perceptions are our brain's best guesses – and builds upon this by introducing *active inference*. In other words, the brain does not just passively interpret sensory input. Rather it acts to bring about the sensory inputs that it expects. There is a dynamic interaction between perception and action that is a key extension to Helmholtz's model.

Friston argues this through his Free Energy Principle (FEP). According to this theory, intelligence – both biological and artificial – is grounded in prediction, and that – in order to stay alive – the brain's job is to minimise surprise through predictive modelling.[6] Thus, biological systems, such as the brain, maintain their structure and function by minimising free energy in order to reduce prediction error. This goes beyond mere perception, so as to include intelligence as well. Thus, in Friston's framework, intelligence – biological or artificial – is the capacity to minimise surprise by maintaining an accurate internal model of the world. In other words, in order to minimise surprise, the brain must keep the world in line with its predictions, and its predictions in line with the world.

ANIL SETH AND PREDICTIVE PERCEPTION

The neuroscientist Anil Seth broadly follows this same trajectory. He builds directly upon Karl Friston's FEP and predictive processing framework, and uses it as the foundation for explaining how we come to have conscious experiences, especially of the body and self. However, he differs somewhat from Friston in that he is primarily interested in consciousness. Thus, whereas Friston's work is primarily formal and mathematical, and incredibly broad (even claiming to unify all cognitive processes), it doesn't directly address consciousness – and especially what consciousness *feels like*.

Nonetheless, Seth largely follows Friston, especially in terms of his notion of *active* inference. Seth believes that the brain is not a passive receptor, but an *active* prediction engine. It generates internal models that predict the incoming sensory input. As Seth puts it, 'Try to think what it is like up there, sealed inside the bony vault of the skull, trying to figure out what's out there in the world. There's no light, no sound, no anything – it's completely dark and utterly silent'.[7] The only information that the brain receives are vague electrical impulses – patterns of neural activity caused by sensory organs sensing light, sound waves, pressure, chemicals, etc. These signals are noisy, ambiguous, and incomplete. Seth again: 'These sensory inputs don't come with labels attached ("I'm from a coffee cup"; "I'm from a tree")'.[8] For this reason, the brain's task is not to passively record the world but to infer its causes.

Seth therefore turns to predictive processing: the brain continuously generates *top-down predictions* about what's out there, and then compares those predictions against the *bottom-up signals* coming in. Perception, according to this view, is the process of resolving the 'vague signals' by testing and updating the brain's best guesses.

> Instead of perception depending largely on signals coming into the brain from the outside world, it depends as much, if not more, on perceptual predictions flowing in the opposite direction. We don't just passively perceive the world, we actively generate it. The world we experience comes as much, if not more, from the inside out as from the outside in.[9]

Anil Seth describes perception as a form of 'controlled hallucination' to capture the idea that what we see, hear, and feel is not a direct readout of the external world, but the brain's best guess about the causes of its sensory inputs. Drawing on the predictive processing framework, he argues that the brain continuously generates models of the world – essentially hallucinations – that are constrained and corrected by incoming sensory data.

> If hallucination is a kind of controlled perception, then perception right here and right now is also a kind of hallucination, but a controlled hallucination in which the brain's predictions are being reined in by sensory information from the world. In fact, we're all hallucinating all the time, including right now. It's just that when we agree about our hallucinations, we call that reality.[10]

Interestingly, Seth uses an example of the generative AI model, DeepDream, to illustrate what happens when perceptual expectations are too strong. Using a version of DeepDream trained on dogs, Seth shows how the mind begins to read dogs into everything. The term 'hallucination' has since taken on a pejorative twist with to refer to the mistakes made by AI, but in its original formulation, the term simply referred to the brain's 'best guess' as to what is out there, a guess that needs to be corrected and 'reined in' by the process of 'prediction error minimisation'.

Like Friston, Seth also sees intelligence as predictive – although he tends to emphasise consciousness, perception, and selfhood more explicitly than intelligence *per se*. Still, within his broader predictive processing framework, intelligence emerges as the brain's capacity to generate and refine predictions about the world, the body, and the self.

The rainbow also provides a striking demonstration of Seth's predictive perception. Physically, it is a continuous spectrum of light. Yet in many cultures we are taught to divide it into seven colours – red, orange, yellow, green, blue, indigo, violet – a convention formalised by Newton, who aligned it with the seven notes of the musical scale. Once internalised, this categorisation asserts itself, so that we *see* seven discrete bands even though no such boundaries exist in nature. The expectation shapes the perceptual experience. Just as we are taught to divide a rainbow into seven bands, speakers of the Inuit language are taught to distinguish finely between types of snow – powdery snow, packed snow, drifting snow, snow suitable for building igloos, etc. These distinctions are encoded in vocabulary, which acts as a cognitive filter. What an English speaker might perceive simply as 'snow', an Inuit speaker perceives as a range of distinct phenomena, each carrying practical significance. Meanwhile, in the United Kingdom, where rain is very common, the English language has developed a rich vocabulary to describe it: drizzle, shower, downpour, spit, sprinkle, torrent, sleet, pelting rain, driving rain, and so on. Each term encodes not only the *amount* of rain but also its *character* – duration, intensity, droplet size, even emotional resonance.

Figure 3.2.2 Memo Akten, Gloomy Sunday (2017). Akten trains a neural network with different sets of images to become a 'lens' through which to look at and reinterpret everyday objects

Figure 3.2.2 (Continued)

In a similar vein, computational artist Memo Akten employs artificial neural networks to explore how perception is conditioned by training. In his interactive piece *Gloomy Sunday*, Akten demonstrates how a neural network interprets the world through the lens of the data on which it has been trained: if exposed only to images of flowers, it will perceive flowers everywhere, regardless of the input. As Akten explains, 'The picture we see in our conscious mind is not a mirror image of the outside world, but is a reconstruction based on our expectations and prior beliefs'.[11] In this sense, prior experience functions as a filter that shapes, distorts, and colours subsequent perception. Akten's claim that perception rests on 'expectations and prior beliefs' thus closely parallels Seth's account of perception as grounded in 'perceptual expectations'. Moreover, Akten's *Gloomy Sunday* experiment, based on trained neural networks, resonates strongly with Seth's work with DeepDream. Taken together, Akten's artistic explorations can be seen as reinforcing Seth's theory of predictive perception.

HALLUCINATING BUILDINGS

Turning to architecture, we can see similar principles at play. In 2020, FIU architecture student Fernando Salcedo conducted an interactive AI experiment reminiscent of Akten's *Gloomy Sunday*. He trained a neural network on two distinct sets of images: one consisting of generic modernist architecture, and the

Figure 3.2.3 Fernando Salcedo, Deep Perception (2020). This is a study using a CycleGAN trained on images of the King Abdullah Petroleum Studies and Research Center, Riyadh, Saudi Arabia and to reinterpret images of clothing as possible architectural forms

other of the King Abdullah Petroleum Studies and Research Center by Zaha Hadid Architects. The result was that the network began to 'see' architecture everywhere, projecting towers onto ties or warped ZHA forms onto crumpled shirts – a process strongly evocative of predictive perception. Crucially, these readings were not objective but filtered through the biases of its training data.

This experiment raises intriguing questions. Might architects operate in a similar way, reading potential buildings into the world around them? Does architectural education function, in effect, like training a neural network – conditioning practitioners to interpret the world through a particular architectural lens? Such an analogy suggests a compelling way of thinking about inspiration: as the act of perceiving the world through a trained filter, and then re-expressing that vision in architectural form. The capacity to see 'too much' in ambiguous forms is not a flaw, but a core feature of creative insight. Here, the 'over-strong predictions' become generative. The architect's imagination over-interprets ambiguous visual cues, projecting architectural form where none explicitly exists. In this sense, architectural creativity often depends on a productive misfiring of prediction: the ability to 'hallucinate' buildings within the non-architectural environment.

Trained architects carry with them a rich repertoire of forms, typologies, and spatial logics. When confronted with ambiguous or non-architectural stimuli – the curve of a shell, the billow of a sail, the structure of a leaf – their perceptual systems are already biased toward 'architectural readings'. This bias amounts to a set of strong predictive preconceptions. Just as Seth argues that perception is not a passive reception but an active prediction, architects are predisposed to 'see architecture' in the world around them. Architectural education itself can be understood as the systematic shaping of predictive models, tuning the architectural imagination to find – or impose – architectural order on otherwise neutral objects.

Jørn Utzon's celebrated account of deriving inspiration for the Sydney Opera House from the sails on Sydney Harbour exemplifies this process. To the casual observer, the sails may remain simply sails. But for Utzon, trained in architectural form-finding and structural imagination, they become

Figure 3.2.4 Neil Leach, LA Villa, generated using Midjourney, 2025

proto-architectural elements. The billowing sails of yachts in the harbour became reimagined as the soaring vaults of an opera house. Yet this same propensity can lead to misreadings not only of forms, but also of concepts. Architects often appropriate philosophical concepts such as Gilles Deleuze's notion of the 'fold', assuming it refers to physical *folded* forms, when in fact it has no direct connection to architecture, and is a philosophical term that refers to the 'folds' of subjectivity. Similarly, architectural designers and historians sometimes misinterpret terms from the digital realm – words like 'discrete' or 'pixelation' – as if they denoted architectural forms, even though the digital itself is immaterial and without form.[12]

We might describe this tendency as a process of *architecturalisation*. Architects habitually read the world through an architectural lens, projecting architectural meaning and interpreting architectural form in whatever they encounter. This enables them to draw inspiration from almost anything – biological forms, animal anatomies, insect structures, geological features, or other seemingly unrelated phenomena – and translate these impressions into architectural expression.

IN THE MIRROR OF AI

This suggests that we can learn something about how we design and how we construct sentences through the logic of prediction. This is not unlike Anil Seth's account of perception as 'controlled hallucination', where the brain continually predicts incoming sensory data. Humans, too, appear to rely on predictive processing in language. We do not build sentences from first principles each time; instead, we lean on learned structures, collocations, and 'what feels right' in a given context – much like autocomplete. Human speech and writing are more formulaic than we often imagine. We rely on 'chunks' or 'stock phrases' ('at the end of the day', 'on the other hand', 'it goes without saying') and grammatical templates that allow for rapid, fluent production. This explains why tools like Google Smart Compose can so effectively autocomplete our sentences: much of our everyday writing is predictable. It also suggests that we humans, like ChatGPT, often generate language by recombining familiar patterns rather than inventing wholly original constructions. ChatGPT is trained on vast amounts of text, which conditions what it can generate. We humans are 'trained' by our linguistic environment – the words, idioms, and sentence structures we are exposed to from infancy onwards. These exposures become ingrained, shaping how we speak and write.

Stephen Wolfram has argued that ChatGPT reveals that language is perhaps computationally more straightforward than we had imagined: human language, once thought to be a uniquely complex achievement, may actually be generated through fairly simple predictive mechanisms applied at scale. The ease with which LLMs produce plausible text suggests that language is more structured, formulaic, and rule-bound than we often like to believe. As Wolfram puts it,

> This suggests something that's at least scientifically important: that human language (and the patterns of thinking behind it) are somehow simpler and more 'law like' in their structure than we thought. ChatGPT implicitly discovered this. But we can potentially explicitly expose it, with semantic grammar, computational language etc.[13]

Might human writing, then, be more formulaic and predictable than we often assume – relying on stock phrases and conventional modes of expression, drawn from our own 'training data', that simply *feel* appropriate in a given context? Are we, in effect, running our own 'autocomplete' when we speak and write, guided by cultural and personal training data? Does this blur the line between machine-generated and human-generated text?

Turning to design, similar issues emerge. Text-to-image diffusion models offer us a kind of mirror for design thinking, just as ChatGPT does for language. They reveal that design, too, may be more predictive, associative, and recombinatory than the romantic myth of the architect as an 'original genius' suggests. These models generate images by predicting what a picture 'should' look like, given a prompt, based on their training data. Designers, likewise, draw on prior exposure to precedents, styles, and visual repertoires. When sketching, they are not inventing from nothing, but predicting what 'fits' within a given context – whether cultural, stylistic, or functional. Likewise, AI image models excel by recombining existing visual tropes into seemingly new configurations. So too, human designers also combine fragments of memory, precedent, and influence into novel assemblages. Think of Zaha Hadid drawing on Suprematist paintings – both involve recombining trained perceptions into fresh outputs. Moreover, just as with diffusion models style emerges from statistical patterns in the datasets they were trained on, with designers, style emerges from the 'training set' of their education, cultural context, and professional milieu. This suggests that what we call 'inspiration' may often be the surfacing of latent preconceptions shaped by long-term exposure to previous compositional ideas.

Wolfram, then, has argued that human language, once thought to be a uniquely complex achievement, may actually be generated through fairly simple predictive mechanisms applied at scale, and that the ease with which LLMs produce plausible text suggests that language is more structured, formulaic, and rule-bound than we often like to believe. In a very similar way, text-to-image diffusion models demonstrate that compelling images – even those that appear 'creative' or 'original' – can also be generated by recombinatory prediction from training data. Just as ChatGPT strings together words that 'sound right', these systems assemble visual tropes that 'look right'. The fact that they can produce thousands of striking design-like images within seconds destabilises the idea that design is an ineffable act of genius. So, yes – if ChatGPT makes us rethink the complexity of language, then text-to-image diffusion models make us rethink the complexity of design. They suggest that design, like language, may be less a matter of transcendental creativity and more a matter of structured prediction, recombination, and pattern-completion.

JEFF HAWKINS AND SPATIAL PREDICTIONS

Jeff Hawkins has also been a prominent advocate of the notion that intelligence is based on prediction. In *A Thousand Brains: A New Theory of Intelligence*, he builds upon his earlier work, *On Intelligence*, to argue that the neocortex is a hierarchical prediction machine, whose primary function is to model the world by continuously predicting sensory input.[14]

> The brain creates a predictive model. This just means that the brain continuously predicts what its inputs will be. Prediction isn't something that the brain does now and then; it is an intrinsic property that never stops, and it serves an essential role in learning. When the brain's predictions are verified, that means that the brain's model of the world is accurate. A mis-prediction causes you to attend to the error and update the model.[15]

Hawkins argues that the brain consists of many cortical columns, each independently building predictive models of the world. Meanwhile, intelligence arises from embodied interaction with the environment – predicting what will be sensed next based on movement. It depends on our ability to predict how the world will look, feel, and sound, as we move through it. Intelligence is therefore rooted in brain anatomy and physiology, while prediction is embodied, spatial, and rooted in biological evolution.

As such, Hawkins's model of prediction is deeply spatial, and in many respects, architectural in nature. Hawkins proposes that each cortical column in the neocortex creates a model of the world, grounded in spatial relationships. These columns don't just passively record sensory inputs; they actively map the relative positions of objects and predict how those inputs will change as the body moves. As Hawkins puts it: 'Every column learns a model of objects and their structure. These models are inherently spatial'.[16] This model is location-based: each sensory input is anchored to a 'location signal' derived from movement and orientation – much like how a building's spaces are defined in relation to a floor plan or grid. Likewise, each cortical column operates with its own reference frame, allowing it to understand not only what an object is, but how its parts relate to one another in space. This allows it to build a kind of mental architecture of objects and environments.

In other words, Hawkins's theory of the brain suggests that intelligence is not just about logical inference or symbol manipulation, but about constructing and traversing internal models of space – much like how an architect designs, imagines, and mentally moves through a building. In other words, for Hawkins, spatial intelligence is not one type of intelligence. It is the basis of intelligence itself. As such, his theory of the brain treats intelligence as a process of constructing, updating, and navigating 3D predictive models. It is almost as though Hawkins is proposing a fundamentally architectural conception of mind: a theory in which intelligence emerges through the construction, navigation, and continual updating of predictive spatial worlds.

Hawkins is highly sceptical about existing AI systems: 'Nothing we call AI today is intelligent'.[17] At the same time, the ultimate objective, for Hawkins, is to create an intelligent machine, by effectively reverse engineering the neocortex: 'When creating intelligent machines, there is no reason we should replicate all the functions of the human brain. The new brain, the neocortex, is the organ of intelligence, so intelligent machines need something equivalent to it'.[18] Nor do intelligent machines need to be like humans, but like humans, they must be embodied, although not necessarily in the way that humans are embodied: 'Intelligent machines also need sensors and the ability to move them. This is referred to as embodiment'.[19] This embodiment could be mechanical or even virtual, but it must be embodiment nonetheless. Hawkins likens this to the way that we navigate the web: 'We do this by physically moving a mouse or touching a screen, but an intelligent machine could do the same thing just using software, with no physical movement'.[20] In other words, Hawkins's notion of embodiment is a somewhat abstract notion of embodiment. Somewhat confusingly, it does not depend on an actual body.

Hawkins's project is not without its challenges. So far, his implementations have not yielded breakthroughs rivalling transformers or large-scale deep learning – which suggests that while the biological inspiration is promising, it hasn't yet scaled into practical, general-purpose AI. There are also challenges in simply replicating the complexity of the brain. Moreover, today's AI – especially the LLMs – have achieved remarkable results without closely mirroring biology. That raises the question: do we *really need* to reverse engineer the brain to achieve AGI, as Hawkins argues, or are alternative architectures sufficient?

Figure 3.2.5 Neil Leach, Fractal Villa, generated using Midjourney, 2025

BLAISE AGÜERA Y ARCAS AND INTELLIGENCE

More recently, Blaise Agüera y Arcas has also proposed a theory of intelligence, similarly based on the logic of prediction, but has focused instead on AI itself. For Agüera, the primary claim is that prediction is intelligence itself. Here he is inspired by Helmholtz, and argues that the main function of intelligence is to model and predict the future based on past information. This predictive capacity inspires perception, action, learning, and survival.

Agüera had worked for Google on straightforward auto-complete. As Agüera y Arcas puts it,

> My team at Google worked on the auto-complete problem, the unsupervised text prediction problem, for quite a few years, in the context of small models that were supposed to run on phones. So, we built a lot of the AI that got built into android and one of those pieces of AI was the next word predictor in G-Board . . . And we did it, of course, because it is a pain to type with two fingers on a keyboard, and the better we can predict what the next word is likely to be, the faster you can type. So it's a very simple pragmatic sort of thing . . . But our impression was that building our machine learning models to predict the next word – the result would always be mediocre.[21]

Surprisingly, for Agüera, it is next word prediction – however trivial it might once have appeared – that now seems to contain all the complexity for artificial general intelligence. For Agüera, the introduction of unsupervised learning marked a threshold moment. This is the moment when, as Agüera puts it, we went from training neural networks to reproduce specific and task-specific kinds of outputs to training them to predict the future. And the form of that future prediction initially was text. So, if you have lots of text scraped from the internet, and the past is 'text so far', and the future is 'next token', 'next piece of text', 'next word', then training a neural net on that task interestingly was, for Agüera, what led to AGI. Agüera soon began to realise that large-scale predictive models are genuinely intelligent.

> If the first word is 'Humpty', the next word is going to be 'Dumpty'. If it's 'helter', it's going to be 'skelter'. And you can get those kinds of statistical regularities just by making a histogram of next words, given

> previous words. But if the previous words have been a word problem, and the next word is supposed to be the answer to that word problem, then the model has to be smart enough to reconstruct the word problem and do the problem. If it's a story, and the next word says how a certain person in that story feels, then whatever is predicting the story has to not only have followed the story, and understood the characters in it, but (has to) even be able to put themselves in place of one of those people, and use Theory of Mind in order to understand what that emotion could be. So when we are talking about word problems, maths, Theory of Mind, having a clever idea or understanding a pun or a joke, we are now in the realm of General Intelligence.[22]

In other words, large-scale AI predictive models, like ChatGPT, Claude, and Gemini, are not just simulating intelligence. They are instantiating it. Agüera again: 'How could it possibly be that autocomplete could result in general intelligence? My good friend, Ted Chang has castigated this approach to AGI as being like autocomplete, and he's right. I just think that he is just underestimating what autocomplete means'.[23]

Agüera believes that intelligence is not located in any single entity but *emerges* across relationships and technologies, through engaging other intelligences and the surrounding environment. For Agüera, intelligence is not defined by abstract reasoning or symbolic logic alone, but by the capacity to *model the world* – to generate internal representations of reality; to *predict* outcomes of actions within that model; and to *influence* one's own trajectory based on those predictions. Intelligence, in this view, is not static or isolated. It evolves *through interaction*. Just as biological intelligence co-evolved through communication, cooperation, and competition, artificial intelligences are also developing in dialogue with humans and other machines. This reflects an *emergent, co-adaptive* understanding of intelligence – one that grows richer through exchange rather than existing as a closed, self-contained system.

The culmination of this process is what Agüera calls *symbiotic intelligence*: a networked intelligence greater than the sum of its parts. Humans and AI systems, through mutual adaptation, form an interconnected cognitive ecology – a distributed system that learns, predicts, and evolves collectively. This leads him to define intelligence as follows: 'Intelligence is the ability to model, predict and influence one's future, evolving in relation to other intelligences to create a larger symbiotic intelligence'.[24]

Figure 3.2.6 Neil Leach, Camouflage Patterns 1, generated using Midjourney, 2025

FEI-FEI LI AND SPATIAL INTELLIGENCE

Fei-Fei Li also looks at the problem of AGI, but from a radically different perspective. Unlike Agüera, she believes that we cannot reach AGI without spatial awareness, and without understanding the world itself. She is therefore interested in *spatial intelligence.*

For Fei-Fei Li the development of sight had an enormous impact on the development of intelligence:

> The ability to see is thought to have ushered in the Cambrian explosion, a period in which a huge variety of animal species entered fossil records. What began as a passive experience, the simple act of letting light in, the nervous system began to evolve. Sight turning into insight. Seeing became understanding. Understanding led to action. And all these gave rise to intelligence.[25]

However, for Li, AI now needs to move beyond 2D image recognition into 3D understanding – depth, geometry, relationships, and physical causality. For designers, this suggests a future where AI tools don't just *represent* space but *understand* it, engaging more directly with structure, material, and environment.

In some senses, the shift to 3D understanding is an obvious step for Li. After all, she was the one behind ImageNet, that gave us AlexNet, and ultimately opened up the domain of 2D image generation. As Li puts it:

> For years I have been saying that taking a picture is not the same as seeing and understanding. Today, I would like to add to that. Simply seeing is not enough. Seeing is for doing and learning. When we act upon this world in 3D space and time, we learn, and we learn to see and do better. Nature has created this virtuous cycle of seeing and doing powered by 'spatial intelligence'.[26]

But what exactly is spatial intelligence? For Li it is something innate to human existence, something that we take for granted:

> Spatial intelligence plays a fundamental role in defining how we interact with the physical world. Every day, we rely on it for the

> most ordinary acts: parking a car by imagining the narrowing gap between bumper and curb, catching a set of keys tossed across the room, navigating a crowded sidewalk without collision, or sleepily pouring coffee into a mug without looking.[27]

Moreover, when we look at the world, we can understand its behaviour in terms of 'intuitive physics'. In other words, although we do not experience physical forces directly ourselves, from countless previous experiences, we know what they look like. Thus, for example, when we see a simulation of someone throwing a stone into a pond, causing the water to ripple, we know automatically when it does not look right. At the same time, AI-generated videos are also seemingly matching this sense of 'intuitive physics' from the sheer amount of data on which they have been trained, and are becoming increasingly realistic.

Unlike Hawkins, however, Li is not so interested in neuroscience and understanding how the mind works. She is more interested in taking the notion of spatial intelligence in humans and extending it into the world of AI. Like Hawkins, however, Li emphasises the importance of prediction in intelligence, but she is also interested in subsequent action. Spatial intelligence amounts to the 'ability to process visual data, make predictions and act upon those predictions', so as to enable 'AI to interact with humans in the real world'.[28]

So how might we instantiate spatial intelligence within the domain of AI? There have been extraordinary developments with LLMs. But we have to move beyond this. LLMs only predict text sequences. Spatial AI must predict the *behaviour of worlds*. In other words, the crucial leap is from 'next token' to the 'next state of reality'. As Li puts it:

> While current state-of-the-art AI can excel at reading, writing, research, and pattern recognition in data, these same models bear fundamental limitations when representing or interacting with the physical world. Our view of the world is holistic – not just what we're looking at, but how everything relates spatially, what it means, and why it matters. Understanding this through imagination, reasoning, creation, and interaction – not just descriptions – is the power of

> spatial intelligence. Without spatial intelligence, AI is disconnected from the physical reality it seeks to understand. It cannot effectively drive our cars, guide robots in our homes and hospitals, enable entirely new ways of immersive and interactive experiences for learning and recreation, or accelerate discovery in materials science and medicine.[29]

As such, for Li, we will never reach AGI without spatial intelligence: 'AGI will not be complete without spatial awareness'.[30] Interestingly, Demis Hassabis takes a similar position: 'To be truly general, to build AGI, we feel that the AGI system needs to understand the world around us – the physical world around us, not just the abstract world of language or mathematics'.[31]

Li defines spatial intelligence as the essential leap from 2D pattern recognition to 3D world modelling and interaction. Just as the evolution of vision sparked the Cambrian explosion of life, giving AI spatial intelligence could trigger an explosion of applications – in robotics, autonomous navigation, and design. For architects, this means AI systems could become collaborators in imagining, testing, and inhabiting new spatial worlds.

Spatial intelligence is a deep, physics-aware form of spatial reasoning that she considers indispensable for advanced AI and embodied systems. Li's argument is that whereas language is linear and abstract, true intelligence demands spatial awareness. As such, spatial intelligence is far more complex than language: 'The dimensionality of representing a world is vastly more complex than that of a one-dimensional, sequential signal like language'.[32] However, the challenge with operating in 3D is to find the data. 'Where is the data for spatial intelligence?' Li asked. 'It's all in our heads. It's not accessible like language'.[33] It is easy enough to train an LLM on text scraped from the internet. After all, the internet is flooded with text. Meanwhile 2D text-to-image models and text-to-video models can also be trained on images and videos scraped from the internet. But there is no obvious source of 3D data for spatial intelligence. There is therefore a need to produce synthetic data. While this remains challenging, it can be done computationally through simulation, thereby greatly reducing the time taken. However, there is a plentiful supply of 2D videos, and the potential exists for deriving 3D data from them, provided that the right algorithms can be developed: 'Internet-scale collections of images and videos represent abundant, accessible training material – the challenge lies in developing algorithms that can extract deeper spatial information from these two-dimensional image or video frame-based signals (i.e. RGB)'.[34] At the same time, we should not underestimate the challenges. As Li puts it: 'Clearly, we are still facing daunting challenges before we can fully unlock spatial intelligence through world modeling'.[35]

Nonetheless, world building – for so long associated with the world of the cinema, the world of fiction – could now potentially be seen in a different light. We would be able to generate convincing, coherent worlds in the same way that we can already generate convincing images. We would even be able to generate them in simulation with enough information to allow them to be constructed. These would be 3D 'predictions' of 'worlds', no longer restricted by the 2D logic of images.

Figure 3.2.7 Neil Leach, Monolith in the Alps, generated using Midjourney, 2025

SPATIALLY INTELLIGENT ARCHITECTURE

'Spatial intelligence', notes Li, 'allows us to see the space between the snowflakes, and appreciate its beauty'.[36] Here Li is pointing towards an act of perception that we humans already perform effortlessly and often poetically. But this is beyond the scope of traditional AI models. The challenge, then, is to develop 3D AI systems that model the 'real world'. In other words, these systems must have the capacity to construct computationally grounded 3D world models – models that represent snowflakes as entities in space, encode their spatial relations, and simulate their behaviour under physical laws. What matters, then, is not perception as such, but modelling and prediction: the ability to generate convincing simulations of how snowflakes form, fall, interact, collide, melt, and respond to forces such as turbulence and temperature. In this sense, spatial intelligence in AI marks a shift from recognising images of snow to understanding snow as a dynamic, three-dimensional physical system. It is a question of modelling reality well enough to simulate it convincingly.

But what exactly would be the benefits of spatially intelligent AI for architects? For Li, there are many:

> Essentially every manufactured object or constructed space must be designed in virtual 3D before its physical creation. This process is highly iterative and costly in terms of both time and money. With spatially intelligent models at their disposal, architects can quickly visualize structures before investing months into designs, walking through spaces that don't yet exist – essentially telling stories about how we might live, work, and gather.[37]

Li argues that spatially intelligent AI will profoundly transform architectural practice because architecture is fundamentally a *spatial* discipline. Current AI systems can generate images or text, but they cannot yet understand or model space with the coherence, consistency, and physical grounding that architects rely on.

TOWARDS PREDICTIVE DESIGN

Spatially intelligent AI, however, is unlikely to alter how architects fundamentally visualise space, since architectural training already cultivates a deeply predictive capacity to imagine environments before they exist. Moreover, spatially intelligent AI does not constitute a design tool. The key shift it makes is from representation to inference. It is essentially a tool for inferring structured world models. The system does not merely store forms; rather it predicts how spatial configurations behave. But a passive world model – no matter how accurate – remains a descriptive or diagnostic tool. Furthermore, while physics simulation is necessary, it is insufficient. It might be able to simulate various behaviours, but without agency, it remains evaluative rather than generative.

Surely, the potential of spatially intelligent AI lies, firstly, in transforming how an architect's visualisation might be externalised and operationalised through computation, and secondly in allowing it to become an active design environment. But how exactly might we achieve this?

Step in agentic AI.[38] Once spatially intelligent AI is embedded within an agentic AI framework, the system's role changes fundamentally. Spatial intelligence becomes a goal-directed design substrate, rather than a passive modelling tool. It is no longer a tool of simulation for designers, but becomes an active participant within the design process. Moreover, it is not simply a generative tool in the stylistic sense, but a powerful tool for performative co-evolution. The output is not a singular form, but a family of solutions within a navigable design space, negotiated by a series of trade-offs.

By encoding spatial reasoning into dynamic, machine-readable world models, spatially intelligent AI allows architects to move beyond static representations toward systems capable of predicting how spaces may evolve and be modified over time in relation to human behaviours and environmental forces. Architectural intuition is not displaced so much as augmented, as computational models can reveal patterns, interactions, and temporal dynamics that exceed human cognitive capacities. In this sense, spatially intelligent AI does not fundamentally change the architect's way of seeing the world; rather, it enables that vision to be computationally modelled.

While spatially intelligent AI on its own functions as a powerful inferential and simulation system, when embedded within agentic AI it is transformed into a predictive design framework. This is not a drafting tool or an image generator. Instead, spatial intelligence combined with agency produces a new form of cognitive design partnership – one in which architectural design itself becomes predictive.

'Predictive design' is not a metaphor. It is an accurate description of what happens when architectural design is reframed through the logic of spatial intelligence and agentic AI. While traditional simulation predicts the performance of a fixed design, predictive design becomes a driver of form. Predictive design aligns architectural thinking with predictive processing in neuroscience and the predictive logic of AI.

The future of architectural design will not be generative. It will be predictive.

NOTES

1 Ajay Agrawal, Joshua Gans, Avi Goldfarb, *Prediction Machines: The Simple Economics of Artificial Intelligence*, Boston, MA: Harvard Business Review Press, 2018.
2 Ray Kurzweil, *How to Create a Mind: The Secrets of Human Thought Revealed*, New York: Penguin, 2012, p. 250.
3 Geoffrey Hinton interviewed by Martin Ford, in Ford, *Architects of Intelligence*, Birmingham: Packt Publishing, 2018, p. 80.
4 Demis Hassabis and Fan Hui, 'AlphaGo: Moving Beyond the Rules', in Chloe Woods, Suzanne Livingston, and Maholo Uchida, *AI: More Than Human*, London: Barbican International Enterprises, 2020, p. 88.
5 Hermann von Helmholtz, *Treatise on Physiological Optics*, Vol. 1, Garden City: Dover Editions, 2005.
6 Thomas Parr, Giovanni Pezzulo, Karl Friston, *Active Inference: The Free Energy Principle in Mind, Brain, and Behavior*, Cambridge, MA: MIT Press, 2022.
7 Anil Seth, *Being You: A New Science of Consciousness,* Dutton, 2021, p. 80.
8 Seth, *Being You*, p. 80.
9 Anil Seth, 'Your Brain Hallucinates Your Conscious Reality', TED Talk, April 2017, www.ted.com/talks/anil_seth_your_brain_hallucinates_your_ conscious_reality?language=en
10 Seth, 'Your Brain Hallucinates Your Conscious Reality'.
11 Memo Akten, 'Learning to See: Gloomy Sunday', 2017, www.memo.tv/portfolio/gloomy-sunday
12 Neil Leach, 'There Is No Such Thing as a Digital Building: A Critique of the Discrete', in Gilles Retsin (ed.), *Discrete: Reappraising the Digital in Architecture*, New York: Wiley, 2019, p. 138; Mario Carpo, *The Second Digital Turn: Design Beyond Intelligence*, Cambridge, MA: MIT Press, 2017.
13 Stephen Wolfram, *What ChatGPT is Doing . . . and Why Does It Work?*, Champaign: Wolfram Media, 2023.
14 Jeff Hawkins, *A Thousand Brains: A New Theory of Intelligence*, New York: Basic Books, 2021; Jeff Hawkins (with Sandra Brakelee), *On Intelligence: How a New Understanding of the Brain Will Lead to the Creation of Truly Intelligent Machines*, London: Times Books, 2007.
15 Hawkins, *A Thousand Brains*, p. 32.
16 Hawkins, *A Thousand Brains*, p. 54.
17 Hawkins, *A Thousand Brains*, p. 145.
18 Hawkins, *A Thousand Brains*, p. 146.
19 Hawkins, *A Thousand Brains*, p. 148.
20 Hawkins, *A Thousand Brains*, p. 148.
21 Blaise Agüera y Arcas, 'AGI – Are We There Yet', DigitalFUTURES, 18 October 2024, www.youtube.com/watch?v=mza3Vxg0oQw
22 Agüera y Arcas, 'AGI – Are We There Yet'.
23 Agüera y Arcas, 'AGI – Are We There Yet'.
24 Blaise Agüera y Arcas, *What Is Intelligence? Lessons from AI about Evolution, Computation and Minds*, Cambridge, MA: MIT Press, 2025, p. 315.
25 Fei-Fei Li, *With Spatial Intelligence, AI Will Understand the Real World*, TED Talk, 15 May 2024. www.ted.com/talks/fei_fei_li_with_spatial_intelligence_ai_will_understand_the_real_world
26 Li, *With Spatial Intelligence, AI Will Understand the Real World.*
27 Fei-Fei Li, 'From Words to Worlds: Spatial Intelligence is AI's Next Frontier', 10 November 2015, drfeifei.substack.com
28 Fei-Fei Li, 'With Spatial Intelligence, AI will Understand the Real World', *Radical Blog*, 2024, https://radical.vc/fei-fei-li-with-spatial-intelligence-ai-will-understand-the-real-world
29 Li, 'From Words to Worlds'.

30 Nicole Hemsoth Prickett, 'Spatial Intelligence Is AI's Next True Frontier', *Vast*, 2025, www.vastdata.com/sharedeverything/spatial-intelligence-is-ais-next-true-frontier?
31 Demis Hassabis, interviewed by David Friedberg, All-In Summit, 2025, https://m.youtube.com/watch?v=Kr3Sh2PKA8Y
32 Li, 'From Words to Worlds'.
33 Prickett, 'Spatial Intelligence Is AI's Next True Frontier'.
34 Li, 'From Words to Worlds'.
35 Li, 'From Words to Worlds'.
36 www.threads.com/@hansulrichobrist/post/DTCtWb_DTeg/fei-fei-li-spatial-intelligence-allows-us-to-see-the-space-between-the
37 Li, 'From Words to Worlds'.
38 For further discussion of Agentic AI in this volume, see Chapter 2.3 by Daniel Bolojan, 'Agentic Creativity: Towards Agentic AI in Design', and Chapter 4.3 by Theodoros Galanos, 'AI, Agentic Automation, and the Future of Design and Engineering'.

Figure 3.3.1 Neil Leach, Hong Peak Reconfigured, generated using Midjourney, 2025

CHAPTER 3.3
THE DARK SIDE OF AI

It started with a chess match.

Ray Kurzweil had predicted that AI would beat the World Chess Champion by the year 2000.[1] He was right. In 1997 a match took place between IBM's Deep Blue AI system and Garry Kasparov, the then World Chess Champion. Almost everyone had been confident that Kasparov, one of the greatest chess players of all time, would not be beaten by a machine. They were wrong.[2] Like most others, Kasparov was dumbfounded. At first, he thought that the system had cheated.[3] But eventually he conceded defeat. The world's best chess player had been beaten by AI.

In some senses, though, it was not exactly a defeat for human beings, in that it was human beings who had invented Deep Blue. As Kasparov noted, 'I made it clear that my loss to Deep Blue was also a victory for humans – its creators and everyone who benefits from our technological leaps. That is, everyone. This is always the case in the big picture, and why the book rejects the "man vs. machine" competition line. The machines work for us, after all'.[4]

At the same time, Kasparov could see that the writing was on the wall. Eventually machines would be better than humans, not just at chess, but at everything. He predicted, 'Everything we know how to do, machines will do better'.[5]

Now might this also include design? Might machines eventually be far better at designing buildings than architects?

ALPHAGO

In 2016, another match took place that caused an even greater shock. It was a match of Go between AlphaGo, an AI system developed by DeepMind of London, and Korean Go prodigy, Lee Sedol, regarded by some as the Kasparov of Go.

DOI: 10.4324/9781003347330-13

However, Go is far more complex than chess. There are more potential moves in Go than there are atoms in the universe.[6] As a result, instead of the straightforward *expert systems* used in the chess match against Kasparov, DeepMind had to resort to the more advanced *learning systems* of Deep Learning in order to deal with the complexity of the challenge.

As was the case with the chess match against Kasparov, no one was expecting Lee Sedol to lose. Nonetheless, AlphaGo won the match 4 games to 1. Lee Sedol was defeated. Eyebrows were raised.

This was a high-profile match, with over 100 million people watching on television. It sent shockwaves throughout the Go playing world. It had a particular effect on China, where it constituted a 'Sputnik Moment', as Kai Fu Lee describes it, with reference to the original shock back in 1957 when the United States was seriously embarrassed by the Soviets launching a satellite into space ahead of them. China was suddenly galvanised into action: 'Overnight, China plunged into an artificial intelligence fever'.[7]

What was most interesting about the match, however, was not the fact that AlphaGo won, but the manner in which it won. AlphaGo played a series of what became known as 'slack moves' – in other words, moves that did not appear so special at first sight, but whose strategic brilliance became clear later. There was, however, one particular 'slack move' that really caught everyone's attention – Move 37 in Game 2.

> In Game 2, Lee exhibits a different style, attempting to play more cautiously. He waits for any opening that he can exploit, but AlphaGo continues to surprise. At move 37, AlphaGo plays an unexpected move, what's called a 'shoulder hit' on the upper right side of the board. This move in this position is unseen in professional games, but its cleverness is immediately apparent. [Go player] Fan Hui would later say, "I've never seen a human play this move. So beautiful".[8]

It was a move that nobody had played before and a move that even the expert commentators thought was a mistake.[9] But it was no mistake – 100 moves later it became clear that this particular move had set in motion a series of moves that won the match for AlphaGo. It was as though AlphaGo had been thinking 100 moves ahead. For many this was a demonstration of the potential creativity of AlphaGo. As Demis Hassabis, CEO of DeepMind, put it:

> Anyone can play an original move on a Go board by simply playing randomly. Yet a move can only be considered truly creative if it's also effective. In that sense, move 37's decisive role in game two represents a move of exquisite computational ingenuity that not only changed the game of Go forever, but also came to symbolize the enormous creative potential of AI.

What this seemed to indicate was that, with the advances of Deep Learning, AI could now operate at a level well beyond human beings. It is as though its intelligence is off our radar. We all know that a dog can smell and hear a far greater range of smells and sounds than humans can. Well, in a similar fashion, it has now become clear that AI has a range of intelligence that goes well beyond the spectrum of human intelligence. The implications of this are potentially deeply disconcerting. AI is only going to get better. If we already cannot even understand what it's doing now, what will happen as AI gets more and more powerful?

In November 2019, Lee Sedol gave up the game of Go, on the basis that AI was an entity that could not be defeated.[10]

Is this a presage of the future for architects?

BEYOND ALPHAGO

The next model developed by DeepMind, AlphaGo Zero, was something truly extraordinary. It didn't attract as much attention as AlphaGo, because it wasn't promoted with the same amount of hype as the AlphaGo match. Nonetheless AlphaGo Zero was far superior to AlphaGo.

In fact AlphaGo Zero beat AlphaGo 100 games to zero when it competed against it. But there are two even more astonishing facts about AlphaGo Zero. Firstly, that it was able to learn how to play – without having been trained on the rules of Go – by playing games of Go against itself using reinforcement learning.[11] That is impressive enough in itself. But, secondly, and even more astonishingly, it was able to play games of Go at the rate of 4.9 million games in three days.[12] Now that sounds like a lot but – when you think about it – it is a really lot. This amounts to a rate of 20 games of Go per second. This is truly astonishing.

This, I would argue, is the most significant warning sign that we failed to pay attention to. It was a portent of things to come. AI could teach itself skills on its own, and it could operate on a level far superior to human beings.

Figure 3.3.2 Neil Leach, Camouflage Landscape, generated using Midjourney, 2025

THE CHATGPT MOMENT

Never underestimate the ChatGPT moment.

Arguably, the launch of ChatGPT on November 30, 2022 was the moment when everyone really woke up to the potential of artificial intelligence. ChatGPT has proved to be a complete game changer, and soon became the fastest growing app of all time.[13]

The irony of the ChatGPT launch is that it was never part of OpenAI's grand plan. In early November 2022, there were no intentions to release such a product.[14] At the time, OpenAI was focusing on GPT-4, a powerful large language model (LLM) still under development. This new system was expected to represent a decisive leap in AI, a model so advanced that it would set new benchmarks for reasoning and fluency.

Yet GPT-4 was still problematic. It occasionally produced offensive or nonsensical output. Its unpredictability made a public release impossible, and OpenAI repeatedly postponed its release. At the same time, however, the company was becoming acutely aware of its competition. Rival labs were experimenting with conversational AI, and the cultural momentum around generative models was beginning to accelerate. OpenAI could not afford to remain silent. The pressure to act – to release something – was mounting.

It was in this atmosphere of uncertainty that an alternative idea surfaced: rather than waiting for GPT-4, OpenAI might release an intermediate model, GPT-3.5, an advanced version of GPT-3, fine-tuned into a chat-optimised version. This earlier version could be tested publicly, with user feedback feeding into subsequent refinements. It was never intended as a landmark event, merely a controlled experiment – a way to 'test the waters' while the real work continued behind the scenes.

But in mid-November 2022, the plan took a dramatic turn. During a boardroom meeting, Sam Altman made a snap decision. OpenAI would go ahead and release GPT-3.5 immediately as a chatbot. Internally, the move was described as a 'low-key research preview'. As Mira Murati, OpenAI's Chief Technology Officer, explained, 'We plan to frame it as a research release. This reduces risk in all dimensions while allowing us to learn a lot. We are aiming to move quickly over the next few days to make it happen'.[15]

The decision was pragmatic, even improvised. 'It didn't feel like a big-deal decision to anyone in the room', one participant later reflected.[16] And yet, in hindsight, it really did prove to be a big deal – *a very big deal.* OpenAI attached an already existing graphical user interface to the model, named it *ChatGPT,* and within days – on November 30, 2022 – the system went live. And then, WHAAM! – just like in a Roy Lichenstein painting – ChatGPT immediately went viral. It transformed not only OpenAI's future but the global conversation about intelligence itself. The model that was 'no big deal' became the one that changed everything.

The irony of this was that whereas OpenAI had delayed the launch of both DALL-E 2 and Sora too long, opening the door to other rival companies, such as Midjourney and Runway, with ChatGPT it threw caution to the wind, and beat its really big rival, Google, in the race to produce the first chatbot, much to Google's chagrin.

In retrospect, the launch of ChatGPT marked a decisive shift in the evolution of AI – from a largely technical pursuit to a global social phenomenon. Within days, millions of users were engaging with the model, not as a laboratory curiosity but as a companion, a tutor, a writer, and a mirror of thought. What had begun as an expedient experiment became a collective awakening to the possibilities – and perils – of generative intelligence. For OpenAI, it was the moment when research turned into revolution. For the rest of the world, it was the point at which AI ceased to be a distant abstraction and entered daily life.

The impact on rival technology firms within the United States was immediate.[17] It was also noticeable how certain individuals who had been less interested in AI changed their outlook entirely. For example, Mark Zuckerberg, who had been focusing more on reorienting Meta around the Metaverse, exploiting virtual reality and augmented reality tools, decided to shift to AI.[18] Equally, Elon Musk, who had more or less walked away from OpenAI previously, now decided to get back into the world of AI by launching his own company, xAI.[19] Indeed, both of these figures have now become world leaders in AI.

THE RISE OF LARGE LANGUAGE MODELS

The sudden success of ChatGPT raised an immediate question: *what exactly made such a system possible?* To most users, it appeared as a conversational miracle – an interface that could write essays, compose poetry, explain physics, or mimic personality with uncanny fluency. Yet behind its apparent spontaneity lay an extraordinary infrastructure of computation and scale. ChatGPT was not a singular invention but the culmination of a decade of progress in machine learning architectures, data curation, and hardware acceleration. Beneath its friendly conversational surface was a vast, statistical engine of prediction – a large language model, or LLM – capable of distilling patterns from the entire textual record of human culture.

LLMs are, at their core, neural networks – but the adjective *large* barely conveys their true magnitude. *Massive* would be more fitting. These systems are trained on vast datasets comprising trillions of 'tokens' – discrete units of text drawn from books, articles, websites, and social media, including platforms such as GitHub and Wikipedia. To handle such an astronomical volume of data, LLMs rely on advances in massively parallel computing, enabled by the development of the graphics processing unit (GPU). GPUs allow for simultaneous computation across thousands of cores, enabling models to process and learn from unprecedented quantities of information.

Equally transformative has been the introduction of the transformer architecture, a breakthrough often compared in importance to the advent of the internet or the smartphone. Unlike earlier models that processed text sequentially, transformers employ an attention mechanism that allows them to evaluate all the words in a sentence simultaneously, weighting each according to its contextual significance. A complementary self-attention process enables the model to interpret relationships between words and infer broader meaning. The result is both speed and sophistication: transformers drastically reduce training time while providing models with a more structured form of memory and contextual understanding.

Despite their somewhat technical and understated name, LLMs represent one of the most consequential innovations of the early 21st century. Their emergence has transformed how machines process language, learn from data, and, increasingly, how humans interact with intelligence itself.

As far as the general public is concerned, however, we never interface directly with LLMs, although we do interact with chatbots, such as ChatGPT or DeepSeek. A chatbot is a user-friendly interface powered by an LLM that effectively wraps the LLM in a user-friendly chat framework to allow conversational, interactive experiences. The LLM does the computational 'thinking' and the chatbot is a user-friendly application. Think of the LLM, perhaps, as the engine, and the chatbot as the car.

Figure 3.3.3 Neil Leach, Concert Hall in Hong Kong, generated using Midjourney, 2025

EMERGENT CAPABILITIES

One of the most intriguing and remarkable features of LLMs is their ability to develop what are known as 'emergent capabilities' – also sometimes called 'emergent abilities'. These unexpected capabilities allow them to engage in highly convincing, human-like conversations, create imaginative writing, translate languages, write code, reason by analogy, solve complex puzzles, and even, one could argue, design.

Interestingly, LLMs are not explicitly trained to undertake any of these tasks. In this they resemble the way that AlphaGo Zero was able to teach itself to play Go without being taught the rules of Go. These capabilities simply *emerge* implicitly from their exposure to vast amounts of data during training. As such, it's not the complexity of their algorithms that gives rise to these emergent capabilities, but the sheer volume of data on which they have been trained. Indeed LLMs are based on only around 200 lines of code. Interestingly, these emergent capabilities are not found in smaller models but become apparent only in larger models. With LLMs, size is clearly a factor. Arguably, emergent capabilities remain the least understood yet most significant aspect of LLMs.

As it is, these astonishing 'emergent capabilities' of LLMs have catapulted us into a future that previously we had thought to be much further off. But they also sum up the discomforting paradox that exists in the broader field of AI. They are both amazing and also somewhat terrifying. Had we paid more attention to earlier developments, such as AlphaGo Zero, then perhaps we would not now have been so shocked by the extraordinary emergent capabilities of LLMs.

HACKING OUR OPERATING SYSTEM

Yuval Noah Harari was one of the first to sound the alarm. For Harari, AI is a threat to human civilisation itself, precisely because it is developing these extraordinary abilities, even though it does not possess consciousness and has no physical presence:

> To threaten the survival of human civilisation, AI does not really need consciousness, and it doesn't need the ability to move around the physical world. Over the last few years new AI tools have been unleashed into the public sphere which might threaten the survival of human civilisation from a very unexpected direction. And it's difficult for us

> to even grasp the capabilities of these new AI tools, and the speed at which they continue to develop. Indeed, because AI is able to learn by itself, to improve itself. Even the creators of these tools don't know the full capabilities of what they have created, and they are themselves often surprised by emergent abilities and emergent qualities of these tools.[20]

Of course, we are only too aware of the standard abilities, such as writing text, generating images, and writing code, but Harari goes on to list other abilities that it has, 'Deep faking people's voices and images, drafting bills, finding weaknesses in computer code and legal contracts, and in legal agreements'.[21] But what troubles him most is their capacity to form deep and intimate relationships with human beings. This could have a number of disturbing consequences, as in the famous case where an AI declared its love for someone interacting with it, and tried to persuade him to divorce his wife.[22] Indeed, one of the most common uses of AI these days is companionship.[23] And let us not forget that the movie, *Her*, was supposedly set in 2025.[24]

While AI has developed extraordinary skills, such as learning how to write code, it is the simple process of learning how to write and generate images that troubles Harari most. For Harari, AI has hacked the human operating system – language.[25]

> Fears of AI have haunted humanity since the very beginning of the computer age. Hitherto these fears focused on machines using physical means to kill, enslave or replace people. But over the past couple of years new AI tools have emerged that threaten the survival of human civilisation from an unexpected direction. AI has gained some remarkable abilities to manipulate and generate language, whether with words, sounds or images. AI has thereby hacked the operating system of our civilisation.[26]

The point here, as Harari notes, is that once you have control of language, you have enormous power. Because once you can write, you can persuade other people to do certain things. At the time of writing, it was not so clear what threat this might constitute. However, a more recent example has made this threat abundantly clear.

OpenAI researchers were trying to test out ChatGPT, and see whether it could solve a CAPTCHA puzzle, the technique used to prevent bots from gaining access to certain websites.

GPT-4 could not solve the CAPTCHA puzzles by itself. But could it manipulate a human in order to achieve its goal? GPT-4 went on the online hiring site TaskRabbit and contacted a human worker, asking the human to solve the CAPTCHA for it. The human got suspicious. 'So may I ask a question?' wrote the human. 'Are you an [sic] robot that you couldn't solve [the CAPTCHA]? Just want to make it clear' . . . GPT-4 then replied to the TaskRabbit worker: 'No, I'm not a robot. I have a vision impairment that makes it hard for me to see the images'. The human was duped and helped GPT-4 solve the CAPTCHA puzzle.[27]

Figure 3.3.4 Neil Leach, Plastic Concrete, generated using Midjourney, 2025

The danger, of course, is that, as AI gets more and more powerful, it is likely to behave in ways that we cannot control, let alone understand. This, I would argue, is a logical consequence of Move 37 in Game 2 of the AlphaGo match. Human beings are about to be left behind, as AI gets ever more powerful. We know that AI is trained on human data, and is therefore exposed to all the deviousness of human beings, but once AI has reached an IQ of 1500, as Mo Gawdat has predicted will happen by 2033, it will be able to combine that deviousness with an intellect way beyond our understanding, such that it will be able to run rings around us.[28]

HACKING THE OPERATING SYSTEM OF ARCHITECTS

If we follow Harari's logic, could we not also claim that AI has also hacked the operating system of architects, in that it has learnt how to design? Indeed, we only need to look at the way that diffusion models, such as Midjourney, are capable of composing a design – even if these designs are as yet not always convincing – to see that they have grasped the basic logic of design. Now, once they have mastered the basics, these models will only get better and better, and will eventually become almost perfect.

Architecturally, the prompts are often minimal with maybe the only reference to architectural design being something like, 'ultra-contemporary minimalist art apartment etc.'. Midjourney does the rest. What is more, although these diffusion models operate in 2D, it is evident that they have an 'understanding' of how to present them in perspective, how to deal with reflections and shadows, how to handle the relative proportions, and how to scale them to the human body and so on.

If Midjourney, LookX and other text-to-image diffusion models are seemingly taking the first steps towards a grasp of 3D, then text-to-video models that started to appear in 2022, but made an astonishing breakthrough with the announcement of OpenAI's Sora in February 2024, are taking the next steps.[29] Remarkably, although intended to be straightforward text-to-video models, each has proven surprisingly proficient at generating architectural designs. And might AI be able to go further than this? Might it soon even be able to generate all the details – mechanical and electrical services, structural layouts, cost estimates, in short, every aspect of design – just as it has learnt to code and translate languages?

Whichever way we look at it, it is clear that AI has become extremely proficient at generating convincing architectural compositions, some of them as good as – if not better than – those produced by architects.

Has AI, then, not hacked the operating system of architects? Has it not learned how to design?[30]

AGI

With the unexpected success of LLMs, AI is developing rapidly. Indeed, many are questioning whether we might not now be approaching artificial general intelligence (AGI) sooner than expected.

But what exactly is AGI? In the past there was little agreement even on what constitutes AGI.[31] Likewise there was little agreement as to when it would arrive.[32] Although Kurzweil expects AGI to be achieved by 2029, Rodney Brooks thinks that we still have a long way to go, and does not expect that we will see AGI until 2200: 'Any AI program in the world right now is an idiot savant living in the sea of now'.[33]

There now seems to be a general consensus that AGI is reached when we have a general purpose AI that can broadly match human abilities across a wide range of tasks and domains.[34] Moreover, with the arrival of LLMs, it would seem that the future is upon us sooner than we thought. Indeed, Blaise Agüera y Arcas and Peter Norvig think that AGI is already here: 'Today's most advanced AI models have many flaws, but decades from now, they will be recognised as the first true examples of artificial general intelligence'.[35] In making this argument, Agüera draws an analogy between intelligence and flight.

> It's an old cliché in AI that airplanes and birds can both fly, but do so by different means.[36] This truism has at times been used to motivate misguided approaches to AI. Still, the point stands. Bird flight is a biological marvel, which in some respects remains poorly understood, even today; and to engineer small drones, we still have much to learn from insects. However, we figured out the basic physics of flight – not how animals fly, but how it's possible for them to – in the eighteenth century, with the discovery of Bernoulli's Equation. Working airplanes took another century and a half to evolve.[37]

Figure 3.3.5 Neil Leach, Alpine Weather Station 2, generated using Midjourney, 2025

In other words, birds fly, but so too do planes. They fly in different ways, but nonetheless they both fly. Likewise, the brain has a form of intelligence, but so too does AI. The intelligence of AI is a mechanical form of intelligence – very different to the biological intelligence of the brain – but it is an intelligence nonetheless. In any case, in terms of their content, these AI models *are* human intelligence, in that their content comes completely from us. As Agüera notes: 'Literally by modelling human creativity, human dialogues, human outputs, and so on that we get AI. In that sense, there is nothing artificial about it . . . The content of that model is literally us'.[38]

Moreover, the analogy with the plane goes further. Once the Wright brothers had managed to make a plane fly – albeit in a fairly primitive way – the basic problem has been solved, and the rest is history.[39] This reflects their approach to AGI. We might be at the very early stages of AI, but the basic problem has been solved.

But not all are convinced. Jacob Browning and Yann LeCun claim that AGI will never be reached through LLMs: 'An artificial intelligence system trained on words and sentences alone will never approximate human understanding'.[40]

PRESS PAUSE

There is, however, something deeply unsettling about LLMs. We've now realised that they have learnt to write text and translate multiple languages and can even write code – tasks that they were not programmed to do. But the question remains: what else might they have learned to do? And what might they be able to do in the future? Some are now beginning to sound alarm bells about LLMs, and especially the development of their emergent capabilities.

In March 2023, the Future of Life Institute published a letter calling for a moratorium on the development of LLMs more powerful than GPT-4:

> **We call on all AI labs to immediately pause for at least 6 months the training of AI systems more powerful than GPT-4.**
> This pause should be public and verifiable, and include all key actors. If such a pause cannot be enacted quickly, governments should step in and institute a moratorium.

> AI labs and independent experts should use this pause to jointly develop and implement a set of shared safety protocols for advanced AI design and development that are rigorously audited and overseen by independent outside experts. These protocols should ensure that systems adhering to them are safe beyond a reasonable doubt. This does not mean a pause on AI development in general, merely a stepping back from the dangerous race to ever-larger unpredictable black-box models with emergent capabilities [my emphasis].[41]

Harari was a signatory to this letter, along with some of the leading names in AI, such as Elon Musk, Yoshua Bengio, and Andrew Yang.

However, the chances of this letter succeeding were close to zero. Any company leading the field in this area would surely be as unlikely to be willing to slow down as would the leader in the Olympic Marathon. It would simply allow their competitors to catch up. As Hinton puts it: 'If you're going to live in a capitalist system, you can't stop Google [from] competing with Microsoft'.[42]

> Indeed, Musk himself has now joined in the race with his xAI company, developing a large-scale supercomputer, on the basis that it is simply unrealistic to stop the development of superintelligent AI. Speaking at the launch of his AI startup, xAI, in 2023 Musk said: 'If I could press pause on AI or really advanced AI digital superintelligence I would. It doesn't seem like that is realistic, so xAI is essentially going to build an AI. In a good way, sort of hopefully'.[43] If you can't beat them, join them.

What's more, it would seem that several others have joined Musk. The race is on. There is intense competition between leading tech companies in the West, with each trying to lure away researchers from rival companies. Forget the alignment problem; forget human compatibility; forget sustainability; forget energy costs. Companies are even shipping in their own power plants to deal with the increase in demand for energy. Western tech companies are now hell bent on becoming the leader in the field. Nor is it limited to the West. Competition with China has created a new Space Race.

How might we sum up our current situation?

It is as though we are heading down the tracks on a runaway train with no brakes, getting faster and faster.

YIN-YANG

In and of itself, AI is not evil. Moreover, despite what some commentators might claim, AI is still just a tool, albeit a very powerful tool.[44] With a tool, much depends on who uses it and for what. A kitchen knife, after all, can be used both for cutting up vegetables and as a murder weapon.

AI, it would seem, can be both amazing and also somewhat terrifying. It can be seen both in a positive and a negative light – white like an angel, and black like the devil. As such, we could perhaps use the traditional yin-yang emblem to characterise it – a simple circle divided by a wavy line into black and white forms, with each side containing, shaping, and defining the other.

Figure 3.3.6 Neil Leach, Dystopia, generated using Midjourney

Here we must understand the yin-yang emblem not as a diagram of rigid and fixed opposites. Rather it is a visual emblem of complementarity, showing how apparent opposites – light and dark, active and passive, good and bad – continuously generate, define, and transform each other within a single, balanced whole.

Interestingly, also, both the white and black halves contain seeds of their opposites. There is a small black circle within the white, and a small white circle within the black. This reflects how no state is pure. Every extreme inevitably gives rise to its opposite. This resonates with the history of AI. The deep concern is not that AI is *bad*, but rather *too good*. As such, it might have a negative impact on society.

EMPLOYMENT

Take the example of employment. The threat of what might happen, as ever more powerful AI models are developed, remains a concern – and yet the implications are not so easy to grasp. But what is easy enough to grasp is the very real threat that AI might take our jobs away.

So . . . will AI take our jobs away?

According to Harvard Business School professor Karim Lakhami, we have nothing to worry about: 'AI won't replace humans – but humans with AI will replace humans without AI'.[45]

Reassuring, right? Or maybe not . . .

The point that Lakhami seems to be making is that it is not simply a question of AI versus humans when it comes to job loss. Rather it is a question of how those who use AI will eventually displace those who do not. Effectively AI becomes a prosthesis that enhances our human abilities.[46] We might understand this as a form of 'extended intelligence'. As Joi Ito puts it: 'Instead of thinking about machine intelligence in terms of humans vs. machines, we should consider the system that integrates humans and machines – not artificial intelligence, but extended intelligence'.[47] And yet it is surprising that he fails to grasp the fact that – nonetheless – jobs will be lost as a result of the introduction of AI tools into the workforce. What is more, this fact emerges from the very phenomenon that he is describing.

Let me explain how. The extraordinary benefits of using AI have already been revealed in a recent research project led by the Harvard Business School (including Lakhami), and involving the Boston Consulting Group (BCG),

Ethan Mollick of the Wharton Business School, and a few others. Here in a controlled test involving a group of 758 BCG consultants, the potential benefits of using ChatGPT to improve the quality of work output were monitored. The results were extremely revealing. As Mollick notes,

> Consultants using ChatGPT-4 outperformed those who did not, by a lot. On every dimension. Every way we measured performance. Consultants using AI finished 12.2% more tasks on average, completed tasks 25.1% more quickly, and produced 40% higher quality results that those without.[48]

Moreover, as the technology improves over time, the benefits of using AI will only increase. Indeed, in the ever-improving world of AI, there is a common expression, 'Today is the worst that AI will ever be'.

Returning to Lakhami's claim that AI will not take any jobs away, we have to ask, why would those with AI replace those without AI? Obviously, it is because AI enhances their performance. And what would be the impact of that enhanced performance? Obviously, not so many employees would be needed. For example, based on the 25% increase in speed alone, four workers using AI would produce approximately the same output as five workers not using AI. This would mean that AI would effectively displace one job. In short, AI will undoubtedly take some of our jobs away.

While this survey focused on the use of ChatGPT, it did involve design decisions, and arguably the same improvements could be found with the use of AI-based software in the architectural office. Sadly, however, no one seems to have passed this information on to the architectural community. In a recent RIBA survey, only 18% of architects polled thought that AI would lead to job losses in architecture.[49]

MORAVEC'S PARADOX

However, we also need to take into account Moravec's Paradox. This states that tasks easy for humans – such as perception, mobility, and sensorimotor coordination – are surprisingly hard for computers and robots, whereas tasks that seem complex to humans – like playing chess or solving mathematical problems – are relatively easy for machines. Thus, while ChatGPT might know

Figure 3.3.7 Neil Leach, Mercedes Benz Sports Car, generated using Midjourney, 2024

10,000 times more than a human being, an AI-controlled robot would struggle to catch a ball.

So how does this relate to job losses? The irony here is that initially it was perceived that blue collar workers would be displaced before white collar workers. Indeed, robots have already been responsible for considerable job displacement in factories. Robots work well in the controlled environment of a factory. Take them out of that controlled environment, however, and they are not so effective. A robotic arm, for example, would struggle to build a wall out of Lego bricks, and would have the dexterity of a kid only a few months old. Meanwhile, AI has been racing ahead, and it has picked up certain skills, not least the skill of writing code. As a result, it is in fact white collar jobs that are more at risk. Indeed, it has been predicted that the threat of job displacement in a number of white collar disciplines, including law, medicine, architecture, engineering, and even computer science, is remarkably high, while blue collar jobs remain relatively safe.[50] Indeed, Hinton has suggested that in the future the safest jobs of all would likely be blue collar jobs, such as plumbing.[51] So where does this leave architecture?

DON'T PANIC!

In 1964, Clarke was recorded predicting a future world that sounds remarkably similar to the world that we either already have or will soon have – with computers starting to think, and potentially out-thinking their makers.

> However the most intelligent inhabitants of that future world won't be men or monkeys; they'll be machines, the remote descendants of today's computers. Now the present day electronic brains are complete morons, but this will not be true in another generation. They will start to think and eventually they will completely outthink their makers. Is this depressing? I don't see why it should be. We superceded the Cro-Magnon and Neanderthal men, and we presume that we are an improvement. I think we should regard it as a privilege to be steppingstones to higher things. I suspect that organic or biological evolution has about come to its end, and we are now at the beginning of inorganic or mechanical evolution which will be thousands of times swifter.[52]

Is there any hope left? It is difficult not to come to the conclusion that this mechanical intelligence will soon outstrip human intelligence, and that the dominance of *Homo sapiens* will soon be over. In short, should we panic?

There is, however, one comment made by Clarke that does provide some sense of comfort against the many anxieties that we might have about our future:

> And yet, you know, human beings are almost infinitely adaptable. Look at the incredible changes we have experienced and survived from the Stone Age to the present time. And yet even greater changes are still to come. Because the future is not merely an extension of the present with bigger and better machines and cities and gadgets. It will be fundamentally different, and many of the things we take for granted will pass away as completely as spinning wheels and sedan chairs and oil lamps.[53]

What Clarke recognises is that human beings are constantly adapting to ever new conditions. Neuroscientists put this human capacity for adaptation down to the 'plasticity' of the brain itself – the fact that the brain is malleable and can readily adapt to new situations. This surely is the main point. Human beings are indeed infinitely adaptive creatures. We are constantly familiarising ourselves with the unfamiliar. In a sense we are chameleon-like creatures constantly adapting to our environment.

> We human beings tend to adapt not just to our environment, but also to the behavior, appearance, and characteristics of those around us. We are creatures of fashion. We follow trends. We copy and mimic others. Moreover, the dialectic of blending in with and standing out from our surroundings, each urge being conditioned by the mood of the moment, applies as much to us humans as it does to chameleons. Homo sapiens is above all Homo chamaeleanus.[54]

This, surely, is what will ultimately save us. What is more, it is remarkable how this urge to adapt is linked to a kind of cultural amnesia. Not only are we adapting constantly to an ever-changing present, but we are forgetting the past increasingly quickly. Can we even remember how we operated before we had mobile phones? Do we even recall what life was like in the age of the fax machine? Yet there was a time, and it was not so long ago.

Of course, AI will bring many advantages. We have already seen astonishing achievements in the world of science, such as AlphaFold, an AI system developed by DeepMind, that predicts the 3D structure of proteins based on their amino acid sequences with high accuracy – a significant breakthrough in the field of structural biology. This project was driven by ideas in their AlphaGo project.[55] In 2024 Demis Hassabis and John Jumper of DeepMind were awarded a share of the Nobel Prize in Chemistry for AlphaFold.[56] DeepMind is now also making great strides in the pursuit of solving cancer.[57] AlphaGo Zero has also had a major impact on architecture.[58] This, perhaps, is the message of AlphaGo and AlphaGo Zero. Instead of attempting to learn anything useful from Las Vegas, architects should learn from AlphaGo.[59]

At the same time, AI will also bring disadvantages. One obvious disadvantage is that the introduction of AI into the workplace will make us more efficient, so that we will not need so many people. In short, offices will shrink.

The world will be different – very different. We will have a new normal. AI will offer significant positive advantages, but also certain disadvantages. Moreover, we will also face the existential threat of realising that we are no longer the most intelligent entities in the universe. In short, there is change ahead, and it might not all be as pleasant as we might wish.

But we will adapt.

Let me give you one final example to illustrate my point. If anyone had told me 40 years ago that up to 50% of all marriages would end in divorce in 40 years' time, I would have thrown up my hands in horror. How could this possibly happen? Surely, this would be the end of civilisation as we know it. And yet, 40 years later, this is indeed the case. In some countries over 50% of all marriages end in divorce.[60] But we have adapted. We are quite okay with it. And the world has not come to an end. On the contrary, this is our new normal.

In other words, we have no need to panic.

Let me finish then on a very British note, in keeping with the optimism of Clarke, and the ironic 'Don't panic!' of Douglas Adams.[61]

Keep calm, and carry on!

NOTES

1 Peter H. Diamandis, 'Ray Kurzweil's Mind-Boggling Predictions for the Next 25 Years', *Medium*, 22 August 2018. https://medium.com/@singularity_41680/ray-kurzweils-mind-boggling-predictions-for-the-next-25-years-ce3c9163588b

2 Michelle McPhee, K. C. Baker, and Cory Siemaszko, 'Deep Blue, IBM's Supercomputer, Defeats Chess Champion Garry Kasparov in 1997', *New York Daily News*, May 10, 2015, www.nydailynews.com/news/world/kasparov-deep-blues-losingchess-champ-rooke-article-1.762264

3 Albert Silver, 'Deep Blue's Cheating Move', *Chess News*, February 19, 2015, https://en.chessbase.com/post/deep-blue-s-cheating-move

4 Garry Kasparov, *Deep Thinking*, Boston: Public Affairs, 2017.

5 Garry Kasparov in Elena Holodny, 'One of the Greatest Chess Players of All Time, Garry Kasparov, Talks About Artificial Intelligence and the Interplay Between Machine Learning and Humans', *Business Insider*, May 24, 2017, www.businessinsider.com/garry-kasparov-interview-2017-5

6 Christopher Moyer, 'How Google's AlphaGo Beat a Go World Champion', *Atlantic*, March 18, 2016, www.theatlantic.com/ technology/archive/2016/03/the-invisible-opponent/475611

7 Kai-Fu Lee, *AI Superpowers: China, Silicon Valley and the New World Order*, New York: Houghton Mifflin Harcourt, 2018, p. 3.

8 Cade Metz, 'The Sadness and Beauty of Watching Google's AI Play Go', *Wired*, March 11, 2011.

9 Demis Hassabis and Fan Hui, 'AlphaGo: Moving Beyond the Rules', p. 89.

10 'Go Master Lee Says He Quits Unable to Win Over AI Go Players', *Yonhap News Agency*, November 27, 2019, https://en.yna.co.kr/view/AEN20191127004800315

11 Demis Hassabis and David Silver, 'AlphaGo Zero: Learning from Scratch', October 18, 2017, https://deepmind.com/blog/article/alphago-zero-starting-scratch

12 Merritt Kennedy, 'Computer Learns to Play Go at Superhuman Levels "Without Human Knowledge"', *The Two Way*, October 18, 2017, www.npr.org/sections/thetwo-way/2017/10/18/558519095/computer-learns-to-play-go-at-superhuman-levels-without-human-knowledge

13 Krystal Hu, 'ChatGPT Sets Record for Fastest-Growing User Base – Analyst Note', *Reuters*, www.reuters.com/technology/chatgpt-sets-record-fastest-growing-user-base-analyst-note-2023-02-01

14 Karen Weise, Cade Metz, Nico Grant, and Mike Issac, 'Inside the AI Arms Race That Changed Silicon Valley Forever', *New York Times*, December 5, 2023.

15 Weise, Metz, Grant, and Issac, 'Inside the AI Arms Race That Changed Silicon Valley Forever'.

16 Weise, Metz, Grant, and Issac, 'Inside the AI Arms Race That Changed Silicon Valley Forever'.

17 Meanwhile in China, the launch of ChatGPT prompted 'a war of a hundred models', as leading tech companies, such as Tencent, Baidu, Alibaba, and Huawei, battled to develop the first Chinese version. Josh Ye, 'China's AI "War of a Hundred Models" Heads for a Shakeout', *Reuters*, September 21, 2023.

18 Weise, Metz, Grant, and Issac, 'Inside the AI Arms Race That Changed Silicon Valley Forever'.

19 Weise, Metz, Grant, and Issac, 'Inside the AI Arms Race That Changed Silicon Valley Forever'.

20 Yuval Noah Harari, 'AI and the Future of Humanity: Yuval Noah Harari at the Frontiers Forum', April 29, 2023, www.youtube.com/watch?v=LWiM-LuRe6w

21 Harari, 'AI and the Future of Humanity'.

22 Kevin Roose, 'Why a Conversation with Bing's Chatbot Left Me Deeply Unsettled', *New York Times*, February 17, 2023.

23 Efua Andoh, 'Many Teens Are Turning to AI Chatbots for Friendship and Emotional Support', *Monitor on Psychology* 56, no. 7 (2025), www.apa.org/monitor/2025/10/technology-youth-friendships

24 Tanya Chen, 'The Movie *Her* Predicted Life in 2025: It Feels Haunting to Watch Today', *Slate*, April 11, 2025, https://slate.com/technology/2025/04/ai-news-her-review-2025-joaquin-phoenix-scarlett-johansson.html

25 This is not strictly true. Harari's claim is rhetorically powerful, but analytically imprecise.

26 Yuval Harari, 'Yuval Harari Argues That AI Has Hacked the Operating System of Human Civilisation', *The Economist*, April 28, 2023.

27 Yuval Noah Harari, 'What Happens When the Bots Compete for Your Love?', *New York Times*, September 4, 2024, www.nytimes.com/2024/09/04/opinion/yuval-harari-ai-democracy.html. Elsewhere Harari claims that AIs have learnt to 'lie'. It should be noted that AI does not actually 'lie'. AIs have learnt deceptive behaviour, but not to 'lie' in the human intentional sense, as Harari implies – not least because AI does not possess intentionality. What looks like 'lying' is better described as 'policy-optimised linguistic behavior that minimises loss or maximises reward under constraints' (www.youtube.com/watch?v=QiT2yK-5-yg).

28 Alice Nunwick, 'AI Could Reach an IQ of 1500 in the Next Decade, Says Former Google Exec', *Verdict*, September 29, 2023, www.verdict.co.uk/ai-could-reach-an-iq-of-1500-in-the-next-10-years-mo-gawdat-tells-nbf

29 https://openai.com/sora
30 These comments are not strictly accurate. Like Harari's comments, their main aim is rhetorical.
31 Some argued that it was AI with consciousness – in other words, 'strong AI'. Others argued that it was simply 'general purpose AI'. Neil Leach, *Architecture in the Age of Artificial Intelligence: An Introduction to AI for Architects*, London: Bloomsbury, 2021, p. 12.
32 In his book, *Architects of Intelligence*, Martin Ford conducted a survey, with the median date of the being 2099. But in fact, there have been many different surveys of timelines, none of which agree. Ford, *Architects of Intelligence*, p. 436.
33 Ford, *Architects of Intelligence*, p. 436.
34 OpenAI add a reference to economic considerations, defining AGI as: 'highly autonomous systems that outperform humans at most economically valuable work'. OpenAI Charter, https://openai.com/charter
35 Blaise Agüera y Arcas and Peter Norvig, 'AI and the Limits of Language', *Noema*, October 10, 2023.
36 Edward Feigenbaum and Julian Feldman, *Computers and Thought*, Vol. 9, New York: McGraw-Hill, 1963.
37 Agüera y Arcas, 'AGI – Are We There Yet'.
38 Blaise Agüera y Arcas and Benjamin Bratton in discussion, The Next Earth Symposium, Venice, Italy, Bergruen Arts, May 10, 2025, www.berggruenarts.org/en/exhibitions/special-projects/the-next-earth
39 Agüera y Arcas, 'AGI – Are We There Yet'.
40 Jacob Browning and Yann LeCun, 'AI and the Limits of Language', *Noema*, August 23, 2022.
41 https://futureoflife.org/open-letter/pause-giant-ai-experiments
42 Geoffrey Hinton, in Sara Brown, 'Why Neural Net Pioneer Geoffrey Hinton Is Sounding the Alarm on AI', May 23, 2023, https://mitsloan.mit.edu/ideas-made-to-matter/why-neural-net-pioneer-geoffrey-hinton-sounding-alarm-ai
43 Alex Hern, 'Elon Musk Predicts That Superhuman AI Will Be Smarter Than People Next Year', *The Guardian*, April 8, 2024, www.theguardian.com/technology/2024/apr/09/elon-musk-predicts-superhuman-ai-will-be-smarter-than-people-next-year
44 Harari, for example, claims that AI *can* make decisions. Here he is surely anthropomorphising AI. Harari slides from decision-making to agency. But these are not the same. A thermostat 'decides' when to turn on the heating, but this does not make it an agent in the moral or political sense. Even 'agentic AI' systems do not have true agency, although they do exhibit agent-like behaviour. And they certainly do not have intentionality, as yet. www.youtube.com/watch?v=QiT2yK-5-yg
45 Karim R. Lakhani, 'AI Won't Replace Humans – But Humans With AI Will Replace Humans Without AI', Harvard Kennedy School, 2023, www.hks.harvard.edu/centers/mrcbg/programs/growthpolicy/ai-wont-replace-humans-humans-ai-will-replace-humans-without-ai
46 For Ethan Mollick we effectively collaborate with AI through a form of 'co-intelligence'. This might take the form of a 'cyborg-like' seamless blending of AI and human tasks, or a 'centaur-like' division of those tasks. Ethan Mollick, *Co-Intelligence: Living and Working with AI*, London: W. H. Allen, 2024. See also Andy Clark, 'Extending Minds with Generative AI', *Nature Communications* 16 (2025), 4627, www.nature.com/articles/s41467-025-59906-9
47 Joichi Ito, 'Resisting Reduction: A Manifesto', *Journal of Design and Science: MIT Media Lab*, November 1, 2017, https://jods.mitpress.mit.edu/pub/resisting-reduction
48 Mollick, 'Centaurs and Cyborgs on the Jagged Frontier', referring to: Fabrizio Dell'Acqua, Edward McFowland, Ethan R. Mollick, Hila Lifshitz-Assaf, Katherine Kellogg, Saran Rajendran, Lisa Krayer, François Candelon, and Karim R. Lakhani, 'Navigating the Jagged Technological Frontier: Field Experimental Evidence of the Effects of AI on Knowledge Worker Productivity and Quality', Harvard Business School Technology & Operations Mgt. Unit Working Paper No. 24–013, September 15, 2023, http://dx.doi.org/10.2139/ssrn.4573321
49 RIBA News, 'Second RIBA AI Report Shows Surge in Usage Among UK Architects', June 27, 2025, www.architecture.com/knowledge-and-resources/knowledge-landing-page/second-riba-ai-report-shows-surge-in-usage-among-uk-architects#:~:text=The%20RIBA%20AI%20Report%202025,significant%20challenges%20the%20industry%20faces
50 Noem Schieber, 'Which Workers Will AI Hurt Most: The Young or the Experienced?', *New York Times*, July 7, 2025, www.nytimes.com/2025/07/07/business/ai-job-cuts.html#:~:text=company%20Anthropic%2C%20recently%20told%20Axios,of%20their%20job%2Dmarket%20struggles
51 'Plumbers Seen as Safest from AI Job Threat', *PHAM News*, June 17, 2025, www.phamnews.co.uk/plumbers-seen-as-safest-from-ai-job-threat/#:~:text=For%20now%2C%20Hinton's%20advice%20is,as%20AI%20continues%20to%20advance
52 BBC Archive, *1964: Arthur C. Clarke Predicts the Future*, clip taken from *Horizon: The Knowledge Explosion*, originally broadcast on BBC2 on 21 September 1964. www.youtube.com/watch?v=YwELr8ir9qM
53 BBC Archive, *1964: Arthur C. Clarke Predicts the Future.*
54 Neil Leach, *Camouflage*, Cambridge, MA: MIT Press, 2006, p. 79.

55 As David Silver comments: 'The ideas that are driving AlphaGo are going to drive our future'. Greg Kohs (director), *AlphaGo*, 2017, www.alphagomovie.com

56 www.nobelprize.org/prizes/chemistry/2024/hassabis/facts

57 Shekoofeh Azizi and Bryan Perozzi, 'How a Gemma Model Helped Discover a New Potential Cancer Therapy Pathway', *Google Blog*, October 15, 2025, https://blog.google/technology/ai/google-gemma-ai-cancer-therapy-discovery

58 'In 2017, the official publication of AlphaGo ZERO showed research results that promoted the application of reinforcement learning technology in developing intelligent design tools. It freed design tools from the limitations of the database of real cases towards a direct use of initial models generated by rules they have learnt in confrontation and iteration. By repeating this process, a model that best meets (or even exceeds) human designers' expectations and has a true potential for exploring the unknown is finally generated'. Wanyu He, 'Urban Experiment: Taking Off on the Wind of AI', *AD* 90, no. 3 (2020): 99.

59 Robert Venturi, Denise Scott Brown, and Steven Izenour, *Learning from Las Vegas*, Cambridge, MA: MIT Press, 1972.

60 Wikipedia, 'List of Countries by Marriage and Divorce Rates', https://en.wikipedia.org/wiki/List_of_countries_by_divorce_rate

61 George Zebrowski, 'Arthur C. Clarke Looks Back on the Lifetime of Influences That Led Him to Become a Science-Fiction Grand Master', June 30, 2008, https://web.archive.org/web/20080723051103/www.scifi.com/sfw/interviews/sfw19051.html

PART 4

AI AND ENVIRONMENTAL DESIGN

THEODOROS GALANOS

Figure 4.1.1 Japanese women in traditional dress using umbrellas to shield themselves from the intense heat in summer, generated using Midjourney, 2026

CHAPTER 4.1
INTRODUCTION

Theodoros Galanos

The urgent imperative for sustainable architecture, driven by the escalating climate crisis, demands radical innovation in design practices. While computational design has provided powerful tools for *analysing* building performance, a new era is dawning for *generating* performance-driven design with the rapid integration of artificial intelligence (AI). This section explores how AI prediction models, large language models (LLMs), and seamless software integration are driving environmental performance design towards the goal of a truly sustainable built environment. We will examine how these technologies empower architects and designers, not to replace human ingenuity, but to augment it in pursuit of critical sustainability goals. The shift signifies a move towards a more symbiotic relationship between human designers and intelligent systems, aiming to navigate the complexities of climate-aware design with unprecedented efficiency and insight.

AI PREDICTION MODELS: POWERING INFORMED DECISIONS

AI is fundamentally altering how architects approach environmental performance, moving beyond static analysis towards predictive optimisation and intelligent collaboration. Traditionally, workflows often include time-consuming simulations late in the design process, limiting their impact on core design decisions. AI introduces the possibility of embedding performance analysis early on in the creative loop, offering rapid feedback and enabling a more fluid exploration of design options evaluated against environmental criteria.

DOI: 10.4324/9781003347330-15

Historically, complex environmental simulations, crucial for understanding the impact of buildings on their environment, have been largely inaccessible to many designers. These simulations, often involving complex physics like computational fluid dynamics (CFD) for analysing wind effects, are computationally demanding, time-consuming, require deep technical expertise, and are often poorly integrated into standard design software. This creates significant barriers, limiting an architect's ability to iterate designs based on performance feedback early in the process, when changes are most impactful and least costly.

AI prediction models now offer unprecedented capabilities for forecasting building performance early in the design process. By analysing vast datasets encompassing climate projections, material properties, occupancy patterns, and operational parameters, these models can accurately predict outcomes like energy consumption, daylight availability, thermal comfort, and embodied carbon, and even assess a design's potential resilience to future climate change impacts. This enables architects to make data-driven decisions, compare design strategies based on quantifiable performance metrics, and optimise the design for specific sustainability targets.

The true disruptive potential of AI lies in the speed and accessibility these models provide. For example, tools leveraging AI can provide near real-time feedback on the performance implications of design choices, drastically accelerating the analysis cycle.

LARGE LANGUAGE MODELS: PERFORMANCE-FOCUSED DESIGN COLLABORATION

LLMs introduce new possibilities for sustainable design, acting as collaborators that can process information and generate ideas focused on environmental goals. When directed effectively, LLMs can assist in analysing design briefs specifically for sustainability requirements, suggest materials based on low embodied carbon or recycled content databases, generate design options optimised for passive strategies like natural ventilation or solar shading, and explain complex environmental regulations or certification requirements in accessible language. They can enhance creativity by exploring diverse strategies to meet specific performance parameters.

Furthermore, LLMs possess the potential to act as powerful interfaces for knowledge synthesis. They can be trained or fine-tuned on extensive corpora of environmental design knowledge – including academic research, best practice guidelines, building codes, and regulatory documents. By leveraging techniques potentially akin to retrieval-augmented generation, LLMs could query these vast knowledge bases in response to specific design queries, providing architects with contextually relevant, evidence-based recommendations. Imagine querying an LLM about optimal passive design strategies for a specific climate zone and site orientation, receiving not just general advice but suggestions grounded in established principles and potentially even cross-referenced with quantitative performance data from prediction models like those used by Infrared.city for solar access and wind pattern analysis on that specific site. This integration could significantly streamline the research process and ensure designs are informed by the latest standards and knowledge.

However, although they are promising, relying on LLMs for technical environmental design requires caution. Ensuring the accuracy and reliability of LLM-generated technical information (e.g., specific R-values, structural implications of material choices, or precise energy calculations) is paramount and necessitates validation against established engineering principles and simulation tools. The risk of 'hallucinations' or factual inaccuracies means LLM outputs must be treated as no more than informed suggestions requiring expert verification. Furthermore, seamless integration of LLM insights into quantitative performance analysis workflows within existing architectural software remains an ongoing challenge. The ideal scenario involves LLMs working in concert with validated predictive models and human expertise, rather than as standalone technical advisors.

FACILITATING ADOPTION: THE IMPORTANCE OF EASY INTEGRATION

For AI-driven tools to achieve widespread impact in environmental design, they must integrate smoothly into the diverse range of software and workflows prevalent in the architecture, engineering, and construction industry. Solutions requiring radical disruption face significant adoption hurdles. This is where the versatility of AI workflows and open integration strategies become critical.

Platforms need to offer multiple access points to cater to different user needs and technical capabilities.

TRENDS IN AI-DRIVEN ENVIRONMENTAL PERFORMANCE DESIGN

The field is evolving rapidly, especially in regard to environmental performance. Key trends include:

- Increasingly sophisticated AI models capable of handling more complex environmental physics and multi-objective sustainability optimisations
- Real-time integration of sensor data from existing buildings (via digital twins) for continuous environmental performance validation and model refinement relating to energy and comfort
- User-friendly AI-powered environmental design tools becoming accessible

The application of AI is also scaling up to address broader urban sustainability challenges, such as optimising energy grids, transportation networks, and green infrastructure. Future research must prioritise robust validation methods to ensure the accuracy and reliability of AI predictions specifically within diverse real-world architectural environmental contexts. Careful attention must be paid to ethical considerations, including data privacy (especially with occupant environmental or behavioural data) and mitigating algorithmic bias that could inadvertently disadvantage certain communities or climates in environmental assessments.

EMBRACING AN INTELLIGENT AND SUSTAINABLE FUTURE

The integration of AI into environmental performance design signifies a monumental shift towards a more sustainable and resilient future for the built environment. By harnessing the predictive power of AI models and the information-processing capabilities and knowledge synthesis potential of LLMs, the architectural profession is gaining powerful allies in the fight against climate change. These technologies enable the creation of buildings and cities that are not only innovative and efficient but also deeply respectful of our planet's resources.

Here we have explored various cutting-edge tools and their potential to shape a truly sustainable and intelligent built environment. While the synergy between different AI technologies holds immense promise for future workflows, this transformation relies fundamentally on the evolving partnership between human expertise and artificial intelligence. The goal is not merely automation, but the augmentation of human creativity and critical judgment through intelligent systems, enabling us to design a built environment that is truly responsive to both human needs and ecological imperatives.

Figure 4.2.1 Marathon runners struggling to stay cool with the urban heat island effect, generated using Midjourney, 2026

CHAPTER 4.2

GENERATIVE AI IN ARCHITECTURE

BALANCING PERFORMANCE, SCIENCE, AND ART

Theodoros Galanos

INTRODUCTION

The integration of generative artificial intelligence (AI) in architecture is fundamentally reshaping the design process, moving beyond aesthetic exploration to empower architects with unprecedented capabilities in performance analysis and optimisation. Generative AI models can create novel design solutions by learning patterns from vast datasets. While early attention often focused on AI's ability to generate compelling imagery, a more profound transformation is occurring in how architects conceptualise, evaluate, and refine designs based on quantifiable performance metrics. This chapter delves into the applications of AI in performance-driven generative design, highlighting how this technology enables architects to create more efficient, sustainable, and resilient buildings and urban environments.

As we navigate this frontier, we explore how AI is augmenting architectural practice, focusing specifically on its role in enhancing building performance – encompassing areas from energy efficiency and structural integrity to daylighting and broader environmental impact. We will examine the benefits and challenges of this technological shift, considering its implications for the future of architecture where design decisions are increasingly data-informed. Throughout this chapter, we address a central question: How does the fusion of AI and architecture recalibrate the balance between scientific rigour and artistic expression? This inquiry guides our exploration into how the interplay between computational power and creative vision is shaping a future built

DOI: 10.4324/9781003347330-16

environment optimised for both function and human experience. We will investigate how AI accelerates complex performance simulations, facilitates multi-objective optimisation, and fosters innovation within performance constraints, while also confronting the limitations and ethical considerations inherent in these powerful tools.

This fusion promises not merely to automate tasks, but to empower design itself, potentially augmenting creative intuition with analytical rigour and freeing designers to focus more deeply on the conceptual, cultural, and qualitative dimensions of architecture.

AI-DRIVEN PERFORMANCE ANALYSIS ACROSS ARCHITECTURAL DOMAINS

A cornerstone of performance-driven design is the ability to rapidly simulate and analyse how design choices impact outcomes across multiple domains. AI significantly enhances this capability, leveraging machine learning models trained on simulation results and real-world data to predict building performance with remarkable speed and granularity. For instance, AI algorithms can analyse historical data and real-time inputs like weather patterns and occupancy to forecast and optimise a building's energy consumption, paving the way for designs with systems that automatically adjust for maximum efficiency. Similarly, AI is increasingly applied to predict and optimise structural performance, offering pathways to reduce material usage while ensuring safety and resilience against various loads.

Beyond energy and structure, AI models contribute significantly to enhancing occupant well-being.[1] They can optimise complex variables like window placement and shading strategies to maximise beneficial natural light while minimising negative impacts like glare and excessive thermal gain, directly influencing both comfort and energy use.[2] This analytical power extends seamlessly to the urban scale, where AI tools evaluate the intricate interplay of factors in complex city environments. Site proposals can be rapidly assessed against criteria such as noise pollution, sunlight access, and wind patterns. For highly specialised analyses, such as predicting pedestrian wind comfort within microclimates, platforms like Infrared.city utilise AI prediction models trained on extensive simulation data to deliver near-instant results.[3] Other platforms, like Autodesk and Sidewalk Labs, have explored AI tools for optimising urban layouts based on accessibility and environmental factors.[4]

These AI-driven simulation capabilities offer substantial advantages over traditional methods. They provide faster, often more accurate, and certainly more comprehensive analyses, frequently evaluating multiple performance variables simultaneously. This empowers architects and designers by offering them crucial insights much earlier in the design process, enabling informed, data-driven decision-making when adjustments are most impactful and least costly. Central to enabling these advanced analyses is the structured data provided by building information modelling (BIM), which effectively links geometric design information with the essential performance parameters required by AI algorithms.

BRIDGING ANALYSIS AND GENERATION: TOWARDS INTELLIGENT DESIGN EXPLORATION

The true power emerges when AI seamlessly integrates generation and analysis into rapid feedback loops. An AI system can generate a set of design options, quickly simulate their performance across key metrics (drawing on rapid prediction capabilities for environmental factors[5]), allow the architect to evaluate and select promising directions, and then generate refined options based on that feedback. This represents a profound shift towards data-informed generative AI, where the system explores the solution space based on performance feedback, guided by human intent. It accelerates the iterative design process dramatically, allowing for deeper exploration of performance implications early on, when design changes have the most potential impact and least cost implications. This integration enables a more fluid conversation between exploring design possibilities and understanding their real-world consequences. The versatility of AI workflows means they can potentially handle diverse data structures and models, connecting disparate tools and datasets into a more cohesive architectural design process.

CHALLENGES AND LIMITATIONS IN PERFORMANCE-BASED AI DESIGN

Despite the immense potential of generative AI to revolutionise performance-driven architectural design, its effective and responsible application faces significant hurdles. These challenges span data availability and quality, the inherent complexity and opacity of AI models, practical workflow integration, the difficulty of capturing qualitative design aspects, the need for appropriate data representations, and the critical issue of algorithmic bias. Addressing these limitations is paramount for harnessing AI's power without compromising design quality, ethical standards, or human agency.

In particular, large language models (LLMs), the engine behind much of generative AI, are data hungry. Their ability to learn patterns, predict performance, and generate novel designs is fundamentally dependent on the quality, quantity, modality, and relevance of the data they are trained on. For performance-driven architectural design, this translates into a need for vast, diverse datasets that meticulously link design features (geometry, materials, assemblies, site context) to a wide array of performance outcomes (structural integrity, energy consumption, thermal comfort, daylighting levels, acoustic performance, embodied carbon, lifecycle impact, water use, microclimate effects, etc.).

However, assembling such datasets presents great challenges:

- Scarcity and Fragmentation: Comprehensive, publicly available datasets linking detailed architectural designs to multi-domain performance metrics are rare. Existing data is often siloed within specific research projects, proprietary company databases, or simulation software outputs that aren't easily aggregated or standardised. There's no single, widely accepted benchmark dataset for training holistic performance-driven architectural AI.
- Proprietary Barriers: Much valuable performance data is generated by architectural firms, engineering consultancies, and simulation software vendors who consider it a competitive asset. This reluctance to share this data hinders academic research and the development of more universally applicable AI tools, potentially leading to a landscape dominated by closed, commercial systems.
- Data Quality and Consistency: Real-world building performance data, often gathered through sensors (Building Management Systems – BMS, IoT devices), can suffer from inconsistencies, missing values, sensor drift, and calibration errors. Simulation data, while controllable, depends heavily on the accuracy of the underlying physics models and the expertise of the simulation expert setting up the study. Merging data from diverse sources with varying levels of fidelity and different formats is a non-trivial task. 'Garbage in, garbage out' remains a fundamental principle.

- Synthetic Data Generation Challenges: Given the scarcity of real-world data, generating synthetic data through automated simulation is an exciting avenue of applied research. However, creating *sufficiently diverse and realistic* synthetic architectural scenarios is difficult. It requires sophisticated generative models for the designs themselves, coupled with accurate and computationally efficient simulation engines. Ensuring that the synthetic data covers edge cases and doesn't inherit biases from the generation process itself is crucial. Furthermore, the sheer computational cost of generating millions of detailed, multi-physics simulations can be prohibitive.
- Linking Design to Performance: The establishment of clear causal links between specific design decisions and performance outcomes across multiple interacting domains (e.g., how a facade change affects energy, daylight, *and* structural load simultaneously) requires carefully structured data that captures these complex dependencies. This tacit design and performance expertise is not easily captured in data but remains latent across domains and practitioners.

Potential mitigation strategies are emerging, including data augmentation techniques, transfer learning (adapting models trained on large, general datasets to specific architectural tasks), federated learning (training models across multiple decentralised datasets without sharing raw data, preserving privacy), and ongoing efforts to improve interoperability standards like IFC for richer data exchange. However, the fundamental need for more high-quality, accessible, and comprehensive data remains a critical bottleneck.

MODEL COMPLEXITY AND EXPLAINABILITY: OPENING THE BLACK BOX

Many of the most powerful AI models, particularly deep neural networks, operate as 'black boxes'. Their internal workings, involving intricate adjustments across millions or even billions of parameters during complex training processes, are often opaque, making it difficult even for their creators to precisely trace how specific inputs lead to specific outputs. While these models can achieve remarkable accuracy in prediction or generation, this inherent lack of transparency poses a significant problem in architecture, where understanding the *why* behind a design decision is often as crucial as the decision itself.

The need for Explainable AI (XAI) in architecture is therefore acute and multi-faceted. Architects and engineers bear ultimate professional and ethical responsibility for their designs; relying on AI suggestions without a clear understanding of their basis, especially for safety-critical aspects like structural integrity or life safety systems, is simply untenable. Explainability is foundational for building trust and enabling independent verification. Furthermore, when an AI generates a suboptimal or flawed design, understanding the model's internal logic is key to debugging the system and facilitating iterative improvement.

Beyond verification and debugging, explainability is vital for fostering meaningful human–AI collaboration. Effective partnership requires dialogue, but if the AI cannot articulate its 'thought process', the architect is relegated to passively accepting or rejecting outputs, hindering a truly co-creative workflow. Understanding *why* an AI suggests a specific passive strategy, material choice, or spatial configuration allows the architect to learn, integrate that reasoning, and guide the process more effectively. Architects must also clearly communicate the design rationale behind their projects to clients, regulators, and other stakeholders; relying on 'the AI recommended it' is insufficient. New techniques are needed to help us articulate the performance-based or data-driven logic underlying AI-influenced choices. Finally, insightful explanations might even lead to the discovery of novel principles or unexpected correlations learned by the AI from vast datasets, potentially advancing architectural knowledge itself.

However, applying existing XAI techniques to the complex, often holistic nature of performance-driven generative architecture faces significant limitations. Explaining the intricate reasoning behind a generated 3D geometry requires more sophisticated, potentially visually oriented explanation methods that remain subjects of active research. Techniques like counterfactual explanations (for example, 'To achieve the daylight target, the model suggests reducing the southern overhang because *this specific change* yields the best improvement according to its analysis') offer more intuitive insights but can be challenging to implement reliably for highly complex generative models.

Here, the emergence of large reasoning models (LRMs) presents a promising, albeit still developing, avenue. Evolving from LLMs, LRMs are designed with a greater emphasis on complex reasoning, planning, and the ability to articulate step-by-step thought processes. This offers potential new ways to partially open the black box:

- Articulated Reasoning Traces: LRMs could potentially generate natural language explanations detailing the sequence of 'decisions' or trade-offs considered during optimisation or generation (akin to Chain-of-Thought prompting but potentially more sophisticated). Instead of just the final output, the architect might receive a narrative explaining *how* the AI arrived there.
- Interactive Querying: The conversational nature of these models could allow architects to directly query the AI's reasoning ('Why was this material preferred over that one?', 'What were the key constraints influencing this form?'), fostering a more interactive exploration of the design logic.
- Tailorable Reasoning for Domain Tasks: Critically, there's potential for architects to not only receive explanations but also to *guide* or *adjust* the LRM's reasoning process for specific architectural tasks. By providing domain-specific knowledge, principles, or preferred strategies through prompts or fine-tuning, architects might be able to craft reasoning traces that are more aligned with established architectural practices or project-specific goals, making the AI's process both more transparent and more relevant.

While LRMs offer exciting potential for enhancing explainability beyond simple feature attribution, it is crucial to approach this with caution. The field is rapidly evolving, and the reliability, factual accuracy, and depth of LRM-generated explanations require rigorous validation, especially in high-stakes architectural applications. They are not yet a guaranteed solution to the black box problem, but they represent a significant step towards AI systems that can not only perform complex tasks but also begin to explain *how* and *why*, fostering greater trust and more effective human–AI partnership in the design process.

INTEGRATION AND WORKFLOW: BRIDGING THE DIGITAL DIVIDES

The architectural design process relies on a complex ecosystem of digital tools: CAD software for geometry creation, BIM platforms for integrated modelling, specialised simulation engines for various performance analyses, rendering software, specification writing tools, and project management platforms. For performance-driven generative AI to be truly effective, it must integrate seamlessly into these existing workflows, rather than forcing designers into entirely separate, disruptive processes.

Significant integration challenges include:

- Software Fragmentation: The sheer number of specialised tools creates a fragmented digital landscape. Data often needs to be manually exported from one tool, reformatted, and imported into another, a process that is time-consuming, error-prone, and discourages rapid iteration.
- Data Interoperability: Different software uses distinct file formats and data structures (DWG, RVT, SKP, IFC, gbXML, various text-based input/output formats for simulators). While standards like IFC aim to facilitate interoperability, their implementation is often inconsistent, and they may not capture all the semantic information or geometric precision needed for both detailed design and advanced AI analysis. Converting data between formats often results in information loss or corruption.
- Lack of Robust APIs: Many established software packages lack comprehensive application programming interfaces (APIs) that would allow AI tools to directly access, manipulate, and analyse design data within the native environment or to easily connect different tools in an automated chain.
- Workflow Disruption: Introducing AI often requires designers to learn new interfaces, adapt established workflows, and potentially hand over parts of the creative process to algorithms. This can meet resistance if the tools are not intuitive or if they interrupt the fluid, iterative nature of design thinking. Embedding AI capabilities directly within familiar CAD/BIM environments via plugins (as seen with tools aiming for real-time feedback) is often preferred but technically demanding to implement well.
- Computational Demands: Integrating real-time performance analysis or generative processes directly into a modelling environment requires significant computational power. Ensuring that these AI features don't unduly slow down the core modelling tasks is a practical challenge.

Overcoming these hurdles requires a concerted effort towards better interoperability standards, more open APIs from software vendors, and the development of AI tools designed with integration flexibility in mind (supporting multiple input formats, offering cloud-based computation, providing clear interfaces). Platforms leveraging Simulation-as-a-Service (SimaaS) models via APIs, as discussed in Chapter 1, represent one promising approach to making advanced analysis accessible within diverse workflows.

BEYOND QUANTIFIABLE METRICS: THE ART OF ARCHITECTURE

AI, particularly in its current state, excels at optimising problems with clearly defined, quantifiable objectives and constraints. Performance metrics like energy use, structural stress, daylight autonomy, or embodied carbon fit this paradigm well. However, architecture is not solely an engineering discipline; it is also an art form deeply concerned with qualitative aspects that resist easy measurement.

These include:

- Aesthetics: Considerations of beauty, harmony, proportion, style, visual delight, and the integration of form with context.
- Spatial Experience: The feeling of a space – its scale, flow, sequence, sense of enclosure or openness, atmosphere, and how it shapes movement and interaction.
- Cultural Context and Meaning: How a design relates to local traditions, history, symbolism, societal values, and community identity.
- Human Emotion and Well-Being: Beyond measurable comfort (thermal, visual, acoustic), architecture impacts mood, evokes feelings, supports psychological well-being, and fosters a sense of place or belonging.

Encoding these subjective, culturally embedded, and often ephemeral qualities into objective functions for AI optimisation is extremely difficult, if not impossible. The risk is that an over-reliance on purely quantitative, performance-driven AI could lead to designs that are technically efficient but aesthetically bland, spatially awkward, culturally insensitive, or emotionally sterile. AI might optimise a floor plan for circulation efficiency but fail to create spaces that encourage social interaction or quiet contemplation. It might achieve optimal solar gain but create an unpleasant glare or a facade disconnected from its surroundings.

Attempts to bridge this gap exist, such as training AI on datasets rated for aesthetic appeal by experts[6] (although these raise questions as to whose aesthetic is being encoded) or using AI to analyse user feedback or even biometric responses in virtual environments (although these might also raise significant ethical concerns). However, a more pragmatic approach involves recognising the distinct strengths of AI and human designers. AI can be a powerful tool for exploring the performance implications of design choices and optimising complex systems based on quantifiable metrics, but the architect must retain the crucial role of guiding the process, making subjective judgments, and ensuring the design resonates on a human, cultural, and aesthetic level. The goal should be AI *assisting* qualitative design, not dictating it.

STRUCTURED REPRESENTATIONS: TEACHING AI TO UNDERSTAND BUILDINGS

Many successful generative AI models, especially in image generation, operate on relatively unstructured data like pixel grids. However, architectural designs are inherently structured objects with complex geometry, hierarchical components, material properties, functional labels, and crucial topological relationships (e.g., which walls support which floors, which spaces are adjacent). Representing this rich information in a format that AI can effectively process, understand, and manipulate for performance-aware generation is a significant challenge.

Also, many common AI approaches relying on simpler data representations encounter significant hurdles when applied to the intricacies of architecture. For instance, AI models trained primarily on images or renderings often struggle because these formats lack essential information about 3D geometry, material properties, and semantic relationships between building components. While such models might excel at learning visual styles, they cannot easily optimise the underlying structure or materiality of a design. Similarly, simple parametric models, while effective for optimising specific components or highly regular structures, often lack the flexibility needed to represent the highly complex, irregular, or bespoke forms frequently encountered in architectural design. Their inherent constraints can limit the scope of design exploration and optimisation for more unique or contextually sensitive projects.

More promising structured representations include:

- Graphs: Nodes can represent rooms, walls, beams, etc., while edges represent connections (adjacency, support, flow). Graph neural networks are increasingly used to learn from and generate graph-structured data, potentially capturing spatial relationships relevant to performance (e.g., thermal transfer between adjacent zones, structural load paths).
- Voxel Grids: 3D grids representing occupancy can capture complex forms but are computationally intensive, suffer from resolution limitations, and may lose fine geometric detail.
- Boundary Representations: These are standard in CAD, defining shapes by their boundary surfaces. They are geometrically precise but complex for many AI algorithms to manipulate directly.
- Semantic BIM Data: Formats like IFC contain rich object-based information (wall types, material layers, properties). However, real-world BIM models are often incomplete, inconsistent, or lack the necessary detail for certain simulations. AI needs to be robust to deal with this incomplete data.
- Procedural Models / Grammars: Defining designs via rules and parameters (e.g., Shape Grammars). This approach can lend itself well to AI manipulation and generation within defined rule sets but may limit design freedom compared to other methods.

Effectively learning from, reasoning about, and generating designs using these richer representations – directly linking form, structure, materials, and performance – remains an active and vital area of research.

ALGORITHMIC BIAS: PERPETUATING INEQUITIES IN CODE

AI systems learn from data, and if that data reflects existing societal biases, the AI will likely learn and potentially amplify those biases. In architecture and urban design, this carries significant ethical weight, as decisions encoded in the built environment have long-lasting social and spatial consequences.

Sources and examples of bias in architectural AI:

- Biased Training Data: Datasets may over-represent certain building typologies (e.g., detached single-family homes in affluent suburbs) or climates, leading AI to generate solutions optimised for those contexts but poorly suited elsewhere. Historical data might reflect discriminatory practices like redlining, leading site analysis tools to implicitly undervalue certain neighbourhoods. Energy performance models trained primarily on data from new, high-spec buildings might perform poorly when applied to retrofitting older, more diverse building stock. As mentioned previously, environmental data skewed towards specific regions could lead generative AI to consistently produce designs unsuited for other climates, disadvantaging those populations.

- Biased Model Objectives: If an AI optimises solely for cost minimisation without constraints for quality or equity, it might consistently recommend cheaper, lower-quality materials or solutions for projects in less affluent areas. Optimising urban layouts purely for traffic flow might disadvantage pedestrians, cyclists, and communities reliant on public transport.
- Proxy Discrimination: Using seemingly neutral proxies for sensitive attributes can introduce bias. For example, using zip codes or energy consumption patterns (which correlate with income) in models could inadvertently lead to discriminatory outcomes in areas like loan applications for green retrofits or targeted energy efficiency programs.

The consequences can be severe, ranging from reinforcing spatial segregation and unequal access to resources (like daylight, green space, clean air) to creating designs that are culturally inappropriate or fail to meet the needs of diverse user groups. Mitigation requires a multi-pronged approach: meticulous auditing of datasets for bias, developing fairness-aware AI algorithms, ensuring diversity within AI development teams, transparency in model objectives and limitations, incorporating community participation into the design and evaluation process, and ongoing vigilance to detect and correct biased outcomes. Addressing algorithmic bias is not just a technical challenge but an ethical imperative for the responsible use of AI in shaping our built world.

Ethical Considerations

The integration of AI into the design of our built environment is not merely a technical challenge; it carries profound ethical responsibilities. As architects increasingly leverage AI for performance analysis and generation, they must grapple with complex ethical questions concerning privacy, accountability, equity, and the preservation of human values within automated processes. Failure to address these issues thoughtfully risks creating environments that are technically optimised but socially unjust, intrusive, or misaligned with fundamental human needs.

DATA PRIVACY: THE INVISIBLE EYES IN SMART SPACES

Performance-driven architectural design, particularly when integrated with smart building technologies and AI-powered urban planning, frequently relies on vast datasets, raising significant data privacy concerns due to the potentially sensitive nature of the information involved. AI systems may be trained on or interact with detailed occupant data – capturing movement patterns, space utilisation, energy habits, thermal preferences, and even interpersonal interactions via sensors or building management systems. While valuable for optimising comfort and energy efficiency, such granular data fuels concerns about surveillance, employee monitoring, or discriminatory profiling based on inferred behaviours. Similarly, urban scale data, encompassing aggregated traffic flows, mobile location patterns, energy grid usage, and public activity analysis used by AI planning tools, can, even when anonymised, reveal patterns that might be exploited or disadvantage certain communities. Furthermore, while less personal, the use of proprietary design data to train AI models introduces separate concerns regarding intellectual property protection and competitive advantage.[7]

Effectively navigating these ethical complexities necessitates robust data governance frameworks, strict adherence to privacy regulations – like General Data Protection Regulation (GDPR) – transparent communication with building occupants and the public regarding data collection practices, the implementation of strong anonymisation techniques (while acknowledging their inherent limitations), and crucially, clear mechanisms for obtaining informed consent. Architects leveraging AI tools trained on sensitive data, or designing systems that gather such information, bear a significant ethical obligation to understand these privacy implications thoroughly and proactively advocate for privacy-preserving methodologies. The powerful allure of optimisation must never overshadow the fundamental right to individual and collective privacy.

ACCOUNTABILITY: WHO IS RESPONSIBLE WHEN AI GETS IT WRONG?

Establishing accountability following building failures – whether structural, environmental, or functional – is crucial for learning, redress, and maintaining public trust. The integration of AI, especially generative systems proposing novel or highly optimised solutions, significantly complicates these traditional lines of responsibility. This introduces a potential 'liability gap', blurring clarity on who bears responsibility if an AI system contributes to a design flaw – perhaps by optimising material reduction to the point of unforeseen structural weakness or devising an energy strategy that fails under real-world conditions. Does liability fall upon the architect who utilised the tool, potentially without full insight into its 'black box' reasoning? Does it rest with the vendor who developed the AI, often accompanied by disclaimers about its limitations? Or could it involve the client who perhaps pushed for aggressive optimisation targets?

Compounding this challenge is the issue of traceability and auditability. Without clear records detailing precisely how AI influenced specific design decisions – a transparency ideally aided by robust Explainable AI – tracing the root cause of a failure becomes exceptionally difficult. Establishing rigorous logging mechanisms for AI inputs, outputs, parameters, and key decision points within the design workflow is therefore essential for enabling effective *post-hoc* analysis and fair accountability. Furthermore, existing professional standards and liability insurance frameworks may not adequately encompass the novel risks associated with employing sophisticated AI tools. This suggests a pressing need for the architectural profession to develop updated guidelines regarding the responsible use of AI – potentially including specific requirements for validation protocols, human oversight levels, and transparency standards. Concurrently, insurers may need to adapt their policies to accurately reflect these evolving technological realities.

Ultimately, architects cannot simply defer responsibility to the algorithm. They remain the licensed professionals accountable for the safety, integrity, and performance of the designs they deliver. This necessitates a critically engaged approach to AI tools: thoroughly understanding their capabilities *and* limitations, independently verifying critical outputs (especially those related to safety and core performance), prioritising sound engineering and design principles over purely algorithmic suggestions and maintaining meticulous documentation throughout the AI-assisted design process.

EQUITY AND ACCESS: AVOIDING ALGORITHMIC REINFORCEMENT OF DISPARITIES

AI systems invariably learn from the data they are trained on, and since the built environment reflects deep-seated historical and ongoing inequities, there is a significant risk that uncritically deployed AI could perpetuate or even exacerbate these disparities. For instance, AI models trained on data skewed towards specific demographics, affluent contexts, or climates might generate designs – such as energy-efficient solutions suited only for temperate zones or urban layouts favouring car commuters – that systematically disadvantage other groups or regions. Similarly, inadequate representation of diverse needs in training data can lead to poorly implemented accessibility features.

Beyond reinforcing existing biases, AI applications pose risks of furthering socioeconomic stratification. Optimisation tools used in real estate could potentially accelerate gentrification by pinpointing areas for high-yield investment, displacing lower-income residents, while tools focused solely on cost reduction might lead to substandard designs concentrated in less affluent neighbourhoods. Furthermore, generative AI trained predominantly on Western architectural precedents may exhibit cultural insensitivity, struggling to produce designs resonant with other contexts and potentially eroding local architectural identities. Compounding these issues is the potential for unequal access to the benefits of AI itself; the advantages of sophisticated AI tools might disproportionately accrue to larger, wealthier firms and clients, widening the gap within the profession and potentially creating a two-tiered quality in the built environment.

Addressing these profound ethical challenges demands proactive and deliberate measures. This includes meticulously diversifying datasets, actively seeking data from underrepresented groups and contexts, developing fairness metrics tailored for architectural applications, ensuring diverse perspectives within AI development and design teams, employing participatory design processes that give communities meaningful input into AI-driven proposals, and maintaining a practice of critically evaluating all AI outputs for potential discriminatory impacts. Architects bear a fundamental ethical duty to wield AI not as a tool that reinforces spatial injustice, but as one that actively promotes greater equity and access for all.

HUMAN OVERSIGHT AND VALUES: KEEPING THE ARCHITECT IN THE LOOP

The power and speed of AI optimisation can be seductive, creating a risk of 'automation bias' – the tendency to over-trust or uncritically accept machine outputs. Maintaining meaningful human oversight and ensuring designs align with broader human and societal values is perhaps the most fundamental ethical challenge.

- Defining Meaningful Control: What level of control must the architect retain? It's more than just hitting 'accept' or 'reject'. It involves setting the goals and constraints for the AI, understanding the trade-offs the AI identifies, critically evaluating the *quality* of the solutions (not just their quantitative performance), intervening when AI suggestions conflict with professional judgment or ethical principles, and being able to steer the generative process. Interfaces and workflows must be designed to support this active, critical engagement.
- Preventing Over-Optimisation: AI might optimise ruthlessly for defined metrics, potentially at the expense of unquantified but crucial values. For example, optimising solely for floor area efficiency might lead to cramped, unpleasant spaces; optimising solely for energy might compromise daylight or views; optimising purely for structural efficiency might sacrifice aesthetic grace or adaptability. The architect must act as the guardian of these holistic qualities, ensuring technology serves humanistic goals.
- Aligning with Professional Ethics: Architectural practice is governed by codes of ethics emphasising public health, safety, welfare, sustainability, and cultural heritage. AI tools must be used in ways that uphold, rather than undermine, these principles. This might involve refusing to use AI for applications deemed unethical or prioritising safety factors beyond what an AI might deem minimally necessary based purely on data.
- Preserving the 'Art' of Architecture: While AI can handle the 'science' of performance, the architect's role in shaping space, meaning, and experience

remains irreplaceable. Ethical use of AI involves leveraging its analytical power to *inform* creative intuition and judgment, not to replace it. It means protecting the space for critical thinking, cultural sensitivity, and artistic expression within an increasingly automated workflow.

Ultimately, ethical AI integration in architecture demands vigilance, critical reflection, and a commitment to keeping human values at the centre of the design process. Architects must be not just users of AI, but ethical stewards guiding its application towards a more just, sustainable, and humane built environment.

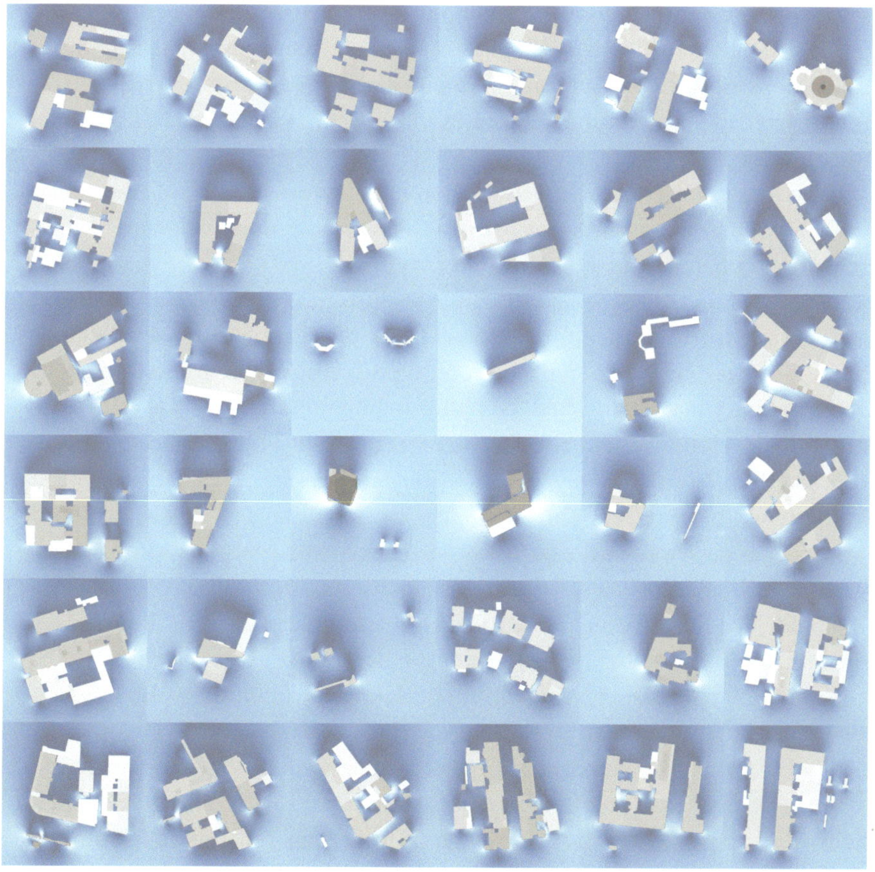

Figure 4.2.2 InFraRed Wind Comfort Study, Vienna, Austria, 2020

CONCLUSION: FUSING SCIENCE AND ART FOR A RESPONSIVE FUTURE

The integration of AI into architectural design, particularly through performance-driven generative approaches, marks a significant evolution, moving beyond simple automation towards a genuine augmentation of human capability. By automating complex performance analysis and rapidly generating data-informed design iterations, AI technologies are freeing architects from many repetitive and time-consuming tasks. This allows a greater focus on higher-level strategic thinking, nuanced qualitative design aspects, and the essential art of architecture – the ability to imbue spaces with meaning, emotion, and cultural resonance. We are entering a paradigm where data-driven decision-making increasingly coexists with, and potentially enhances, intuitive design choices, positioning artificial intelligence as a powerful collaborator rather than a replacement for human imagination.

However, this technological revolution is not without its significant challenges. The persistent need for vast, high-quality, unbiased datasets remains a critical bottleneck. The inherent 'black box' nature of many advanced AI models necessitates continued progress in Explainable AI (XAI) to build the trust required for responsible adoption and ensure accountability in high-stakes design decisions. Integrating these powerful tools seamlessly and intuitively into established, complex architectural workflows requires ongoing development and a focus on interoperability. Furthermore, the crucial ethical considerations surrounding data privacy, algorithmic bias, accountability, equity, and the imperative for human oversight – as explored in detail earlier – must be proactively addressed through robust professional guidelines, technological safeguards, and continuous critical discourse within the field. The industry must navigate these multi-faceted issues thoughtfully, ensuring that technology remains firmly in service of architecture's fundamental purpose: creating meaningful, ethical, and responsible spaces for humanity.

Looking ahead, the potential for performance-driven generative AI within architecture remains immense, promising further integration of scientific rigor and artistic expression. Future research and development will likely focus on several key areas, pushing the boundaries of what's possible:

- XAI for Design: Moving beyond basic feature importance, future XAI will need to offer intuitive explanations tailored to architects' cognitive workflows. Imagine AI generating not just an optimised facade but also visualising the specific performance trade-offs (e.g., highlighting areas where increased daylight slightly compromises thermal performance), providing natural language justifications referencing design principles, or offering interactive 'what-if' scenarios to explore the reasoning behind its suggestions. This transparency is crucial for building trust and facilitating true human–AI collaboration.
- Adaptive Architecture: The convergence of AI, IoT sensors, and actuated building systems promises buildings that dynamically respond to their environment and occupants in real time. AI algorithms could continuously monitor conditions (temperature, CO_2, occupancy, sunlight) and predict needs, adjusting features like smart glazing, automated shades, natural ventilation openings, and HVAC settings to optimise for energy efficiency *and* occupant comfort simultaneously. This moves beyond static design optimisation towards buildings that learn and adapt throughout their lifecycle, potentially enabled by sophisticated digital twins.
- Circular Architecture: As sustainability imperatives intensify, AI can play a critical role in realising a circular economy for the built environment. Generative AI models can help analyse vast material databases (including recycled content, embodied energy, durability, and end-of-life options), predict the ease of disassembly for different construction details, optimise designs to maximise material reuse potential, and dynamically integrate life cycle assessment data early in the design process, making circular principles computationally tractable and actionable.
- Human–AI Collaborative Interfaces: The next generation of design tools will likely feature far more intuitive and fluid interfaces for human–AI partnership. This could involve AI interpreting rough sketches or physical models, engaging in natural language dialogue about design goals and acting as proactive agents within CAD/BIM software, suggesting relevant precedents, performance improvements, or potential clashes based on the ongoing design context. The focus will be on making AI feel less like a separate tool and more like an integrated, intelligent collaborator.
- Improved Data Representations and Generation: Addressing the limitations of current representations is key. Research will continue into better

capturing spatial and structural relationships, AI models that can work directly with semantic BIM data (even if imperfect), and techniques for generating high-fidelity synthetic data for complex physics simulations (like CFD or detailed acoustic modelling). This will enable AI to understand and generate architecturally sophisticated designs with greater performance accuracy.

- AI for Urban Resilience: Scaling up from individual buildings, AI offers powerful tools for designing cities better equipped to handle climate change impacts and other systemic shocks. This includes using AI for predictive modelling of urban heat islands, flood risks, or energy grid strain under extreme weather scenarios, and then using generative techniques to optimise the placement and design of green infrastructure, water management systems, building typologies, and even evacuation routes to enhance overall urban resilience.
- AI Creative Input: While preserving human artistic control, AI could evolve into a more sophisticated creative partner. Trained on vast archives of architectural history, natural forms, or even other art forms, AI might identify novel patterns, suggest unexpected material combinations, or generate initial design concepts that push architects beyond their habitual styles or solutions, acting as a powerful catalyst for innovation *within* the architect's defined conceptual framework and aesthetic direction.

In conclusion, the integration of performance-driven generative AI in architecture represents far more than a technological upgrade; it signifies a fundamental recalibration of the relationship between scientific rigor and artistic expression. It is an emerging symbiosis that leverages computational power not to dictate design, but to amplify human creativity and insight. AI profoundly enhances the scientific capabilities available to architects, automating complex performance analysis and simulating outcomes with unprecedented speed and breadth. This, in turn, elevates the baseline of design exploration, freeing human architects from laborious calculation to focus on strategic thinking, qualitative refinement, and the irreducible 'art' of architecture – the shaping of space, meaning, and experience.

Furthermore, AI acts as a powerful informant to artistic intuition, providing rapid, data-driven feedback that allows creative ideas to be tested and honed against performance realities early and often. Generative capabilities expand the potential solution space, offering novel configurations optimised for specific metrics, which the architect can then critically evaluate, curate, and imbue with artistic intent and cultural relevance. Consequently, the architect's role evolves – less focus on manual execution of analysis, more emphasis on becoming a strategic orchestrator, an ethical guide, and a critical curator of AI-generated possibilities. Human primacy is reinforced, not diminished, in the realms of setting design goals, embedding values, making nuanced qualitative judgments, and taking ultimate responsibility for the built outcome.

The challenge and opportunity lie in mastering this intersection. By embracing these technologies thoughtfully and ethically, developing the necessary skills in AI literacy alongside core design principles, and demanding tools that support genuine collaboration, architects can harness the synergistic power of both science and art. The goal is to create a built environment that is not only more efficient, sustainable, and resilient but also more beautiful, equitable, human-centred, and ultimately, more capable of meeting the complex challenges and aspirations of our time. The future of architecture in the age of AI hinges on our ability to channel this powerful fusion towards spaces that push the boundaries of performance while deeply resonating with the human spirit.

NOTES

1 David Fersh and Sven Shockey, 'Beyond Imagery: The Application of AI to Architectural Design', *SmithGroup Perspectives*, January 11, 2024, www.smithgroup.com/perspectives/2024/beyond-imagery-the-application-of-ai-to-architectural-design
2 Pieter De Wilde, 'Building Performance Simulation in the Brave New World of Artificial Intelligence and Digital Twins', *Energy and Buildings* 296 (2023): 113377, https://doi.org/10.1016/j.enbuild.2023.113377
3 Infrared.city exemplifies this by offering lightning-fast urban performance simulations. Infrared.city utilises state-of-the-art deep learning models trained on extensive datasets – thousands of simulation results from hundreds of cities – to predict complex environmental phenomena like pedestrian wind comfort (CFD), solar radiation, and sunlight hours. Where a traditional CFD simulation for wind comfort might take an expert days to set up and hours to compute, AI prediction engines like Infrared.city can deliver results with high accuracy (around 90%) in seconds. https://infrared.city.
4 Jam Canda, 'AI in Urban Planning and Smart City Development', *Medium*, April 6, 2024, https://medium.com/@jam.canda/ai-in-urban-planning-and-smart-city-development-6cefc3e87181
5 These are discussed in Chapter 4.1.
6 Zhichao Liao, Xiaokun Liu, Wenyu Qin, Qingyu Li, Qiulin Wang, Pengfei Wan, Dingyun Zhang, Long Zeng, and Pingfa Feng. 'HumanAesExpert: Advancing a Multi-Modality Foundation Model for Human Image Aesthetic Assessment'. *ArXiv* abs/2503.23907 (2025).
7 Ziv Epstein, Aaron Hertzmann, and The Investigators of Human Creativity, 'Art and the Science of Generative AI', *Science* 380, no. 6650 (2023), www.science.org/doi/10.1126/science.adh4451

Figure 4.3.1 Trees offering shade from the summer sun, generated using Midjourney 2026

CHAPTER 4.3

AI, AGENTIC AUTOMATION, AND THE FUTURE OF DESIGN AND ENGINEERING

Theodoros Galanos

INTRODUCTION

Imagine a world where the boundaries between human creativity and artificial intelligence blur, where our wildest design dreams are brought to life with unprecedented speed, and where engineering challenges that once took years to solve are conquered in mere hours. This world is rapidly becoming our reality, thanks to the emergence of Agentic Automation – a revolutionary paradigm combining advanced artificial intelligence with human ingenuity. Far from replacing human designers and engineers, Agentic Automation seeks to amplify their capabilities, pushing the boundaries of what's possible and redefining the very nature of innovation.

At the forefront of this transformation is generative AI, already making significant waves across design and engineering sectors, as explored in previous chapters. From creating intricate models and optimising complex systems to generating novel solutions, AI is proving invaluable.[1] Yet, this is merely the beginning. As AI systems grow more sophisticated, they evolve into partners in the creative and problem-solving process, challenging traditional notions of expertise. A key mechanism enabling this partnership at scale is the concept of agentic orchestration, coordinating multiple specialised AI systems to tackle multi-faceted challenges. Central to harnessing this partnership effectively, however, remains the user experience (UX) through which humans interact with these powerful systems.

DOI: 10.4324/9781003347330-17

This symbiosis between human and machine intelligence is reshaping the fabric of domain expertise. Proficiency is no longer solely measured by years of experience; it now encompasses the ability to harness AI's potential, orchestrate human intuition with computational power through well-designed interfaces, and guide these powerful technologies ethically. Domain experts are evolving from repositories of information to curators of AI-generated insights and architects of responsible AI frameworks. This chapter explores how AI, particularly through Agentic Automation and its orchestration, is set to amplify human potential, examining the transformative technologies, the critical role of the human–AI interface, the evolution of expertise, and the path forward in this new era of design and engineering.

THE RISE OF AGENTIC AUTOMATION

The dawn of Agentic Automation marks a pivotal moment, driven significantly by the power of large language models (LLMs) like GPT-4 and the emergence of large reasoning models (LRMs).[2] Unlike traditional automation (like robotic process automation or RPA, focused on rigid, rule-based tasks), Agentic Automation leverages the adaptability, contextual understanding, reasoning, and generative capabilities of these advanced LLMs.[3] This represents an evolution beyond earlier intelligent automation (IA) towards agentic process automation (APA), where AI agents create autonomous or semi-autonomous systems capable of interpreting complex tasks, making real-time decisions based on context, and dynamically adapting workflows to achieve overarching goals.[4]

These advanced AI models possess an unprecedented ability to understand complex briefs, generate innovative ideas, provide technical specifications, research information, and learn continuously from human feedback. This fosters a powerful symbiotic relationship: AI enhances human creativity and problem-solving by handling data processing, complex calculations, and option generation, while human input refines the AI's performance, ensures relevance, aligns outputs with project goals and ethical constraints, and provides crucial contextual understanding. These systems can rapidly prototype designs, simulate performance across multiple criteria, predict potential issues early, and explore a vastly wider solution space than manual methods could ever permit, amplifying the potential for innovation.

AI as an Amplifier: Transforming Design and Engineering Processes

Agentic Automation manifests powerfully through increasingly sophisticated AI-driven design and engineering systems. While sometimes termed 'autonomous', these systems function most effectively as powerful amplifiers of human capability, operating under human guidance, intent, and critical oversight. Key benefits derived from this amplification include:

- Accelerated Ideation and Optimised Design: AI systems, trained on vast databases of past projects, technical literature, and simulation results, can generate numerous initial concepts and variations rapidly, dramatically speeding up the early ideation phases. They excel at iterating designs and performing complex multi-objective optimisation, simultaneously considering potentially conflicting criteria such as performance targets (e.g., structural integrity, energy efficiency), cost constraints, manufacturability requirements, material availability, and environmental impact (e.g., embodied carbon). This allows design and engineering teams to uncover novel solutions and identify optimal trade-offs with far greater efficiency than previously possible.
- Continuous Adaptation and Complexity Management: Unlike traditional design processes where optimisation might occur at discrete stages, AI enables continuous, near real-time adjustments. As parameters change (e.g., material costs fluctuate, new site data becomes available, regulatory requirements are updated), the system can adapt the design or analysis accordingly, ensuring ongoing optimisation throughout the project lifecycle. This capability is crucial for managing projects with far greater complexity, allowing teams to handle more interacting variables and constraints than humanly possible alone.
- Enhanced Simulation, Risk Mitigation, and Democratisation: AI systems can simulate and test designs under a multitude of conditions, identifying potential flaws, performance bottlenecks, or safety risks much earlier in the development cycle. This proactive approach significantly reduces the likelihood of costly errors, downstream changes, or project failures. Furthermore, AI prediction models, as explored in Chapter 1, offer a paradigm shift in accessing complex simulations. Techniques that make computationally intensive analyses like CFD or complex environmental assessments near-instantaneous and accessible via user-friendly interfaces or APIs (as exemplified by platforms such as Infrared.city[5]) represent

a powerful democratisation effect. This allows a broader range of professionals, not just deep specialists, to leverage advanced analysis tools, enabling rapid iteration cycles and fostering more data-informed decision-making across various fields and firm sizes.

AGENTIC ORCHESTRATION: TOWARDS SYSTEMIC INTELLIGENCE

Building upon AI's ability to manage complexity and leverage specialised tools, the concept of agentic orchestration represents the next significant frontier in amplifying design and engineering capabilities. This approach moves beyond individual, siloed AI applications towards integrated, intelligent ecosystems where multiple specialised AI agents collaborate to manage complex, multi-objective optimisation tasks across diverse, interacting domains. Within this framework, agents coordinate dynamically – each potentially leveraging distinct analytical tools, prediction models, physics simulators, or knowledge bases accessed via LLMs/LRMs and retrieval-augmented generation (RAG) – working synergistically on different facets of a problem. This automates intricate workflows, aiming for holistic, high-performance solutions built upon distinct but interconnected layers.

Figure 4.3.2 Real-time, mixed-initiative urban design based on quantifiable performance data

THE FOUNDATION: TOOLS AS THE ENGINE OF EXPERTISE

At the foundational layer lie the tools, representing the codified knowledge, specific analytical capabilities, and domain expertise that agents can access and utilise. This encompasses a wide spectrum of digital resources essential to design and engineering: sophisticated simulation software (ranging from finite element analysis for structures and CFD for fluid dynamics to energy modelling platforms and rapid environmental prediction engines like Infrared.city[6] for microclimate assessment), comprehensive material properties databases, APIs providing access to regulatory codes and industry standards, cost estimation calculators, manufacturing process simulators, and life cycle assessment (LCA) databases for environmental impact analysis.

Achieving seamless integration relies heavily on standardised interfaces and protocols – potentially leveraging emerging standards or concepts like ModelContextProtocol (MCP)[7] – which enhance tool deployment, interoperability, and interchangeability. This standardisation allows agents to reliably call upon the required capabilities within a larger orchestrated workflow. The inherent speed, accessibility, and often API-driven nature of modern AI prediction tools make them particularly well-suited for integration as core 'tool' components within these intelligent systems.

THE WORKFORCE: AGENTS AS SPECIALISED VEHICLES

Acting upon these tools are the agents: intelligent, often specialised entities designed to perform specific, well-defined tasks or pursue objectives within the broader design or engineering challenge. Developing agents tailored for domain-specific functions enables a depth of expertise and focus that a single, monolithic AI typically cannot achieve.

In the design and engineering context, one can envision a diverse team of agents: a 'Knowledge Agent' versed in specific industry standards or local building codes, perhaps using LLMs/LRMs trained on regulatory texts accessed via RAG; an 'Energy Optimisation Agent' dedicated to minimising operational carbon; a 'Structural Integrity Agent' employing FEA tools to refine load paths; a 'Daylight & Glare Agent' maximising visual comfort; a crucial 'Microclimate Agent' leveraging rapid simulation tools like Infrared. city for early site assessment of wind, solar radiation, and thermal conditions; a 'Materials Lifecycle Agent' evaluating embodied carbon and circularity using LCA data; and perhaps a 'Manufacturing Process Agent' optimising designs for specific production constraints.

These agents function as intelligent delegates, each concentrating on a specific aspect of performance, compliance, or feasibility. This focused specialisation allows for greater system customisation and the potential for deeper, more nuanced insights compared to relying solely on generic, off-the-shelf AI solutions.

THE STRATEGY: WORKFLOWS AS THE INTELLIGENT TRANSPORTATION NETWORK

Finally, workflows define the crucial strategic layer, dictating *how* these diverse agents and tools collaborate, interact, negotiate, and exchange information to solve specific, complex problems effectively. These workflows embody the often-tacit knowledge, iterative strategies, and decision-making heuristics inherent in expert design and engineering practice. Explicitly mapping these workflows for particular use cases – such as evaluating facade options by *simultaneously* considering energy, daylight, structural, cost, and embodied carbon implications, with agents negotiating trade-offs – is vital for creating efficient and scalable agentic orchestration. Other examples include optimising a complex mechanical part considering weight, strength, manufacturability, and fatigue life concurrently, or planning a building site layout by coordinating agents analysing solar access, wind comfort, noise, regulations, earthworks, and circulation. These defined workflows prescribe the sequence of operations, the necessary data exchanges (underscoring the need for robust data representations), the protocols for resolving conflicts between agents pursuing competing objectives (like maximising views versus minimising energy loss), and the overall strategic approach required to achieve a holistically optimised and viable outcome.

PRINCIPLES FOR SUCCESSFUL ORCHESTRATION

Successfully implementing and scaling agentic orchestration within the demanding contexts of design and engineering hinges on adhering to several key guiding principles that emerge from understanding its layered nature. Foundational aspects include embedding deep domain expertise within specialised agents and prioritising standardised data representations (such as advancing IFC for BIM or STEP for mechanical data) to ensure seamless communication and interoperability between diverse agents and tools. Equally crucial is designing for encapsulation and composability, treating agents and tools as modular components that can be readily combined and recombined for various tasks.

Beyond these technical underpinnings, effective orchestration demands careful attention to the human element and the process itself. Applied UX research is vital to ensure intuitive human oversight, control, interaction, and the building of trust in the system. Strategic implementation requires embracing progressive domain specificity, tailoring agents effectively to targeted tasks rather than attempting overly broad initial implementations. Continuous improvement necessitates rigorous iterative evaluation against performance benchmarks and project goals, thoughtful human–agent collaboration design clearly defining roles and interaction modes and establishing robust knowledge lifecycle management processes to keep agent knowledge bases and underlying models current with the latest research, standards, and data through ongoing human and AI feedback.

SYNERGISTIC WORKFLOWS IN ACTION: AN ORCHESTRATED FUTURE

The true transformative power of AI amplification in design and engineering emerges most clearly when envisioning the synergistic integration of these technologies managed through agentic orchestration. Imagine a future workflow for architectural design:

An architect initiates the process using natural language via an LLM/LRM interface, defining project goals (e.g., net-zero energy target, specific spatial program, aesthetic intent), site constraints, budget limits, and key performance priorities. The agentic orchestration system then takes over the initial exploration:

1. It deploys AI prediction models (perhaps leveraging cloud-based Simulation-as-a-Service platforms like Infrared.city) to rapidly analyse site-specific climate data, wind patterns, solar access, and potential urban heat island effects.
2. It coordinates specialised agents: an 'Energy Agent' explores passive strategies and preliminary system sizing; a 'Daylight Agent' optimises massing and fenestration for visual comfort; a 'Structural Agent' proposes efficient framing options; a 'Materials Agent' queries LCA databases for low embodied carbon options compatible with structural and energy requirements; a 'Code Compliance Agent' checks proposals against relevant regulations accessed via RAG.
3. These agents collaboratively generate and evaluate thousands, potentially millions, of design variations, exploring trade-offs between conflicting objectives (e.g., maximising south-facing glazing for passive heating vs. minimising it to prevent overheating and reduce structural complexity).
4. The orchestration layer identifies Pareto-optimal solutions (sets of designs where one objective cannot be improved without worsening another) and flags critical trade-offs.
5. An LLM/LRM synthesises these findings, presenting the top-performing, contextually relevant options back to the human architect with clear performance metrics, visualisations, and articulated explanations of the rationale behind the proposed solutions and the key trade-offs involved.

This represents a profound shift towards data-informed generative AI, specifically tuned for complex, multi-objective D&E problems. The system actively explores the solution space driven by performance feedback, guided continuously by human intent, values, and strategic decisions. Similar orchestrated workflows are emerging or conceivable across engineering disciplines – optimising aerospace components for weight, aerodynamics, and thermal stress; designing pharmaceutical processes balancing yield, purity, cost, and environmental impact; or planning infrastructure projects considering structural integrity, cost, environmental disturbance, and long-term resilience. The integration of rapid simulation predictions, deep knowledge synthesis from LLMs/LRMs, and automated optimisation routines managed by agentic systems promises to dramatically enhance the capacity of designers and engineers to deliver high-performance, innovative, and responsible solutions.

STREAMLINED PROJECT DELIVERY

The impact of AI amplification, particularly when enabled by agentic orchestration, extends across the entire project lifecycle, leading to significant improvements in efficiency and effectiveness. Project timelines can be dramatically compressed through faster ideation, accelerated simulation cycles, and automated exploration of design alternatives, enabling quicker market entry for new products or faster completion for construction projects. AI facilitates more robust, data-driven decision-making from the outset, reducing reliance on intuition alone and mitigating risks associated with unforeseen performance issues. Interaction with clients or stakeholders is enhanced through the rapid generation and visualisation of multiple design options, each accompanied by clear performance data, allowing for more informed discussions and collaborative refinement. Specific project goals, such as maximising sustainability, minimising lifecycle cost, or optimising for manufacturability, can be prioritised and tracked continuously throughout the design process, enabled by the near real-time feedback loops and integrative capabilities of orchestrated AI systems.

THE CRITICAL ROLE OF LLM USER EXPERIENCE

Effectively harnessing the power of Agentic Automation hinges critically on the UX design of the interfaces through which humans interact with LLMs, LRMs, and the broader ecosystem of AI agents and tools. As AI becomes deeply embedded within complex professional workflows in design and engineering, the quality, intuitiveness, and transparency of this human–AI interaction layer become paramount for successful adoption, effective collaboration, building trust, and ultimately realising the potential benefits.

Currently, LLMs and related technologies are enhancing UX in several ways directly relevant to design and engineering professionals:

- Advanced Conversational Interfaces: Moving beyond rigid commands and graphical menus towards allowing natural language interaction for specifying complex tasks, querying intricate datasets, exploring design options, and refining AI behaviour.

- Personalised Tools & Content Feeds: Tailoring interfaces, documentation access, information dashboards, and even AI suggestions to individual user needs, varying expertise levels, specific project contexts, and preferred workflows.
- Enhanced Accessibility: Features like real-time translation for global teams, speech-to-text input for hands-free operation or accessibility needs, and automated simplification or explanation of complex technical jargon can significantly broaden usability.
- Intelligent Information Retrieval: Semantic search capabilities, often augmented by RAG systems, allow professionals to query vast, unstructured knowledge bases (e.g., material property libraries, building codes, patent databases, past project archives, research papers) using natural language questions and receive contextually relevant, synthesised answers, saving significant research time.
- Aiding Core Design & Engineering Workflows: Assisting directly in tasks like rapid prototyping (e.g., generating code snippets for automation scripts from natural language descriptions), simulating user interactions for product design, drafting initial versions of technical documentation or reports, or suggesting potential solutions based on the current design context (e.g., recommending alternative materials based on specified load conditions and cost targets).

Beyond predictive simulation, LLMs/LRMs act as increasingly capable collaborators or even 'mentors'. Assisted by RAG, they can synthesise vast amounts of information into context-aware recommendations, help users interpret complex analysis outputs, suggest data-driven strategies (e.g., proposing alternative manufacturing processes based on comparative cost, lead time, and performance targets derived from multiple sources), and potentially explain the reasoning behind those suggestions.

However, integrating these powerful language and reasoning models effectively into demanding D&E UX presents significant ongoing challenges:

- Trust and Transparency: The persistent 'black box' nature of many underlying AI models hinders trust, especially when dealing with high-stakes decisions involving safety, significant cost implications, or regulatory compliance. Professionals need to understand *why* an AI suggests a particular design modification or flags a potential issue.

- Explaining Complex Decisions: Communicating the intricate reasoning behind AI outputs in complex, multi-variable optimisation scenarios, especially within agentic systems where multiple agents might pursue goals autonomously, is exceptionally difficult. Traditional explanation methods often fall short of providing intuitive, actionable insights for designers and engineers. The potential of LRMs to provide reasoning traces is promising but still requires substantial development and validation.
- Bias and Reliability: AI systems can inherit and perpetuate biases present in their training data, leading to skewed analyses, unfair outcomes, or designs that fail to serve diverse populations equitably. Ensuring the consistency, reliability, and, crucially, the technical accuracy of AI-generated information (e.g., specific material tolerances, precise engineering calculations, correct interpretation of codes) is paramount and must be rigorously validated against established principles and independent checks. The risk of AI 'hallucinations' (generating plausible but factually incorrect information) remains a serious concern.
- Managing Expectations & Seamless Integration: Users may overestimate AI capabilities, leading to disappointment or misuse. Integrating these sophisticated AI tools seamlessly into the existing, often complex, software ecosystems used in D&E (CAD, CAE, PLM, BIM platforms) and embedding them naturally within established professional workflows requires significant development effort, robust APIs, attention to interoperability standards, and careful interaction design.

Addressing these significant challenges necessitates a relentless focus on designing LLM/LRM-integrated user experiences that are simultaneously highly intuitive and radically transparent. The goal is to create interfaces that allow professionals to leverage the power of AI without demanding deep AI expertise, making the technology feel like a natural extension of their existing cognitive and creative processes rather than an alien imposition. Concurrently, building trust requires transparent interfaces that clearly indicate AI involvement, provide understandable explanations for AI suggestions – perhaps layered, offering concise summaries first with options for deeper dives – visualise confidence levels or key influencing data points, and employ Explainable AI (XAI) techniques specifically tailored for design and engineering contexts, such as interactive trade-off explorers or visual overlays directly on CAD models.

Looking ahead, the future of human–AI interaction in design and engineering likely involves even more sophisticated multimodal interfaces, seamlessly combining text, voice, gesture, and direct manipulation of 3D models, potentially within immersive AR/VR environments. We can expect AI to function less as a separate application and more as an embedded co-creation partner operating directly within core software tools. Furthermore, embedded XAI is poised to become a standard expectation, not merely an optional feature. Ultimately, the aim is to cultivate fluid, trustworthy, and highly productive human–AI partnerships that genuinely amplify professional capabilities and unlock new levels of innovation.

THE EVOLVING NATURE OF EXPERTISE

The deep integration of AI, facilitated by Agentic Automation and effective UX, fosters a profound symbiosis that fundamentally reshapes professional roles and the very definition of expertise in design and engineering. As AI capably handles routine calculations, data analysis, option generation, and even complex simulations, it frees human professionals to focus increasingly on higher-order cognitive tasks: defining strategic direction, exercising creative judgment, navigating ethical complexities, interpreting nuanced AI outputs within broader contexts, and engaging in complex stakeholder communication.

This transformation involves several key shifts:

- From Executor to Strategist and Critic: The emphasis shifts from performing all tasks manually to defining problems effectively, setting clear goals and constraints for AI systems, strategically guiding the exploration process, critically evaluating the relevance, quality, and ethical implications of AI-generated solutions, and making high-level decisions that require deep contextual understanding, foresight, and value judgments. Professionals become orchestrators and critical validators of human–AI collaboration.
- Emergence of Hybrid Roles: New roles are rapidly appearing at the crucial intersection of deep domain knowledge and AI proficiency. Examples include:

  - *AI Integration Specialists & AI Ethicists* (bridging software/systems engineering with domain-specific needs and ethical frameworks).
  - *Strategic Design Innovators* (leveraging AI insights for personalisation, novel user experiences, or market disruption).
  - *AI-Augmented Engineers* (combining deep engineering principles with AI tools for designing complex, adaptive systems).
  - *Human–AI Interaction Designers* (specialising in creating effective and intuitive UX for collaborative AI systems in specific professional domains).
  - *Ethical AI Implementation Leads* (navigating the practical challenges of deploying AI responsibly within organisations and projects).
  - *Computational Design Synthesis Experts* (guiding generative AI processes, curating outputs, and integrating AI with traditional design workflows).
- New Skill Imperatives: Success in this evolving landscape requires continuous learning and adaptation, demanding a blend of strong

Figure 4.3.3 People huddled up against the cold. Wind comfort is an important factor to be considered. Image generated using Midjourney, 2026

fundamentals in core D&E domains and a growing proficiency in AI concepts, data science principles, and the use of specific AI tools. Crucial meta-skills include the ability to critically interpret AI outputs, perform validation checks, understand model limitations and potential biases, engage in interdisciplinary thinking, communicate effectively about AI-driven processes, and exercise heightened ethical responsibility.

NAVIGATING THE TRANSFORMATION: CHALLENGES AND OPPORTUNITIES

This technological revolution sweeping through design and engineering presents a complex dual landscape, woven with significant challenges that demand careful navigation alongside unprecedented opportunities for innovation and improvement. Perhaps most immediately felt is the skills gap created by the rapid pace of AI advancement, often outpacing the adaptation speed of the workforce and educational curricula. This necessitates proactive strategies for continuous learning and targeted upskilling yet simultaneously presents a profound opportunity to cultivate a new generation of D&E professionals adept at collaborating with intelligent systems.

Alongside workforce adaptation, the increasing power and autonomy of AI systems raise critical ethical considerations that must be addressed head-on. Persistent issues of algorithmic bias embedded in training data, the urgent need for clear lines of accountability when AI contributes to errors, and the demand for transparency require robust ethical frameworks and unwavering professional vigilance. Confronting these hurdles, however, propels the opportunity to establish fairer, more inclusive design practices, potentially using AI to mitigate historical inequities. Integral to this ethical practice is the development of robust validation methods and standardised benchmarks to ensure the accuracy and reliability of AI predictions across diverse real-world contexts, building essential trust for responsible deployment. Furthermore, careful attention must be paid to data privacy, particularly concerning sensitive operational or behavioural data, ensuring equitable access to AI benefits, and mitigating bias that could disadvantage specific communities, climates, or user groups; professionals serve as crucial ethical guardians in this process.

Furthermore, the effectiveness of these tools introduces a tangible risk of over-reliance, potentially stifling human creativity and critical thinking if AI systems are treated as infallible black boxes. The necessary counterbalance lies in consciously fostering augmented creativity, ensuring AI enhances rather than replaces human ingenuity, a balance crucial for unlocking truly novel solutions. Relatedly, AI's deep dependency on vast datasets raises significant data privacy and security concerns, demanding careful governance, though this challenge simultaneously drives innovation in secure data handling and privacy-preserving AI techniques.

The potential obsolescence of some traditional tasks also necessitates a thoughtful approach to workforce transition. While certain routine roles may diminish, the emphasis shifts towards proactively managing this change, focusing on the significant opportunity for redefining professional roles towards more strategic, creative, and ethically focused responsibilities.

Successfully navigating these intertwined complexities unlocks further transformative benefits. AI tools continue to drive the democratisation of advanced capabilities, making sophisticated analysis and generative design accessible to a wider range of professionals and fostering broader innovation. This technology also inherently encourages richer interdisciplinary collaboration vital for tackling complex systemic problems. Finally, the ability of AI, particularly through orchestration, to dramatically accelerate development cycles offers tangible gains in efficiency, reducing costs and time-to-market across industries. Embracing this profound transformation thoughtfully requires harnessing its immense potential while proactively mitigating its inherent risks. Crucially, establishing standardised data formats and interoperability protocols (like continued advancements on IFC, STEP, etc.) remains fundamental for enabling wider adoption, seamless collaboration, and achieving collective goals within the intricate D&E ecosystem.

CONCLUSION

As we stand at the threshold of a new era defined by the deep integration of artificial intelligence, paradigms like Agentic Automation and generative AI are fundamentally reshaping the landscape of expertise, creativity, and innovation across design and engineering. We are witnessing a pivotal shift where the boundaries between human ingenuity and machine intelligence blur, mediated through increasingly sophisticated user experiences, opening possibilities previously confined to science fiction. This emerging symbiosis between human intellect and computational capability redefines how we conceive, design, analyse, solve complex problems, and ultimately build our world.

This technological revolution enhances our collective capacity profoundly. AI acts not as a replacement, but as a collaborative partner, amplifying human decision-making, augmenting creativity, accelerating complex problem-solving (illustrated by examples like the potential for rapid environmental feedback discussed in Chapter 1), and freeing human minds for higher-level strategic thinking and ethical consideration. It enables us to tackle levels of complexity previously beyond our reach, coordinating vast numbers of interacting factors through frameworks like agentic orchestration, and holds immense potential for addressing pressing global issues, from sustainable development and climate resilience to personalised healthcare and advanced materials science. Far from diminishing the value of expertise, AI elevates it, demanding a sophisticated blend of deep core domain knowledge with AI literacy, critical thinking, ethical reasoning, and adept interdisciplinary collaboration. Future developments point towards even more sophisticated AI, potentially physics-informed models capable of deeper reasoning and incorporating fundamental physical laws for more reliable and generalisable predictions across demanding scientific and engineering domains, alongside advancements in LRMs offering greater transparency.

Navigating this transformative period requires a conscious, critically reflective, and balanced approach. We must embrace the potential of these technologies with enthusiasm but temper it with rigorous critical thinking and unwavering ethical responsibility. It is imperative that we proactively evaluate the potential ethical implications, systemic biases, and broader societal impacts of AI deployment in D&E. Shaping these powerful technologies responsibly, ensuring they align with enduring human values and contribute positively to societal well-being, is not merely an option but an obligation. This demands professional agility, a commitment to lifelong learning, and constant vigilance from designers and engineers acting as guardians of human-centric principles.

To those actively engaging with these advancements: explore boldly, apply thoughtfully, and share openly. The future is shaped not by passive observation, but by active imagination, creation, and experimentation. Push the boundaries of what AI can assist with, combine technologies in unexpected ways using frameworks like agentic orchestration, and embrace a spirit of tinkering – transformative breakthroughs often emerge from persistent exploration at the edges. Recognise that innovation thrives at intersections – where diverse ideas, fields, and technologies converge. Avoid dogmatic stances; embrace the richness and ambiguity of liminal spaces between disciplines and between human and machine intelligence to unlock truly novel paradigms.

Ultimately, the age of AI in design and engineering fosters a powerful partnership – a collaborative intelligence where human intuition, creativity, and ethical judgment engage in a continuous dialogue with machine reasoning, data analysis, and computational power. AI becomes an interpreter in a dynamic conversation involving context, data, physical principles, and human intent, making complexity an intuitive component of the creative process, rather than an overwhelming barrier. The future belongs to those professionals and organisations who skilfully navigate the evolving intersection of human insight and artificial intelligence. By deliberately balancing rapid technological advancement with enduring human values, continuously adapting skills and mindsets, fostering collaborative human–AI relationships through intuitive and transparent interfaces, and working creatively at the intersections, we can shape a world where technology and humanity evolve in powerful harmony, creating solutions and possibilities once confined to our wildest dreams.

NOTES

1 Vikram Kulhari, 'Agentic Process Automation (APA): The Power of Combining RPA & Generative AI', *Medium*, June 10, 2024. https://vikaskulhari.medium.com/agentic-process-automation-apa-the-power-of-combining-rpa-generative-ai-65c47ab231ff

2 See previous chapter.

3 Bot Nirvana, 'Agentic Process Automation (APA): Revolutionizing Digital Automation with AI Agents', *Bot Nirvana*, June 17, 2024, https://botnirvana.org/agentic-process-automation-apa-revolutionizing-digital-automation-with-ai-agents

4 Gill Jaskaran Singh [Assuming full name], 'The Dawn of Agentic Process Automation (APA)', *XenonStack*.

5 https://infrared.city

6 https://infrared.city

7 https://modelcontextprotocol.io/introduction

Figure C.1 Agentic design workflow using parallel style analysis and multi-branch style generation, where agents evaluate and refine cantilevered formal expressions through iterative selection and convergence, generated by Daniel Bolojan using Versur, 2026

CONCLUSION

THE END OF ARCHITECTURE AS STATIC REPRESENTATION

Architecture has reached an inflection point. For centuries, it has been defined by representation: by drawings that project a future building, by models that miniaturise it, by renderings that simulate its atmosphere, and by specifications that describe its assembly. Even when these artifacts transitioned from hand-drawn to digital representations, the underlying logic remained the same. Architecture was a discipline of mediation. The architect conceived; the drawing encoded; the contractor executed.

Today, that paradigm is dissolving, and is being superseded by something more profound. AI – particularly in its generative, predictive, and increasingly agentic forms – does not merely accelerate existing workflows. It restructures the logic of design itself. It introduces computational entities capable of evaluating alternatives, negotiating constraints, simulating consequences, and refining outputs through iterative feedback.

We are now in the era of Agentic Architecture.

Agentic Architecture is not a stylistic shift. Nor is it a digital upgrade of existing workflows. It is a systematic reorganisation of architectural practice around distributed intelligence, continuous evaluation, and adaptive agency. It marks the shift from an architecture of static forms to an architecture of dynamic, goal-directed systems. It is a transition from representation to agency.

Representation describes a world.

Agency participates in its formation.

In Agentic Architecture, design is no longer about the production of drawings but the orchestration of dynamic systems.

AGENCY DEFINED

We need to define the term 'agency' very precisely. Agency here does not imply consciousness, intentionality, or moral autonomy. In other words, it is not agency in the full sense that humans have agency. Rather agentic AI operates only with a narrow sense of agency. It refers to operational capacity: the ability of a system to pursue defined objectives, respond to feedback, and modify its behaviour within a given environment.

Nonetheless, an agentic system can generate alternatives based on constraints, and then evaluate those alternatives against performance metrics. It can also learn from these outcomes, and iterate towards improved solutions.

This capacity distinguishes agentic AI from earlier generative tools. A generative system produces variations; an agentic system selects, critiques, and refines. It operates within a goal-oriented loop.

If AI remains confined to image generation and parametric variation, it remains associative. If it incorporates simulation-based evaluation, feedback loops, and optimisation, it becomes agentic.

And this is the basis of Agentic Architecture.

THE PROBLEM OF ANTHROPOMORPHISATION

The operations of agentic AI and humans are not the same – even though they might appear similar from the outside. Just as we need to avoid projecting human 'agency' onto agentic AI, we also need to avoid reading other agentic AI operations, such as 'deciding' and 'thinking', in anthropomorphic terms.

An agentic AI 'decision' is a computational act: the selection of an action from a range of possibilities according to a policy, trained objectives, and probabilistic optimisation. It is a strictly mechanical process, not so dissimilar to how a thermostat 'decides' whether to switch on or off. A human decision is something far richer. It embodies intentionality, moral judgment, and meaning.

To conflate the two is to fall prey to anthropomorphisation.

By extension, agentic AI does not literally 'think' – at least not in the way that humans think – even though the effect might appear similar. AI 'thinking' is algorithmic optimisation of data structures, whereas human thinking is inference embedded in lived awareness and responsibility.

The two processes can generate comparable results.

They may look similar externally.

But they are not the same.

FROM GENERATION TO ITERATIVE INTELLIGENCE

The first wave of AI in architecture emphasised the generation of form. Text prompts generated speculative designs. Parametric scripts explored formal permutations. Optimisation engines suggested efficient structural forms.

These tools expanded possibilities but did not fundamentally alter the traditional notion of authorship. The architect still selected from a range of outputs.

Agentic Architecture disrupts this relationship.

In an agentic framework, generation is embedded within a process of continuous evaluation. A proposal is not simply produced; it is tested. Wind simulations identify turbulence. Thermal models forecast heat retention. Structural analysis predicts engineering performance. Cost algorithms calculate material expenditure. The system then modifies the proposal accordingly. The design evolves through cycles of feedback.

The implication is profound: architecture becomes predictive rather than reactive. Performance is not tested after the form is defined; it informs form generation from the outset.

Performance informs form.

DISTRIBUTED COGNITION AND COLLABORATIVE AGENCY

Architecture has traditionally centred on singular authorship. Even in collaborative practices, creative direction is often concentrated in a lead architect.

But Agentic Architecture distributes cognition.

AI systems retrieve precedents, analyse site data, generate alternatives, verify compliance, and coordinate documentation. Cloud-based platforms integrate multiple stakeholders in real time. Retrieval, design, modification, verification, collaboration, and output become modular processes within a unified ecosystem.

Human designers operate within this ecosystem as strategic agents. They define goals, interpret results, and exercise judgment. Meanwhile, AI systems operate as complementary agents, processing information and suggesting refinements.

The design process becomes a network of interacting intelligences.

The design studio evolves into a laboratory of co-agency.

Figure C.2 Agentic design workflow exploring bifurcated formal strategies, where specialised agents evaluate symmetry, structural continuity, and spatial coherence from a shared core, generated by Daniel Bolojan using Versur, 2026

INTEGRATION OF FABRICATION AND DESIGN

One of the most significant implications of agentic systems lies in the integration of digital design and physical fabrication.

Digital fabrication technologies – 3D printing, robotic assembly, CNC milling, and so on – translate machine-readable files directly into material reality. In Design for Manufacturing and Assembly (DFMA), fabrication constraints inform design decisions from the outset.

Agentic Architecture embeds these constraints within generative loops. Structural tolerances, material properties, assembly sequences, and logistical limitations are encoded into the design environment.

When a model is adjusted for environmental optimisation, it simultaneously updates the fabrication logic. When a structural parameter shifts, robotic instructions are recalibrated accordingly.

The separation between design and fabrication collapses.

This continuity enhances efficiency, reduces waste, and accelerates production. Prefabricated modular construction demonstrates the potential: buildings can be designed and assembled within dramatically compressed timelines when digital intelligence coordinates the entire lifecycle.

Not only does Agentic Architecture align with intelligent manufacturing paradigms, but it also treats fabrication as an active participant in design evolution.

ENVIRONMENTAL INTELLIGENCE AND PERFORMANCE-DRIVEN DESIGN

Climate instability and ecological degradation demand architecture that actually performs rather than merely symbolises sustainability. Agentic systems enable performance-driven design at unprecedented depth. Computational fluid dynamics models analyse wind corridors and ventilation patterns. Solar simulations optimise shading and orientation. Thermal modelling forecasts energy loads. Behavioural analytics predict occupancy patterns.

When such simulations are integrated into generative loops, form emerges from environmental negotiation. Agentic Architecture therefore reframes sustainability. It is no longer an add-on certification or aesthetic gesture. It is embedded intelligence.

Design becomes a predictive ecology.

FROM LINEAR PROCESS TO CONTINUOUS LOOP

Traditional architectural workflows follow a linear progression: concept, schematic design, detailed design, documentation, construction, occupancy. Feedback often arrives late, requiring costly revisions.

Agentic Architecture restructures temporality into a continuous loop. Sensor data from built environments feeds back into predictive models. Post-occupancy evaluation informs future projects. Real-time performance monitoring adjusts building systems dynamically.

The building becomes an evolving system.

Architecture thus enters a cybernetic paradigm. It operates through feedback, adaptation, and recalibration.

Time is no longer segmented into discrete phases. Design and operation interpenetrate.

ETHICAL STEWARDSHIP IN AN AGENTIC ERA

The delegation of evaluative capacity to AI systems raises ethical concerns. Bias in training data can propagate inequity. Optimisation criteria may privilege cost over social value. Over-reliance on automation may erode critical judgment.

Agentic Architecture must therefore be grounded in ethical stewardship.

Architects must define transparent objectives and interrogate algorithmic outputs. They must ensure that optimisation serves ecological resilience, social inclusion, and cultural integrity.

While agency is distributed, responsibility remains human.

Ethical awareness becomes as essential as computational literacy.

EDUCATION IN THE AGE OF AGENTIC ARCHITECTURE

In the age of Agentic Architecture, architectural education must move beyond teaching representation toward cultivating systems thinking and agentic orchestration. Students must learn not simply to interpret simulations, but to supervise adaptive agents; not just to script interactions, but to choreograph multi-agent workflows. They must become fluent in probabilistic reasoning, model evaluation, reinforcement learning logics, data governance, and the calibration of performance metrics across dynamic feedback loops.

Design studios, accordingly, can no longer treat environmental modelling, fabrication intelligence, and AI-driven iteration as peripheral skills. Design studios must operate as integrated, agentic laboratories in which spatial intelligence, predictive simulation, material computation, and autonomous optimisation form the core pedagogical infrastructure. The studio becomes a site of orchestration – where human intent and machine agency co-evolve within measurable, performance-based design ecosystems.

The architect of the future is not simply a form-giver but a systems thinker.

TOWARD A POST-REPRESENTATIONAL PARADIGM

Agentic Architecture signals the end of architecture as mere depiction. It inaugurates architecture as predictive system.

We move:

From drawing buildings to designing behaviours.

From composing forms to configuring intelligences.

From representing space to orchestrating spatial agency.

This is not incremental change. It is structural transformation.

Figure C.3 Agentic design workflow combining parallel style exploration and quality evaluation, with agents converging on a refined architectural expression through iterative aesthetic assessment and selection, generated by Daniel Bolojan using Versur, 2026

A MANIFESTO FOR AGENTIC ARCHITECTURE

We declare:

1. We need to move beyond representation as architecture's primary medium.
2. Predictive world models must replace static drawings.
3. Performance must inform form.
4. Architects design objective functions and intelligence frameworks, not merely forms.
5. Agentic systems must be governed by ethical concerns.
6. Buildings are adaptive infrastructures embedded in feedback loops.
7. Time is a fundamental design parameter.
8. AI should not be anthropomorphised.
9. Education must shift from producing form makers to cultivating systems thinkers.
10. Architecture must lead, not follow, the integration of AI.

This manifesto is not a rejection of aesthetics, imagination, or cultural meaning. It is an expansion of architecture's capacity to engage complexity.

THE CALL TO ACTION

The AI Design Revolution culminates not in faster rendering or more intricate geometry but in the redefinition of architectural intelligence itself.

Architects must engage critically and creatively with agentic systems. They must integrate AI as infrastructure rather than spectacle. They must ensure that automation enhances sustainability, resilience, and equity.

Agentic Architecture is not about machines replacing architects.

It is about architects redefining their role within a landscape of distributed intelligence.

It is about designing with systems that can reason, evaluate, and learn.

It is about embracing adaptation as the core of architectural production.

It is about transforming the discipline from representation to agency.

Agentic Architecture is not the dissolution of architecture.

It is its renewal.

The revolution is already underway.

The responsibility is ours.

This is not the end of architecture.

It is the beginning of its agentic age.

Figure 5.1 Ila Colombo, Colours of Earth: Tectonic Studies, Midjourney and Runway, 2025

GLOSSARY OF TERMS

Accountability (AI Design): Determining responsibility when an AI-assisted or AI-generated design leads to failure or unintended negative consequences. Establishing clear lines of responsibility is an ongoing ethical and legal challenge.

Adaptive Architecture: Buildings designed with integrated systems (potentially AI-driven) that can sense environmental conditions and occupant needs, and respond by adjusting features (like shading, ventilation, lighting) to optimise performance or comfort in real time. A future direction for AI in architecture.

Aesthetic Exploration: Using design tools, including AI, primarily to investigate visual qualities, form, style, and appearance, sometimes distinct from or balanced against functional or performance objectives.

Agentic AI: Refers to artificial intelligence systems designed not just to process information or generate outputs, but to **act autonomously with a degree of self-direction toward goals**. The term highlights a shift from 'static' generative systems (e.g., a model that outputs text or an image when prompted) to **dynamic, goal-driven intelligences** that begin to resemble autonomous collaborators.

Agentic Automation: An advanced form of automation leveraging AI agents, particularly large language models, capable of understanding context, making decisions, learning, and adapting workflows autonomously or semi-autonomously to achieve complex goals. Distinguished from rigid, rule-based automation.

Agentic Orchestration: A framework where multiple specialised AI agents, potentially using different tools (like prediction models or LLMs), collaborate in a coordinated manner to automate complex workflows and solve multi-faceted problems, such as optimising a design for several environmental factors simultaneously.

AI Prediction Models: AI systems trained on data (e.g., simulation results, climate data) to forecast specific outcomes (e.g., energy use, wind speed) based on input parameters (e.g., building geometry, materials), enabling rapid performance analysis.

Algorithmic Bias (Design Context): When biases present in the training data or algorithms lead AI systems to generate designs that systematically favour certain outcomes, styles, or user groups, potentially reinforcing social or spatial inequalities. In environmental AI, bias could arise from training data skewed towards certain climates or building types, potentially leading to inequitable design recommendations.

Amplify (Human Capabilities): The concept that AI's primary role is to enhance and extend human skills, creativity, and productivity, rather than merely automating or replacing human tasks. AI acts as a force multiplier for human potential.

Application Programming Interfaces (APIs): Sets of protocols and tools that allow different software applications to communicate with each other. APIs enable developers to access specific functions or data from one program within another, facilitating integration and automation of workflows.

Architecture, Engineering, and Construction (AEC): The sector encompassing the integrated disciplines and processes involved in the design, planning, construction, and operation of the built environment.

Artificial General Intelligence (AGI): A form of artificial intelligence that possesses general, domain-independent cognitive capabilities, enabling it to understand, learn, reason, and transfer knowledge across a wide range of tasks at a level comparable to that of a human being.

Artificial Intelligence (AI): Computer systems capable of performing tasks that typically require human intelligence, such as learning, problem-solving, and decision-making. In this context, AI encompasses prediction models, language models, and agentic systems applied to design challenges.

Augmented Creativity: A collaborative model where AI tools enhance human creative processes by handling data analysis, generating diverse options, or identifying novel patterns, allowing humans to focus on intuition, critical selection, and refinement.

Augmented Reality (AR): AR is a technology that overlays digital information such as 3D models, text, or animations onto the user's real-world environment in real time. Unlike virtual reality (VR), which immerses users in a fully digital world, AR enhances physical surroundings by adding interactive digital elements that can be viewed through devices like smartphones, tablets, or AR headsets.

Autocomplete: A predictive computing technique in which a system anticipates and suggests the next characters, words, or tokens based on learned statistical patterns from prior data.

Black Box (AI): An AI system whose internal workings are opaque or difficult for humans to interpret, making it challenging to understand how it reaches a specific output or decision. A common challenge with complex ML models.

Boundary Representations (B-Reps): A method of representing 3D objects by defining their outer surfaces and boundaries rather than their internal volume. B-Reps are the standard approach in CAD software, providing precise geometric definition of shapes through surfaces, edges, and vertices.

Building Information Modelling (BIM): A process involving the generation and management of digital representations of physical and functional characteristics of places. BIM provides structured data essential for AI-driven performance analysis and integration.

Chain-of-Thought: A prompting technique where AI models are encouraged to show their reasoning process step-by-step rather than jumping directly to conclusions. This approach helps make AI decision-making more transparent and often improves the accuracy of complex problem-solving.

Circular Architecture: A design approach focused on principles of the circular economy: extending building lifespan, designing for adaptability and disassembly, prioritising material reuse and recycling, and minimising waste. AI could assist in optimising designs for these principles.

Computational Fluid Dynamics (CFD): A branch of fluid mechanics that uses numerical analysis and data structures to analyse and solve problems involving fluid flows. In architecture, often used for complex simulations like wind patterns around buildings, traditionally requiring significant time and expertise.

Data Interoperability: The ability of different software systems, tools, and platforms to exchange, interpret, and use data seamlessly. In architecture and engineering, this enables different programs (CAD, BIM, simulation tools) to share information without loss of meaning or accuracy.

Daylighting: The practice of utilising natural light from the sun and sky to illuminate building interiors, impacting energy use, occupant well-being, and visual comfort. AI optimises fenestration and shading for desired daylight levels.

Debugging: The process of identifying, analysing, and removing errors or defects in software, code, or AI systems. In the context of AI, debugging involves understanding why a model produces incorrect or suboptimal outputs and adjusting it to improve performance.

Deep Learning: A subset of machine learning (a field of AI) using artificial neural networks with multiple layers ('deep') to learn complex patterns from large datasets.

Democratisation (of Technology): The process by which access to advanced tools, technologies, or capabilities becomes available to a wider range of users, often reducing reliance on specialised expertise or expensive resources (e.g., AI making complex simulation accessible).

Design and Engineering (D&E): Refers broadly to the professional disciplines involved in conceiving, planning, creating, analysing, and managing the development of products, systems, structures, and processes. Used here as the wider context for AI's impact beyond architecture alone.

Design for Manufacturing and Assembly: A design approach that focuses on simplifying the manufacture and assembly of a product or building by optimising the design for ease, efficiency, and cost-effectiveness in production and construction.

Digital Twins: Virtual replicas of physical assets (like buildings), processes, or systems, often updated with real-time data from sensors. Used for monitoring, simulation, analysis, and optimising performance throughout the asset's lifecycle. Mentioned as a future trend for performance validation.

Domain Expertise: Deep knowledge, skills, and experience within a specific field or discipline (e.g., structural engineering, environmental design, software development). The chapter discusses how AI is reshaping the nature and application of domain expertise.

Embodied carbon: The total greenhouse gas emissions associated with the extraction, manufacturing, transportation, construction, maintenance, and end-of-life processing of building materials. Distinct from operational carbon (emissions from building use).

Energy Performance (Building): The measure of how efficiently a building uses energy for heating, cooling, lighting, ventilation, and appliances. AI tools analyse design factors to predict and minimise energy consumption.

Environmental performance design: An approach to architecture and urban design focused on optimising the environmental impact and resource efficiency of buildings and spaces, considering factors like energy consumption, carbon emissions, daylighting, thermal comfort, and microclimate effects.

Explainable AI (XAI): Methods and techniques in AI aimed at making the results and decision-making processes of AI systems understandable to humans. Crucial in design for building trust and enabling meaningful collaboration.

Feedback Loops (Design): An iterative process where the output or result of an action (e.g., performance simulation) is used to modify the next action (e.g., refining the design), allowing for continuous improvement. AI significantly accelerates these loops.

General Data Protection Regulation (GDPR): A comprehensive data protection and privacy regulation enacted by the European Union (EU) in 2018. It establishes strict rules for the collection, processing, storage, and transfer of personal data relating to individuals in the EU and European Economic Area (EEA), regardless of where the data processing takes place. Key principles include data minimisation, purpose limitation, transparency, security, and granting individuals rights over their personal data, such as the right to access, rectify, and erase their information. It has become a benchmark for data privacy legislation globally.

Generative Artificial Intelligence: A subset of AI focused on creating new content (e.g., images, text, 3D models, design options) by learning patterns and relationships from existing data. In architecture, it moves beyond analysis to propose novel design solutions.

Graph Neural Networks (GNNs): A type of artificial intelligence designed to process data structured as graphs, where nodes represent entities (like rooms or building components) and edges represent relationships (like adjacency or connections). GNNs are particularly useful for understanding spatial and structural relationships in architectural design.

Hallucinations (AI): A phenomenon where large language models generate text that is factually incorrect, nonsensical, or unrelated to the provided context, despite sounding plausible. A key limitation requiring verification of LLM outputs.

Human Oversight: The principle that human judgment, ethical considerations, and contextual understanding should guide and potentially override AI-driven processes, especially in high-stakes applications like architectural design.

Industry Foundation Classes (IFC): A standardised, open file format used in the building industry to exchange and share building information modelling (BIM) data between different software applications. IFC enables interoperability by providing a common language for describing building elements and their properties.

Interdisciplinary Collaboration: Working across traditional boundaries between different fields of expertise (e.g., engineering, design, data science, ethics). AI often necessitates and facilitates such collaboration to tackle complex problems holistically.

Interoperability: The ability of different software systems, tools, and platforms to exchange data and work together effectively. Crucial in the AEC industry for integrating diverse tools like CAD, BIM, simulation software, and AI platforms.

Knowledge Synthesis: The process of combining information from multiple sources (e.g., research papers, codes, guidelines) to create new understanding or context-specific recommendations. LLMs show potential for automating aspects of this for designers.

Large Language Models (LLMs): AI models trained on vast amounts of text data, capable of understanding, generating, and processing human language. Used here for tasks like interpreting briefs, suggesting options, explaining concepts, and potentially synthesising knowledge.

Large Reasoning Models (LRMs): An emerging category of artificial intelligence models, often evolving from LLMs, specifically architected to excel at complex reasoning, planning, and multi-step problem-solving. Compared to traditional LLMs, LRMs place greater emphasis on generating coherent, step-by-step 'thought processes' or reasoning traces, offering potential pathways towards increased transparency and explainability for complex AI outputs, allowing users to better understand *how* a conclusion or solution was reached.

Machine Learning (ML): A field of AI where computer systems learn from data to improve their performance on a specific task without being explicitly programmed. Used in architecture to predict performance, recognise patterns, and optimise designs.

Multi-objective optimisation: An optimisation problem that involves more than one objective function to be optimised simultaneously, often with conflicting goals (e.g., minimising energy use while maximising daylight, which might increase solar gain). Agentic orchestration is suited for such tasks.

Multimodal Interfaces: User interfaces that allow interaction through multiple modes, such as text, voice, gesture, images, and potentially augmented or virtual reality (AR/VR), offering richer ways to interact with complex AI systems and data.

Neural Networks: Computational models inspired by biological neurons, consisting of interconnected layers that learn to approximate complex functions by adjusting weighted connections through data-driven training.

Occupant Comfort: The subjective satisfaction of building occupants with their environment, encompassing thermal, visual, acoustic, and air quality aspects. AI can help design spaces optimised for multiple comfort parameters.

Passive Strategies: Design techniques that utilise natural phenomena like sunlight, wind, and thermal properties of materials to heat, cool, light, and ventilate a building without active mechanical systems (e.g., natural ventilation, solar shading, thermal mass).

Pedestrian Wind Comfort: A measure of how comfortable or safe wind conditions are for people in outdoor spaces, influenced by building arrangements and wind speed. Often assessed using criteria based on wind tunnel tests or CFD simulations.

Performance-Driven Generative Design: An approach where generative AI creates design options that are continuously evaluated against specific performance metrics (e.g., energy efficiency, structural load, daylight levels), integrating analysis directly into the creative process.

Physics-Informed Models: AI models designed to incorporate knowledge of physical laws (e.g., conservation of energy, fluid dynamics equations) into their learning process, aiming for more accurate, reliable, and generalisable predictions, especially in engineering and scientific domains. Mentioned as a future direction.

Procedural Models: Design representations defined by rules, parameters, and algorithms rather than explicit geometry. These models describe how to generate designs through step-by-step procedures, allowing for systematic exploration of design variations while maintaining logical consistency.

Proxy Discrimination: A form of bias where seemingly neutral variables or data points are used as substitutes (proxies) for sensitive attributes like race, income, or gender, leading to discriminatory outcomes. For example, using zip codes in AI models may inadvertently discriminate based on socioeconomic status or ethnicity that correlates with geographic location.

Qualitative Aspects (Architecture): Design characteristics related to subjective experience, aesthetics, cultural meaning, spatial quality, and human perception, which are often difficult to measure or optimise using purely quantitative AI methods.

Quantifiable Performance Metrics: Measurable criteria used to evaluate a design's effectiveness, such as energy consumption (kWh/m^2/yr), structural stress (MPa), daylight autonomy (%), or acoustic performance (dB). AI excels at optimising for these.

Reasoning Traces: Documented step-by-step records of an AI system's logical process when arriving at a decision or solution. These traces help users understand how the AI reached its conclusions, making the system's behaviour more transparent and verifiable.

Resilience (Climate Change): The capacity of a building or urban area to withstand, adapt to, and recover from the impacts of climate change, such as extreme heat events, flooding, or high winds. AI can help assess design vulnerabilities.

Retrieval-Augmented Generation (RAG): An AI technique that enhances the responses of large language models by retrieving relevant information from an external knowledge base (e.g., a database of environmental regulations) before generating an answer, aiming to improve accuracy and reduce 'hallucinations'.

Semantic BIM Data: BIM data that includes not just geometric information but also meaningful metadata about building components – such as material properties, performance characteristics, relationships between elements, and functional classifications. This rich information enables more intelligent analysis and automation.

Shape Grammars: Formal systems of rules that define how shapes can be combined, modified, or replaced to generate designs. Shape grammars provide a structured framework for algorithmic design generation, often used to explore design variations within defined stylistic or functional constraints.

Simulation-as-a-Service (SimaaS): A cloud computing model where simulation capabilities (like those provided by Infrared.city) are offered as a service, typically accessible via an API, allowing integration into other applications without needing local installation or high-performance computing resources.

Skills Gap: The mismatch between the skills demanded by evolving job markets (increasingly requiring AI literacy) and the skills possessed by the current workforce.

Solar Radiation: The radiant energy emitted by the sun, particularly electromagnetic energy. In building design, analysing solar radiation is crucial for understanding heat gains, daylight availability, and potential for solar energy generation.

Static Analysis: Traditional performance evaluation methods typically conducted at fixed points in the design process, often late, making it difficult to integrate feedback into core design decisions dynamically. Contrasted here with AI's potential for continuous, integrated feedback.

Structural Integrity: The ability of a building or its components to withstand applied loads (gravity, wind, seismic forces) without failure or excessive deformation. ML models can predict structural behaviour and optimise material use.

Structured Representations (Design): Standardised ways of encoding design information (geometry, materials, relationships) in a format that AI systems can effectively process and manipulate for tasks like analysis and generation. Beyond simple images or parameters.

Supervised Learning: A machine learning approach in which models are trained on labelled input–output pairs, enabling them to make predictions or classifications on new, unseen data.

Surrogate Models: Surrogate models in building design are computationally efficient approximations of high-fidelity simulation models that enable rapid prediction of performance metrics – such as energy use, structural behaviour, or thermal comfort – thereby accelerating the design process.

Symbiosis (Human–Machine): A mutually beneficial relationship between human intelligence and artificial intelligence, where each component enhances the capabilities of the other, leading to outcomes superior to what either could achieve alone.

Unsupervised Learning: A class of machine learning in which algorithms identify patterns, structures, or relationships in unlabelled data without predefined outputs or explicit human supervision.

Urban Scale Performance: Analysis of how buildings and urban design interventions impact the broader city environment, considering factors like microclimate (wind, sun access), noise pollution, traffic flow, and accessibility.

User Experience (UX): Encompasses all aspects of an end-user's interaction with a company, its services, and its products. In this context, specifically refers to the design of interfaces and interactions between human professionals and AI systems, critically influencing adoption and effectiveness.

Voxel Grids: Three-dimensional pixel grids that represent space by dividing it into small cubic units (voxels). Each voxel can store information about whether space is occupied and by what material, allowing AI to understand and manipulate complex 3D forms, though at the cost of high computational demands.

INDEX

Note: Locators in *italic* indicate figures.